STUDIES IN JAPANESE BUDDHISM

AUGUST KARL REISCHAUER, M.A., D.D., 1879–

Seventh Lecturer upon Deems Foundation
Professor of Philosophy and Systematic Theology, Meiji Gakuin, Tokyo, Japan

STUDIES IN JAPANESE
BUDDHISM

BY

AUGUST KARL REISCHAUER

AMS PRESS
NEW YORK

Reprinted from the edition of 1917, New York
First AMS EDITION published 1970
Manufactured in the United States of America

Library of Congress Catalog Card Number: 73-107769
ISBN: 404-05237-1

AMS PRESS, INC.
New York, N.Y. 10003

To

MY WIFE

PREFATORY NOTE

THE present volume contains the seventh course of lectures offered by New York University upon the foundation known as the Charles F. Deems Lectureship of Philosophy. The University contracted April 15, 1895, with the American Institute of Christian Philosophy, a corporation chartered December 1, 1891, that the University would maintain said lectureship for at least twenty years by securing biennially a Lecturer, eminent in Science and Philosophy, who should treat in not less than six lectures some one of the most important questions of Science and Philosophy, with a special reference to its relation to the revealed truths of the Holy Scriptures and to the fundamental principles of Theistic Philosophy.

The Lecturer was to be chosen by the University's Committee upon the Charles F. Deems Lectureship, which was to consist of the Chancellor of the University, two members of the Faculty of Arts and Science and two members of the University Council, to be named as the Council may direct. The subject for each year's lectures was to be agreed upon between this Committee and the Lecturer.

The University provided, free of charge, a room for the lectures, and at its own expense, made due public announcement of the time and place of each lecture. The University was to publish, in book form, each series of lectures, and put the same on sale with one or more reputable book firms, provided this could be done without further expense than could be met by the accumulation of income over and above the expense of maintaining the lectures.

The several volumes of lectures upon the Deems Foundation have been published as follows:

1. "Theism in the Light of Present Science and Philosophy," by James Iverach, M.A., D.D.: The Macmillan Company, New York and London.

2. "Theism," by Borden P. Bowne, D.D., Professor of Philosophy in Boston University: American Book Company, New York, Cincinnati and Chicago.

3. "Religions of Eastern Asia," by Horace Grant Underwood, D.D.: The Macmillan Company, New York.

4. "The Teaching of Paul in Terms of the Present Day," by Sir William Mitchell Ramsay, D.C.L.: Hodder & Stoughton, London New York and Toronto.

5. "Ethics and Modern Thought — A Theory of Their Relations," by Rudolf Eucken, Professor of Philosophy, University of Jena: G. P. Putnam's Sons, New York and London.

6. The failure of the health of the late Principal Fairbairn of Oxford, England, after the delivery of his lectures, prevented the preparation of them for the press.

7. The present volume published by The Macmillan Company, the seventh and concluding volume of the first series of lectures, is from the pen of the youngest of the seven lecturers upon this Foundation.

Dr. August Karl Reischauer was born in Jonesboro, Illinois, September fourth, 1879, and was therefore in his thirty-fourth year when he lectured upon the Deems Foundation, being the first of the lecturers who was under forty years of age. He studied at Hanover College, Indiana, and the McCormick Theological Seminary, Chicago; and after his ordination in 1905, went at once to Japan to teach Ethics and Philosophy in the mission college in the south part of the city of Tokyo, the school being called Meiji Gakuin, in honor of the Meiji era of the history of Japan, which was ushered in in the year of 1868 by the abolition of the government of the Shoguns and the replacing in supreme power of the Mikado, who had for centuries been kept in subjection to the military Shogunate. He has published in

Japan a catechism on Buddhism of the Shin Sect, Buddhist Gold Nuggets, and a treatise on personal immortality. Dr. Reischauer's lectures on the Deems Foundation have not appeared earlier because he did not return to Japan for some months after their delivery and required considerable time for preparing them for the press. No libraries outside of Japan contain more than a mere fraction of the Buddhist authorities from whose writings the material of these lectures was obtained.

The lecturer in his first lecture presented Buddhist Origins. In the second he traced the development of Primitive Buddhism into the Mahayana Buddhism, this form of Buddhism having the lead in Japan. He presented in his third lecture the historical development of Japanese Buddhism. His fourth lecture discussed the Buddhist Canon. In his fifth he sketched the Japanese Sects and their chief tenets and in the sixth Buddhist Ethics. The closing lecture presented, in comparison with Buddhism, the strength of Christianity in Japan.

The twenty years' contract between the American Institute of Christian Philosophy and New York University having expired by limitation, these two parties are now considering the question of renewing the same. It falls to me as both a member of the University Committee and President of the Institute of Philosophy to supply this prefatory statement.

HENRY MITCHELL MacCRACKEN.

University Heights,
New York City.

AUTHOR'S PREFACE

In sending this book forth to the public I am keenly aware of the fact that the magnitude of the subject with which it deals is such that it may seem absurd to try to cover it in such a short space. Any one chapter might easily be expanded into a large volume without even then going into very great details. And yet I feel that a general, brief survey of the subject, such as this book tries to give, is on the whole the wisest plan when one considers the present degree of interest in Oriental religions and philosophies on the part of Western readers. There is still so very little in English books on Japanese Buddhism of even a general character that no author can hope to get much of a hearing who does not confine himself largely to merely the outstanding facts and characteristics of his theme. Then further should it be said that even the interested student who enters this field must ever be on his guard lest in the multiplicity of the details — and in Japanese Buddhism there is a wealth of this — he lose sight of the main trend of the subject.

As stated in the preface by Dr. H. M. MacCracken, this volume comprises the Deems Lectures for the year 1913, but it should be said that the lectures as originally given have been almost entirely rewritten and considerably expanded. The form of the lectures has, however, determined in general the main trend of thought in the book

Naturally I feel myself indebted to a great many writers and to other friends with whom I have talked on this great subject during my eleven years of residence in Tōkyō. This, as far as books written in European languages are concerned, has been partly acknowledged, but I wish to make special mention here of the late Professor Arthur Lloyd, whose pioneer work was of great value to me at the beginning of my studies

when Japanese authors were still "closed books." My debt
to these Japanese writers is such that I shall not even attempt
to acknowledge it properly. In closing I only wish to mention the names of Professors G. Kato and M. Nagai of the
Tōkyō Imperial University and Professor S. Tajima of Meiji
Gakuin for their kind assistance in preparing the bibliography
of Japanese books, which it is hoped may prove of help to
the student who desires to pursue further his studies in this
immense, and to the Western scholar practically unknown,
field.

                    AUGUST KARL REISCHAUER.

MEIJI GAKUIN,
    TōKYō.

CONTENTS

xiii

STUDIES IN JAPANESE BUDDHISM

STUDIES IN JAPANESE BUDDHISM

INTRODUCTION

NOT many years ago there was on exhibition in an art gallery of Tokyo a remarkable picture. The picture was not exactly a masterpiece, but its subject matter was exceedingly suggestive. In the center stood a child, and grouped around it were four men, each beckoning it to follow. On the face of the child was an expression of bewilderment, of apparent perplexity as to what it should do. The child was meant to represent Japan, and the four men represented a Shintō priest, Confucius, Gautama Buddha and Jesus. The average visitor to the gallery gave this picture little more than a passing glance, but to the student of modern Japan it was of deep interest.

If there is anything characteristic of the life of the rising generation in Japan, especially of its thought-life and the realm of things spiritual, it is bewilderment and confusion; for Japan is the meeting place of four great religions, viz., Shintō, Confucianism, Buddhism and Christianity, not to mention other thought and life currents which have been pouring into this land from all parts of the world during the last fifty or sixty years. It is not strange that the youth of Japan especially should be like the child in the picture — confused and perplexed as to whom or what they should follow. On the one hand are the voices and beckonings of the past — the thought-currents and life habits and customs of their fathers. These they would follow instinctively. But on the other hand they hear the persistent callings of the new and more alluring voices of the present and the future, wooings of western life and civilization. These seem to promise more than the old, but threaten if followed unreservedly to make too great the chasm between the Japanese people of to-day and past generations.

There is, of course, no insuperable difficulty in readjusting the old habits and customs to fit in with the new in the realm of the physical, though even here it is not as simple as it might seem to the outsider. To stand, for instance, at a modern railway station and listen to the clatter of the wooden clogs as the crowds hurry up and down the stairs suggests very forcibly that one is hearing something of the "clash of civilizations." Or to see aëroplanes and dirigibles speeding over paddy fields in which poor peasants are using implements as primitive as those used by Abraham makes one feel that modern Japan has still great chasms to bridge in even the physical realm. And even where they are being bridged the limited resources of the country tends to make the economic readjustments a very painful process. But, after all, it is in the realm of the spirit, in the higher and deeper sentiments and feelings, that the real difficulty of readjustment lies for the present generation. And what adds to the difficulty is the fact that among the so-called leaders in the thought-life of the nation there are so very few who really understand the nature of the forces that are at work. On the one hand are the old-fashioned leaders, who would keep the rising generation bound down to the things of the past. On the other hand are the apostles of the new, who apparently think that they have done all that is required of them when they have doled out to their followers the contents of the latest book that has appeared. Those who are successfully bridging the chasm between the old and the new are few indeed, and it is no wonder that there should be so much confusion in the thought-life of modern Japan.

But it is not so much the general thought-life of Japan that we wish to consider here as it is the more distinctively religious life of the nation, if it is possible to separate this from the general. The picture, we said, represented four great religions as aspiring to give leadership to young Japan. This is hardly accurate, for as a matter of fact the three old religions of Japan are not separate and distinct from one another. Shintō, as we shall show in Chapter III, though the native religion of old Japan, was virtually incorporated into Buddhism about a thousand years ago, and while it was officially separated from the latter in the modern period it is impossible to draw any clear line between the two. And Confucianism really never existed as an independent religion in Japan, but was fostered largely by Buddhist leaders as a part of their own system. It is true that the Neo-Confucianism of the Tokugawa period had a measure of independence and even opposed Buddhism to some extent, but even this was introduced and propagated first by Buddhists and was itself as much Buddhism as Confucianism. As a matter of fact the three old religions of Japan have interpenetrated each other so completely that the average Japanese for centuries has regarded himself as more or less of an adherent of all three. It is Buddhism, however, which has supplied the matrix which holds the various elements together and so it may be said to represent all three in one. It has so completely adapted itself to things Japanese and incorporated everything that it found in its way that one can be a good Buddhist and not be disloyal to anything for which the other two ever stood.

When it comes, however, to the fourth religion, the religion of Jesus Christ, the matter is very different, for no Japanese Christian in good and regular standing would regard himself as anything but a Christian, though he would insist that as such he can retain all that is good in the other three and all that is essential to make one a true and loyal citizen of the empire. And on the other hand few good Shintōists, Confucianists or Buddhists would pretend to be also good Christians, for it was the fashion for almost three centuries to look upon Christianity as an enemy of things Japanese; and so the line between it and the old religions is drawn rather sharply. It would therefore be more correct to say that in the realm of religion there are two that aspire to guide the spiritual destiny of this great nation.

One naturally wonders whom of these spiritual guides the child of Japan will follow. There was a time a few years ago — and it is not altogether past now — when it almost looked as if the expression on the child's face was changing from one of confusion and bewilderment to one of indifference. Japan had followed the old guide for many centuries, sometimes very eagerly and at times only from afar. But during the last fifty years or so, as the rising tide of intelligence has made it impossible for many to rest content with the beliefs and practices of the past, there developed a surprising indifference to the old religious ideals, and in fact an indifference to religion as such. But no one familiar with human nature or human history can regard this save as a passing phase, for man is "incurably religious" and even a Comte must have at least a "Religion of Humanity," though he may regard the historic religions as phases of life which the race should outgrow as it advances. There are abundant signs that this indifference to religion so characteristic of young Japan a few years ago was only a temporary phenomenon. There is now again a remarkable interest in spiritual things, though it is perhaps too early to say to whom on the whole Japan will turn for leadership.

There are those who hold that Japan will neither follow her old religious guides nor turn to the old religion of the West newly introduced, but that there will have to be a New Religion if her allegiance is to be won. This new religion may borrow some things from the old but not exclusively from any one of them or all of them. It will have to be a sort of syncretism made up from the best elements that can be gotten together, no matter from where they come. Just as in other spheres Japan has borrowed the best that could be found and adapted these things to her needs; so she must do in religious matters. One can only smile at the ignorance of the nature of religion and religious history which underlies this view, for while it is quite possible for a New Religion to arise, it is rather certain that it will not come into existence as a result of a few wise heads getting together and saying to one another, "Come now, let us tear down our old religions and from the best fragments let us build up something new which will fit our case better."

Then again there are those who would seek to harmonize the claims of the existing religions by emphasizing the thought that all religions are but different forms of one and the same phenomenon, and that therefore at bottom they are essentially the same. And since all religions are made of essentially the same stuff, there ought to be no insuperable obstacle in fusing them into one grand whole; if not into an organic union, then at least into one great coöperative enterprise for promoting righteousness and peace.

In so far as these broad-minded leaders would do away with the bitter jealousies and strifes between the existing religions, one cannot but have profound respect for their good intentions; but when their efforts are based on the assumption that all religions are essentially one in their great fundamentals and differ only on minor points or expression, one can only pity their lack of understanding. Of course, there is a sense in which all historical religions may be said to be but different forms of Religion, i.e. different aspects of one and the same reality, but this is true only in such a general sense that the statement is practically meaningless. The very fact that it is almost impossible to make a definition of religion which is anything but an empty generalization which includes all only because it includes really nothing very vital of any, should be sufficient proof. Even in such advanced religions as Buddhism and Christianity the radical differences in fundamentals ought to be apparent to any one who is at all familiar with their central teachings. It is inconceivable that the two could ever be merged into one without one or the other giving up some of its essential characteristics. Of course, it is quite possible that Buddhism would be willing to compromise with Christianity and seek to absorb it just as it has done with other religions with which it has come into contact, but that is only possible because Japanese Buddhism really stands for nothing definite and is made up of the most glaring contradictions in even fundamentals. It is impossible to think that intelligent Christians would be willing to be merged into a system which would both affirm and deny at one and the same time everything vital for which they stood. Not only does Christianity differ from Buddhism in the answers which it makes to the great problems of life, but because of this difference the atmosphere in which Christians live their daily life and do the work of the world is not that of the typical Buddhist. This will appear as we proceed with our study of Japanese Buddhism in these pages. Here we simply wish to state that those who regard Buddhism and Christianity as in substantial agreement on the fundamentals of religion may be nearer the truth than the old-fashioned polemists who conveniently marked all religions other than their own as false, but they are not very much nearer.

Now in the third place there are representatives of the old religions of Japan who, realizing that their religion has lost a good deal of ground in recent years, nevertheless believe that the situation can be redeemed by making certain reforms and so winning back the affection of the people. Thus there are signs on all hands of a certain kind of vitality both in Shintō and in some of the more progressive sects of Buddhism. These reforms, however, are little more than patching up a few glaring defects of the old by borrowing certain strong points from Christianity, and they do not go deep enough to make the old religions adequate for modern conditions. In fact many an adherent of the old is apparently fearful that the great days of his faith are past forever and that the future is very uncertain. That is, there is no very widespread confidence on the part of the adherents of the old in the future of their own religion.

And finally there are the representatives of Christianity who believe that the future belongs largely to them. In fact that is one of the great characteristics of Japanese Christians which distinguishes them from the followers of

the old faiths, they have confidence in the future of their
own religion. The child Japan, they believe, will follow
Jesus Christ as its guide, and it is this faith that is overcoming the difficulties in the way. The measure of success
which Christianity is having in Japan justifies this belief,
but at the same time there is also good reason to believe
that the victory will not be an easy one. The old religions
of Japan are not, as some seem to think, about ready to
give up the field. Though it is true that they do not have
the hold on the hearts of the people they once had, this
does not mean that Christianity therefore has an easy task.
When the late Bishop Honda of the Japanese Methodist
Church was once asked what he thought of the great motto,
"The Evangelization of the World in This Generation,"
he replied very modestly, "It is a good motto, a very good
motto for this generation; and I think it will be a good
motto for the next generation too."

The view that the religions of the Orient are one and
all like tottering castles of antiquity which will soon crumble
to dust betrays a rather shallow knowledge of the real
nature of religion. It seems to regard religion as an external something, a garment which can be cast off as the
style changes. As a matter of fact nothing changes as
slowly as a nation's religion and religious customs. Japan,
e.g., has changed its army and navy from a medieval type
to one thoroughly modern and strictly up-to-date, within the
space of a few decades. Her educational system, her transportation facilities and industrial enterprises have likewise
been revolutionized within that period. But with her religion the matter stands quite different. A Constantine may
make Christianity the state religion overnight, and Japanese officials once thought of doing the same, but that
would be only changing a name. For the thought-life of a
nation and the spirit of a people to be made Christian even
to the extent to which this has been accomplished in some
of our western nations (there is, of course, no such thing
as a Christian nation anywhere), will take decades and
perhaps centuries. Whatever one may think of the place

which the old religions of Japan, and Buddhism in particular, will occupy in the future of this people's life, they are forces with which one must reckon. The influence of a stream is determined not only by the direction in which the water is flowing at any one point and by the speed and volume of water, but also by the drift it scatters in its way. And so even if Buddhism should be a dried-up stream, as many seem to think, the river bed which it has made through Japanese life and the bowlders it has left all over these island fields will determine to a greater or lesser degree the direction and speed of the new currents of life which are flowing into this land from other sources.

But, as we said, it is as yet too early to say to whom Japan will turn for leadership, and it is really not our purpose to discuss this in these pages. Our object is rather to understand better the history and spirit of the old religions, especially Buddhism, and from this obtain, perhaps, a better insight into the present situation and the line of its probable development. We shall confine ourselves almost exclusively to a study of Buddhism, which we regard as the dominant religious force of Japan. Shintō and Confucianism we shall touch upon only here and there, for as we have intimated above both of these are really embodied in the term Buddhism as we know that religion in Japan.

But to understand Japanese Buddhism even in its main outline is not a simple matter. It is not only that in Japan Buddhism has taken up into itself everything which it found in its way, which makes it difficult for the student, but because it had a history of a thousand years before it reached these shores, and during those long centuries it had been winning its victories by this same method of compromise. That is, when Buddhism was introduced into Japan in the sixth century it had passed northwestward from India into the lands east of the Caspian Sea and then turned towards the east, spreading gradually through China and Korea, and all the time gathering up into itself, like a rolling snowball, all that it found on its way. For example, its canonical writings by this time had assumed the dimension of a good-sized library containing upward of 5000 books. The contents of these books, written during a period of a thousand years and by peoples of various stages of civilization, are naturally very varied and often flatly contradictory even in matters fundamental. It is not strange, then, that a leading authority on Buddhism, in trying to define what the religion is, could only say that it is the religion founded by the Buddha. Even this was saying too much, for the Buddhism of China and Japan has perhaps more in it that is contradictory to the religion of the Buddha than what is in agreement with it. In fact Northern Buddhism, considered from almost any standpoint one cares to take, embraces a wider latitude of teachings and practices than any other religious system. Even in regard to its inner spirit and life, which is the true measure of any religion, Buddhism presents a bewildering spectacle. It is more like a junk shop where one can find almost anything — good, bad and indifferent. There is little that has ever entered the heart or mind of man which does not find its counterpart in Buddhism somewhere.

To determine, then, what Buddhism is as a whole, or even what Japanese Buddhism is, may seem like undertaking the impossible. We know how difficult it is to say just what are the essentials of Christianity and perhaps few would agree entirely; but, after all, in Christianity there are a few great outstanding ideas and ideals which would generally be recognized as fundamentals. For example, the belief in a personal God, the Heavenly Father, the belief in Jesus Christ as being in some way the relevation of God's love to man and in the Christlike life as being the Christian's ideal, and finally the great hope that this type of life is one which shall be conserved beyond the grave and the wreck of time, — these are among the great essentials to which all Christians, whether Catholic or Protestant, conservative or liberal, ancient or modern, would cling. But in Buddhism, whether we take the religion as a whole, or simply as we find it in Japan, there are radical differences in even such fundamentals of religion. But this will appear as we proceed with our study. We simply mention it here to indicate how very difficult is our task of trying to understand Japanese Buddhism.

Now in order to have, as it were, a norm by which to measure Japanese Buddhism, it becomes necessary to give at least a general outline of the religion of the founder and a brief sketch of its development into what we call Mahāyāna Buddhism. This shall occupy us in our first two chapters. But before we come to that we must here make a few remarks in order to orient ourselves in Buddhism as a whole.

Ordinarily we divide Buddhism into two great divisions, viz., Southern Buddhism and Northern Buddhism. By the former is meant roughly the Buddhism of Ceylon, Burma, Siam, and French Indo-China; India, the birthplace of the religion, having given up its allegiance to the World-Honored One since about the twelfth century, though, of course, the religious life in India to this day shows his influence. By Northern Buddhism we mean the Buddhism of China (*i.e.* Greater China, including Tibet, East Turkestan, Mongolia and Manchuria), Korea, Japan and the lands on the slopes of the Himalaya Mountains, especially Nepal, Bhutan and Sikkim. The Buddhists of Java and Sumatra, though geographically belonging to Southern Buddhism, in point of historic connection and general type should be classed with Northern Buddhism. This geographical division is therefore very inaccurate and should not be regarded as of much value.

Another way of dividing Buddhism is the classification into Hīnayāna, or Little Vehicle, and Mahāyāna, or Great Vehicle; the former corresponding roughly to Southern Buddhism and the latter to Northern Buddhism, though Northern Buddhism has in its voluminous canon also practically all the teachings found in the Hīnayāna school. We shall explain the meaning of this division more fully in Chapter IV; only here it should be said that Hīnayāna Buddhism is roughly speaking the Buddhism of the Pali scriptures, which have preserved on the whole the purest form of the religion of the founder. Mahāyāna represents in general an expanded and developed Buddhism which in many respects, even in things fundamental, is often radically different from original Buddhism. We do not mean to say that Northern Buddhism has not much in it that goes back to the teachings of the founder and, perhaps, even some things of his life and teachings which are not preserved in the Pali literature; but there is in it so much that is different and even radically opposed to what seems to have been the main thought and life of Gautama's religion that we are ready to accept this time-honored division of Hīnayāna and Mahāyāna.

These great differences in Buddhism are, of course, the result of the growth and expansion which this religion underwent in the course of its history as it marched northward and eastward through China, Korea and Japan. Orthodox Buddhists hold that both these great forms of their religion, in spite of the most glaring contradictions, are the teaching of the master, and they resort to the most elaborate schemes of harmonization to get rid of the obvious difficulties. But modern scholars are seeing more and more clearly that it is impossible that even the main points of Mahāyāna and Hīnayāna Buddhism could have all come from the same mind. It seems rather certain, as we have said, that the Pali scriptures of the south contain on the whole the purest form of the teaching of the Buddha, though they too show a considerable development. Whereas the scriptures of Northern Buddhism, which are written parts in Sanskrit and in a mixed dialect of Sanskrit and Middle Indian, or the Gāthā dialect, parts in Chinese, Tibetan, Mongolian and Japanese, contain not only what is found in the Pali scriptures but a great deal more. It is this extra material which leads the Mahāyāna Buddhists to make the claim that their teachings are superior to the Hīnayāna and that they represent the full mind of the master; but to the unbiased scholar it is rather an evidence of *extra* Buddhist elements which came in as Buddhism readjusted itself to meet the attacks of a revived Brahmanism and as it spread into other countries and tried to absorb the native cults which it met in its way.

It is the northern stream, *i.e.* Mahāyāna Buddhism, that is of interest for our present purpose, for it is this stream which ultimately reached Japan in the middle of the sixth century. But that we may understand more clearly the significance of this northern stream, it becomes necessary, as we said above, to take at least a bird's-eye view of the main points of primitive Buddhism and its development. What, then, was the religion of the Buddha? For only as we answer this question at least approximately can we fully appreciate Northern Buddhism and especially its furthest development in the Buddhism of Japan, which in some of its branches seems Buddhist only in name. This we take up in Chapter I.

CHAPTER I

BUDDHIST ORIGINS

THE main facts of the life of Gautama, the founder of Buddhism, and the chief points of the religion he proclaimed are gradually coming clearer to light from year to year as a result of the patient efforts of a certain group of scholars. Not all that is written on the subject adds to our knowledge; in fact, the majority of the older popular books on Buddhism are often very misleading, especially on the points dealing with the origins of Buddhism. This is largely due to the fact that most of these books do not discriminate sufficiently between early and late sources. Thus we have, *e.g.*, such a book as Sir Edwin Arnold's "The Light of Asia," which, perhaps, has been read more widely than any other book on Buddhism, giving a picture of the Buddha and his religion, not as they were, but rather as they appeared to a devout Buddhist poet who lived several centuries later. What is written about the Buddha and early Buddhism by the great majority of Buddhist writers, especially those of China and Japan, is even more misleading, as they see the founder of their religion largely through the eyes of men who wrote from five hundred to a thousand years after Gautama's day. Not that such pictures are wholly erroneous, but that the careful scholar should seek to construct the picture from the oldest sources available, rather than use the sources indiscriminately, is what we mean. Now it is due, as we said, to the patient efforts of a few careful scholars that gradually a few of the real facts in the case are being brought to the light and cleared from the accretions of the centuries. This does not mean that the students of Buddhism have anywhere near such reliable data for the life of Gautama

13

and early Buddhism as Christian students have for the life of Jesus Christ and early Christianity, but that some of the main points are beginning to assume a fairly definite outline.

This outline, especially of the religion of the Buddha, becomes all the more definite when seen in the light of its historical environment.   In fact, our whole conception of early Buddhism has been revolutionized by our growing understanding of the circumstances under which it arose. Let us state briefly the main features of the times that preceded Gautama's day, especially of the religious life of India.

A. *Gautama's Environment*

When Buddhism sprang into life near the end of the sixth century B.C., India had already passed through several stages of its remarkable religious history.   The Aryan conquerors who invaded India from the northwest by gradual stages during the second or third millennium B.C. had already produced the religion of the Vedic hymns.   In fact, the Vedic hymns and the religion of which they are an expression already lay in the distant past, and the lofty poetry of the Rig-Veda had been forgotten by the people in general and was known only by the priests.   Even these apparently knew these hymns no longer in their purity but rather as broken up into charm-texts, Mantras, by which they exercised authority over evil spirits, and through this gained their power over the people.   That is, the Vedic hymns had been replaced by the Brāhmanas, the prose liturgical texts based upon them.   The possessors of this "divine knowledge" naturally were looked up to by the common people and this, perhaps more than any other factor, gave them the supreme place in India's social organization and gradually led to the caste system which has been such a determining element in every phase of that country's life ever since.

The Brāhmanas, which are primarily nothing more than detailed prescriptions for the performance of religious rites, had in turn been enlarged by the addition of commentaries in which are found frequently theological and philosophical discussions centering largely around the cosmogonic problem. These theological and philosophical subjects were then further elaborated and they form the main themes of the Āranyakas, Forest Books, and especially the older Upanishads, which form appendices to the Āranyakas.

Such is the brief outline of the chief religious literature which had been produced in India before the sixth century B.C., and a mere glance at it is enough to show that it represents many centuries of religious development. All this literature is regarded by Indian orthodoxy as alike divinely inspired, and on these books, especially on the Upanishads, all the orthodox systems of metaphysics profess to base their teachings.

It is impossible and unnecessary in such a hurried review to indicate the contents of this literature. It is not only very varied, but the views on the same subject are often quite diverse, as might be expected when it is remembered that these books record in part at least the religious life of a mixed race covering a period of more than a thousand years. We shall give a summary of only a few points which have special bearing on our main theme. These are the God-idea, the soul-theory including the doctrines of transmigration and Karma, salvation and the religious and social structure of the day.

1. *The God-idea.* — The God-idea is exceedingly varied; not only so when the literature is taken as a whole, but also when one age is taken by itself. Alongside of the highest philosophical speculations, ending sometimes in a semimonotheism and at other times in pantheism, is to be found the lowest form of animism and the most revolting polytheism and demonology.[1] In the later portions of the Rig-Veda collection there are passages which have given credence to the view that the oldest literature of India points to monotheism as the earliest form of the God-idea, but a closer study of the facts will hardly bear this out. There is an elementary pantheism to be found, and sometimes this leans toward monotheism, but, after all, the Vedic gods are many; and as the centuries passed the preëminence of one gave way

to that of another. "The flowers of the garlands he wore are withered, his robes of majesty have waxed old and faded, he falls from his high estate, and is reborn into a new life." When we come to the century in which Buddhism arose, many of the Vedic gods, even those who at one time or another had held unique places, had succumbed to this fate. Only a few of them remained, and new gods had taken the places of the old ones. The thing that impresses one is that the keenest thinkers, both in the Vedic age and the centuries which followed, were trying in one way or another to work their way through the animistic and polytheistic maze which surrounded them to the conception that at the origin of all things there must be a unitary ground of existence. This thought in some writers is expressed by singling out one god of the pantheon and ascribing to him all the characteristics of other popular gods as we have, *e.g.*, later in the cases of Vishnu and Siva. Other writers conceive of this unitary ground of existence in terms less personal and regard it rather as a self-existent principle which is the source of all phenomenal existence, the gods included. Especially when we come to the Upanishads do we see the God-idea assume this monistic form. In the Upanishads this principle is usually called Brahman. Brahman is connected by some with the god Brahmā or with Brahmanaspati or Brihaspati, *i.e.* Brahman manifests itself in a personal god, and so the conception leans toward monotheism; but other thinkers use Brahman in an impersonal sense, *i.e.* in the sense of a first principle which is the source of all empirical reality. Thus we read, "Brahma, verily, was in the beginning this world. It created the gods and assigned them the rule over these worlds — Agni over this earth, Vāyu over the atmosphere, Sūryā over the heaven, and higher gods than these over the higher worlds." These worlds and gods, the writer says, are manifest, but Brahman itself has "retired to the half beyond." That is, the worlds and the gods that rule over them belong to the realm of empirical reality, whereas Brahman belongs to the invisible world of the Noumenon.

This self-existent Brahman is sometimes spoken of as the

Atman, the Self. That is, Brahman is conceived of in terms of the human self; not, however, in the ordinary sense, but rather in the sense of the ideal self, the essential self after the body and the sense-world has been subtracted. The conception is something like Kant's Noumenal Ego as distinguished from his Empirical Ego, though what the nature of such an ego might be remains rather vague. The noumenal ego is not only like the Atman but is identical with it, as the pregnant phrase, "Tat tvam asi," "That art Thou," expresses it. The Brahman-Atman, then, represents the furthest development of the God-idea which Indian thought had reached by the end of the sixth century B.C. It was a monistic conception which had monotheistic affinities, but on the whole it is best classified under the convenient though vague term Pantheism.

The spirit of this pantheism is summed up most pithily in Chhandogya Upanishad, III, sec. 14: "Brahman in sooth is this All. It hath therein its beginning, end, and breath; so one should worship it in stillness.

"Now man in sooth is made of will. As is man's will in this world, so doth he become on going hence. Will shall he frame.

"Made of mind, bodied of breath, revealed in radiance, true of purpose, ethereal of soul, all-working, all-loving, all-smelling, all-tasting, grasping this All, speaking naught, heeding naught, this very Self within my heart is tinier than a rice-corn or a barley-corn or a mustard-seed or a canary-seed or the pulp of a canary-seed. This my Self within my heart is greater than earth, greater than sky, greater than heaven, greater than these worlds.

"All-working, all-loving, all-smelling, all-tasting, grasping this All, speaking naught, heeding naught, this my Self within my heart, this is Brahma, to Him shall I win on going hence. He that hath this thought hath indeed no doubt."

To sum up, then, in a few words the God-idea current in India when Buddhism arose, we may say that as held by the common people it was either animistic or polytheistic; both terms including a very wide range of beings. In the

c

minds of the keener thinkers it is quite likely that the God-idea was polytheistic in their practical life, *i.e.* the gods were regarded as having real existence and must be taken into account; but in their speculative moods such minds penetrated through this plurality of gods to the conception of a unitary source of all existence, the gods included. This unitary source they conceived of either in terms of their own psychic life, or as an unpicturable First Principle which somehow is the ground of all that the empirical world reveals to us. This latter conception, however, was entirely too abstract to satisfy the religious sense. While the mind demanded a unitary source of all existence, the heart needed more than a mere First Principle. It is in the reconciliation of these two demands of mind and heart that we find the origin of the conception of a supreme personal God which we find in the great currents of Sivaite and Vishnuite thought which have divided India into two great camps from Pre-Buddhistic days down to the present time. The latest and most lofty expression of India's approach to a true monotheistic God-idea is to be found in the writings of men like Rabindranath Tagore; though, of course, this is no longer purely Indian but borrows much from western science and Christian thought.

2. *The Soul-theory.* — The Soul-theory current in India before the sixth century B.C. was equally varied, for the God-idea and the Soul-theory are most intimately connected. In fact, nothing seems truer than the statement that man makes gods in his own image.

Nothing is more natural to primitive man than the belief in his own soul. He not only believes in the existence of his own soul, but sees a soul in everything else. This is the real heart of animism. Polytheism, too, is really a soul-theory. The great objects of nature, or groups of phenomena, behave as they do because they have souls something like the soul that controls the human body. And many gods are nothing but deified ancestors. But Indian thought had advanced far beyond these simple assumptions by the end of the sixth century B.C. It had attempted a critical analysis of what constitutes the real nature of the human soul and speculated as to its destiny. According to one of the oldest Buddhist texts there were current at that time no less than thirty-six different soul-theories, especially theories as to the state of the soul after the death of the body. And there was at least one theory which held that the soul dies with the death of the body. The majority of these theories, especially when seen in the light of early Buddhism which rejected them, impress the modern student of psychology as being rather materialistic. The soul is usually thought of as some refined substance which inhabits the body and at death leaves it.

In the Upanishads, however, we find a conception far more advanced. To show that the soul is not a material substance we are told that it is smaller than a mustard-seed or the pulp of a canary-seed and yet greater than earth, sky and all the worlds; in fact, it is of the same essence with Brahman and even identified with It or Him.

In short we may say, then, that at the end of the sixth century B.C. India believed in the existence of the soul as a reality different from the body and surviving the dissolution of the body through death.

3. *Transmigration.* — One aspect of the Soul-theory is the doctrine of Transmigration. This doctrine goes at least as far back as the eighth century B.C. In the minds of the uneducated masses this belief assumed a very crude form. All objects were endowed with souls. At death when the soul seemed to depart from the body, it simply changed its abode from one body to another. The nature of the new abode, it was believed, was somewhat determined by the character and conduct of the soul during its occupancy of the body which it was leaving. This phase of the doctrine is the heart of the Karma doctrine, which is closely associated with the theory of Transmigration. Of this we shall speak later, as it is one of the foundation stones of Buddhism. We only wish to add here that the doctrine of Karma, like that of Transmigration, had been the common possession of the people of India for several centuries before Buddhism arose.

By the end of the sixth century B.C. it had already been raised into an ethical conception even in the minds of the masses and explained most satisfactorily to them both the inequalities of man's present life and the rewards and punishments meted out in a future life.

Now just as the Soul-theory was held in both crude and philosophic forms, so the doctrine of Transmigration and its associated doctrine of Karma were also held in higher forms by the better thinkers before the days of Gautama. We read, *e.g.*, in the Upanishads that "Man in sooth is made of Will. As is man's will in this world, so doth he become on going hence." That is, where the masses held the doctrines of Transmigration and Karma in the crude form that the soul at death simply passes over into another body already prepared for it and of the character which the deeds of the soul justly deserve, the higher form held that the soul is essentially Will, and by its own deeds creates its own future environment. In short, man becomes what he desires and strives to be — a doctrine not far removed from some of our modern biological theories regarding the origin of the varied organisms of Life.

The destiny of the soul as held by Pre-Buddhistic thought is already exhibited by the above remarks on the doctrines of Transmigration and Karma. We only add that India believed in a happy lot for the good and in hells for the evil. Either goal is reached through gradual stages by the law of Karma and by means of transmigrating from one body to another. To the masses heaven was a life of endless bliss conceived of in terms of what seemed pleasant in this life, while hell was a place filled with all the horrors that a fertile imagination could conjure up. To the philosopher, and especially to the philosophers of the Upanishads, the life of bliss was union with the great Source of All Being, the "identity of Brahman-Atman." This was not simply to be realized after death, but was regarded as a present possibility. The blessed state was realized the moment that the soul became aware of the great fact that it is essentially the same as the Great Atman. Hell, on the other hand, was to be in

ignorance of this great truth. It was real separation from
the Great-All through ignorance.

To sum up, then, in a word the Pre-Buddhistic theories
regarding the soul and its destiny which were current in
India, we may say India believed that the soul had a real
existence, that it wandered from body to body, or from state
to state, according to the law of Karma which had reached
the ethical plane. India believed that the final destiny of
the soul was on the one hand a life of happiness with the
gods or in union with Brahman, and that on the other hand
it was for the evil a life of unhappiness in lower realms of
existence and in hell, or a life of separation from Brahman.

4. *General Social and Religious Condition.* — But however
much Indian thought was occupied with the problems as to
the nature of the soul and its destiny, and however much
people were taught that at the end of the long road which
led through many years of ascetic practices there lay the
highest heaven in which one can escape from the Wheel
of Life, these beliefs were, after all, rather shadowy, and the
average Indian preferred to cling to the few pleasures of the
present life rather than count upon the promised greater
happiness of an uncertain future. "It is not good to leave
this world, for who knows whether one shall exist in yonder
world or not." And Yajnavalkya, the real founder of
Brahmanism, says, "Beyond the grave there is no consciousness." In another place he says, "To be sure a tree
cut down sprouts again from the stump; but from what
roots will a dead man grow up anew?   Do not say, 'from
the seed,' for seed is produced only by the living. He who
has died shall not be born anew." The religious life of the
masses in India before Gautama's day dealt largely with
present material blessings or curses rather than with moral
achievements that were to determine future conditions. So
prayers and sacrifices to the gods centered then, as they do
to-day, around the things that will feed and clothe the body,
and they were not much concerned with the "garments of
righteousness" which alone can make men fit companions of
God. The average man lived in fear of demons and spiteful

gods, and these he sought to propitiate that they might become friendly to him and give him what he needed for a present life of happiness and prosperity.   Even the Brahmin priests, the sole possessors of the "divine knowledge," were apparently more concerned with keeping the people in terror of their power, so that they themselves might live the better by their trade, than with saving men's lives from sin and leading them to a better and higher life.   Yea, these guardians of the "divine knowledge" magnified the horrors of hell that their fees for their work of deliverance might be the fatter.

5. *Signs of a Better Day.* — There was, however, in the sixth century B.C. a growing class of men and women who were exceedingly serious and sincere in their religious life. These were the so-called Wanderers and Hermits.   There may have been some impostors among them, but on the whole they seem to have been held in high regard by the people because of their holiness and wisdom.   The Wanderers were holy, wise men wandering up and down India talking informally with any one who cared for religious and philosophical things.   They came largely from the ranks of the people, though it would seem that there were also some Brahmins among them.   Their appearance may be said to have heralded and helped cause the change that was about to come over the religious life of India, for these peripatetic philosophers prepared the way for the greatest of these wandering teachers, namely, the Buddha Gautama.   The Hermits who lived in the tangled forests and barren caves were less numerous than the Wanderers, but still in their silent haunts of self-mortification and meditation they, too, had a definite share in bringing in the religion of the "World-Honored-One" who was soon to appear.

With these few words as to the environment in which Buddhism arose we pass on to a brief sketch of Gautama's life and the essentials of his religious views.

B. *The Buddha's Life and Teachings*

The Buddha or Siddhārtha — to call him by his personal name — was born at Lumbini near Kapilavastu about 560

B.C. and died at Kusināgarā about 480 [2] B.C. His father Suddhodana, Pure Rice, was not a king as is often said, but probably a noble landed proprietor of the Gautama branch of the S'akya clan. Thus the Buddha is sometimes called Gautama and sometimes S'akyamuni,[3] Teacher of the S'akyans. The S'akyan clan at that time occupied a district a few thousand square miles in area lying partly on the slopes of the Nepalese foothills and partly on the plains to the south. The capital was Kapilavastu, situated about a hundred miles due north of Benares. The clan was no longer independent, but had come under the suzerainty of the adjoining kingdom of Kosala, to the east of which lay the rival kingdom of Magadha, whose ruler Bimbisāra became the Buddha's first royal patron. The young Siddhārtha lost his mother when he was only a few days old and was brought up by his mother's sister, whom his father married. His bringing up was probably like that of most young men of his class, being trained more in manly sports and the arts of the chase and war than in the learning of the priests or the wisdom of the Wanderers and the Hermits. In due time he was married and became the father of one son, Rāhula, who became in the course of time a member of the Buddhist order.

Soon after the birth of his son, at the age of twenty-nine, Siddhārtha abandoned his young wife and child and wandered forth "to seek after what was right," like hundreds of others were doing at that time. Many writers, ancient and modern, have given us beautiful pictures of the "great renunciation" of the Buddha and his struggle with the tempter who tried to make him give up his quest; but, of course, such pictures should not be taken too literally. Relying upon the oldest sources available it would seem, however, that the cause that led to this step on Siddhārtha's part was his growing realization that to be "carnally minded is death," and that the pleasures of the life of the senses are extremely fleeting and can never satisfy the heart; yea, that life as a whole seems to have more shadows than sunlight.

Legend gives us several instances in which this truth was brought graphically to the attention of the young man. Thus one day while attending a plowing festival he saw an earthworm cut in two by the plow. Soon after this, while passing through the city he met in rapid succession a beggar, an old man, a sick man, and a corpse being carried through the streets. One of the oldest authoritative texts puts the following words in the Buddha's mouth, " An ordinary unscholared man though himself subject to old age, not escaped beyond its power, when he beholds another man old is hurt, ashamed, disgusted, overlooking the while his own condition. Thinking that that would be unsuitable to me the infatuation of a youth and his youth departed utterly from me." That is, youth, health and the pleasures of life end in old age, sickness and sorrow; and therefore these transitory things can never give permanent satisfaction. And because they cannot give real satisfaction it is better to abandon them lest they become too deep-rooted. Let man seek "that which is right," for this alone can give permanent satisfaction.

This, in short, seems to have been the thought in young Siddhārtha's mind when he went forth from his home and became a Wanderer in search of salvation. At first he seems to have attached himself to two teachers skilled in the art of cultivating trance states; but finding that this led to nothing permanent, he turned to a life of self-mortification in which he showed such zeal that five disciples attached themselves to him. He followed this path of hardships until it brought him to the very verge of death, without, however, leading him to what he really sought. If a life of luxury and sensual enjoyment leads to pain and death, the other extreme of fasting and self-mortification also seems to lead nowhere but to a miserable death. Siddhārtha therefore abandoned the life of the ordinary ascetic, realizing that physical impoverishment is not of itself spiritual enrichment. His five companions in misery forsook him when he departed from what they regarded as the only true path of holiness. Siddhārtha, however, continued his quest until finally, after six or seven years from the time he first went forth, the hour of his Enlightenment dawned upon him and he understood for the first time the cause of the world's miseries and saw the way of escape from earth's sorrows. He had attained Buddhahood and was now prepared to become the teacher of the Way which was to bring salvation to Asia's millions.

What is it that Siddhārtha, or rather the Buddha, the Enlightened One, saw in that hour of enlightenment? for to know this is to know the heart of his religion. And to know the heart of early Buddhism is to have a norm by which to judge the development of early Buddhism into Mahāyāna Buddhism and the evolution of this into the Buddhism of Japan, which is the furthest development of Mahāyāna Buddhism and constitutes the real subject of this book.

It may be difficult to answer this question accurately, but the general outline, after all, seems fairly clear. It is most succinctly stated in what is called the Three Conceptions (Trividyā) or the Three Law Seals, the Four Noble Truths and the Noble Eightfold Path. These are not three entirely different things, but they more or less overlap. The Three Conceptions, or Law Seals, may be said to represent the general philosophical presuppositions of Gautama's religion; whereas the Four Noble Truths and the Noble Eightfold Path represent his specific insight into man's needs and the way of salvation.

1. *The Three Conceptions.* — The Three Conceptions, or the general philosophical presuppositions underlying the Buddha's religion, may be summarized under the following three heads: [4]

The Impermanence of All Individual Existence.

The Universality of Suffering Inherent in Individuality.

The Non-reality of an Ego-principle.

a. The Impermanence of All Individual Existence. — We saw above that Brahmin speculation had advanced to the point where it asserted the existence of an unitary ground of all beings in the One-All, the Brahman. This conclusion was a result of speculation based upon observation, namely, the general observation that no individual existence as such is ever permanent but is subject to change.   If there is permanency in anything it must be in that which somehow underlies the world of change, *i.e.* in the Brahman.   Now while Gautama had little or nothing to say about the One-All, nor even that it was without change, he did share with the philosophers of his day the view that all individual existence, all the world of phenomena, was subject to change, and that the one word Impermanence best describes the world as we know it.   This is true especially of all living things.   The insect lives but for a few days, the span of life of the average animal is only a few years, the plant world is green to-day and withered to-morrow, and while trees may endure for decades and even centuries, it is still true that all of them are undergoing changes from day to day.   The inanimate world seems more permanent, but it, too, is in a constant flux.   Rivers change their courses, they overflow in flood time and dry up in droughts.   Rocks crumble to pieces and are worn away by time.   Even the eternal hills are made low by the passing of the centuries.   And what is true of nature in general is especially true of human life.   The new-born babe soon becomes the active lad, and a few years see him grow into the young man of twenty or thirty.   Only a few more years and the prime of life is reached and passed, and then comes the inevitable old age and decay ending in death.   Beggar and prince alike share this fate; yea, the greater the glory the more speedy seems its end.

> "The boast of heraldry, the pomp of power,
>   And all that beauty, all that wealth e're gave,
>   Await alike the inevitable hour.
>   The path of glory leads but to the grave."

Change and decay is not alone the fate of man and his immediate environment, but this seems to be the lot of the universe as a whole.   Suns, moons, and stars, of all it may be said "Our little systems have their day, they have their day and cease to be."   Worlds are formed and dissolved, and periods of organization and life are succeeded by periods of chaos and death.   Not even the gods that inhabited the higher realms did Gautama exempt from the law of change. They, too, are bound to the great Wheel of Life, and its eternal revolutions will some day bring their happy lot to an end.   Nothing, absolutely nothing in the realm of individual existence is exempt.   The one word Impermanence must be written across them all.

   b.   The Universality of Suffering Inherent in Individuality. — The second great underlying thought of all the Buddha's teachings and the one of which the Four Great Truths are really a fuller exposition is the thought that all individual existence is inherently an existence of suffering.   In fact, the very condition of individuality, *i.e.* the effort to remain an individual means suffering.   There is an elemental force at work which ultimately destroys every individual, as is announced in the doctrine of Impermanence, and therefore any effort on the part of an individual to oppose this elemental force must result in pain.   Individuality implies limitation, limitation leads to ignorance, ignorance leads to sorrow and suffering.   This is especially true of man.   Being an individual, his first instinct is self-preservation.   Self-preservation leads him to make an effort against the forces that oppose him, and so the fight that never can win has begun; for even though man gains what he seeks, his desires far outrun his achievements, and even his achievements soon crumble to dust and compel him to be separated from all that he has won or sought to win.   This second truth, the Buddha's contemporaries, too, recognized in a measure, but they held it in no such absolute form, for the Brahmin philosopher held that as the individual is really identical with the Brahman, the One-All, absolute loss is impossible.   And the common people of India believed that though this is a life of suffering and sorrow, and death robs man of all his worldly possession, there is nevertheless the future life of happiness as a compensation.

   c.   The Non-reality of an Ego-principle. — The third great underlying thought of Gautama's religion is the denial of an ego-principle, or the self.   Individuals are real, of course, in a relative sense; but since all things are impermanent, the self (at least the empirical self), too, must be impermanent.   The effort of man to make provision for his soul in a future life is of all efforts the most vain.   It is as if a rain-drop sought to retain within itself the rainbow colors caused by the rays of the sun falling on it for a moment or two.   The rain-drop inevitably falls to the ground and then, united with others, it flows down the stream into the ocean, there to be lost in the eternal depths of Oneness; and what has become of the drop as a drop or the rainbow colors it hoped to treasure up for all eternity?   That Gautama did not deny a certain sort of continuity beyond death is seen from the doctrine of Karma which he accepted, but of this we shall speak later.

These three doctrines, then, namely, the doctrine of the impermanency of all individual existence, the doctrine of suffering inherent in individuality, and the non-reality of any abiding ego-principle, or the self, constitute the underlying presuppositions of all of the Buddha's teachings.   And we may say that these are not denied by the Buddhists of any school, though, as we shall see in succeeding chapters, many of the sects of Chinese and Japanese Buddhism proclaim teachings that seem practically the opposites of these.

2. *The Four Noble Truths,*[5] *and the Noble Eightfold Path.*[6] — We come now to the Four Noble or Great Truths and the Noble Eightfold Path which we said constitute the Buddha's more specific insight into man's real condition and the way of salvation from this condition.   We have a comparatively short statement of this core of the Buddha's religion in the sermon of Benares, entitled "The Foundation of the Kingdom of Righteousness."

"There are two extremes which he who has gone forth ought not to follow — habitual devotion on the one hand to the passions, to the pleasures of sensual things, a low pagan way (of seeking satisfaction), ignoble, unprofitable, fit only for the worldly-minded; and habitual devotion, on the other hand, to self-mortification, which is painful, ignoble, unprofitable. There is a Middle Path discovered by the Ta-thāgata [7] — a path which opens the eyes, and bestows under-standing, which leads to peace, to insight, to the higher Wisdom, to Nirvāna. Verily! it is the Aryan Eightfold Path; that is to say, Right Views, Right Aspirations, Right Speech, Right Conduct, Right Mode of Livelihood, Right Effort, Right Mindfulness, and Right Rapture."

"a. Now this is the Noble Truth as to suffering. Birth is attended with pain, decay is painful, disease is painful, death is painful. Union with the unpleasant is painful, painful is separation from the pleasant; and any craving unsatisfied, that, too, is painful. In brief, the five aggre-gates of clinging (that is, the conditions of individuality) are painful.

"b. Now this is the Noble Truth as to the origin of suffer-ing. Verily! it is the craving thirst that causes the renewal of becomings, that is accompanied by sensual delights, and seeks satisfaction, now here now there — that is to say, the craving for the gratification of the senses, or the craving for a future life, or the craving for prosperity.

"c. Now this is the Noble Truth as to the passing away of pain. Verily! it is the passing away so that no passion remains, the giving up, the getting rid of, the emancipation from, the harboring no longer of this craving thirst.

"d. Now this is the Noble Truth as to the way that leads to the passing away of pain. Verily! it is this Aryan Eight-fold Path, that is to say, Right Views, Right Aspirations, Right Speech, Conduct and Mode of Livelihood, Right Effort, Right Mindfulness, and Right Rapture."

An explanation of the fuller meaning of this Aryan (Noble) Eightfold Path may be seen in the following as given by Rhys-Davids in his "Buddhism."

"Right Views (free from superstitions or delusions).

"Right Aspirations (high and worthy of the intelligent, worthy man).

"Right Speech (kindly, open, truthful).

"Right Conduct (peaceful, honest, pure).

"Right Livelihood (bringing hurt or danger to no living thing).

"Right Effort (in self-training and in self-culture).

"Right Mindfulness (the active, watchful mind).

"Right Rapture (in deep meditation on the realities of life)."

Now there is a ring of sincerity and practicality about these words of the Buddha which one misses in the speculative systems of many religious teachers. The Buddha speaks from experience, and while we may not agree with his interpretation of life and his way of salvation, we cannot help but feel that he was dead in earnest in his quest and honest in his solution of Life's problem which he offered to the people of India. The two extremes which man is to avoid, he knew from his own bitter experience. They are extremes into which not only the people of ancient India had fallen, but they are present with us to this day. Life, indeed, is an art; and, after all, very few can strike the happy balance between using the things of sense without abusing them, the happy balance of living in the world without sinking to the level of the world. This discovery of the Buddha is a commonplace truth to us moderns, though the actual walking in the Middle Path of sane moderation seems almost as difficult to-day as it did to the ancients.

When we come to the specific content of The Four Noble Truths proclaimed by the Buddha, the Western mind and heart parts company with him, though much that is implied in these Truths, few would hesitate to accept. That life has much in it of sorrow and suffering, every man who knows life at all must have experienced, but it is not all that can be said about life. Though not blind to pain and evil, the Western mind has ever held to a divine optimism which refuses to give a whole-hearted allegiance to the statement of the first Noble Truth that life is essentially sorrow and pain. And the deep-rooted belief in the goodness of a Personal God known through Christ as the Heavenly Father, will always make the Buddha's solution of life's problems seem quite inadequate and too gloomy. Even in non-christian circles there is in the West a sort of belief that life is good. If we are beaten in the struggle and "the cards seem stacked," we at least enjoy the game of life and want to play it to the end.

Gautama began his quest as many others had begun before him. Like others he had found that life as lived by the ordinary man, namely, the life of the senses and physical enjoyment, was fleeting and ended in old age, sickness and death. If there are pleasures, they are impermanent and seem to be overbalanced by sorrow and suffering. Thus he was brought to formulate his first Noble Truth, that human life is suffering and vanity. This, as we have said above, is not exactly a new truth with Gautama, but it must be admitted that perhaps no one had ever held it with quite such universal application, seeing that he applied it to all individual existence, the gods of the highest heavens included.

Now in the second of the Noble Truths, we have what seems to have been an original [8] conception with the Buddha, namely, his explanation of the cause of human suffering. The seat of all suffering, he said, is to be found in man's desires, especially in that craving thirst which seeks satisfaction through the gratification of the senses. That is, man as he is constituted in his ignorance has a thirst for things which really do not satisfy. This thirst keeps him ever seeking satisfaction without finding it. Some seek happiness in a life of luxury, others seek it in what seem nobler ways; and still others, foregoing all earthly pleasures, seek happiness in a life of bliss with the gods in the world to come. But all such seeking can never satisfy nor lead to anything permanent, for the simple reason that it is all a sort of self-seeking, i.e. it is based on the belief that the self is a permanent reality, which, according to the Buddha, is the greatest of all follies, seeing that no individual existence is permanent as such, but is subject to the great law of change.

In the third Noble Truth the Buddha announced his gospel, namely, that there is a way of escape from this life of suffering. The way of self-seeking, in whatever form it may be held, leads only to a fool's paradise. Especially is trust in the popular gods of Brahmanism a vain thing, for how can they save man when they, too, belong to this world of change and are bound to the Wheel of Life? But there is a way of salvation discovered by the Enlightened One. This way is declared in what constitutes the fourth Noble Truth. It is none other than the Noble Eightfold Path which leads man finally into true salvation, into an enlightenment in which he sees things as they are.

And when man is enlightened and sees things as they really are, what does he see? He sees that all things are impermanent and that all individual existence is inherently an existence of suffering, that in order to escape from this life of suffering the truly wise must give up all desires for individuality and the things that go to make up such a life. That is, the Enlightened One sees that what we ordinarily call the self is the greatest of all illusions, and hence to know this is to get free from the bondages of individual existence. Freedom from the bondages of individuality is what constitutes real salvation.

Now this denial of the reality of the self seems very strange, at least to the average Western mind; for at once the thought suggests itself that if the belief in the reality of the self is an illusion, it must be an illusion to something, or some one; and what is that "something, or some one"? And still further, if the Enlightened One knows that the belief in the existence of the ego is an illusion, then what, or who, is it that knows this?

Such questions make it clear that the Buddha either did not think the problem through, or that, after all, he must have believed in the existence of a "something" that knows. We are rather inclined to believe that both these alternates are true, i.e. the Buddha neither thought his position clear through nor did he deny absolutely that there was a "something" that knew, which we have a perfect right to call the true or higher self.[9]

The Buddha himself apparently admitted that he did not think his position clear through, for it seems more and more evident that he had no special fondness for metaphysical problems, and that he rather side-stepped them when he could. What he was primarily interested in was the deliverance of suffering humanity from the bondages of sin and passion. Where others were theorizing about the cosmogonic problem, the nature of the soul and its relation to the Brahman, he was preaching the Noble Eightfold Path of practical ethical conduct which was to free man from suffering. What lay at the end of the road of redemption from suffering, he was not so much concerned with; in fact, he felt that speculations on this subject only kept men from obtaining deliverance. Thus we read in one of the oldest and most authentic passages on the subject as follows:

"Unwisely does one consider, 'Have I existed in ages past, . . . shall I exist in ages to be, do I exist at all, am I, how am I? This is a being, whence is it come, whither will it go?' Considerations such as these is walking in the jungle of delusions. These are the things one should consider: 'This is suffering, this is the origin of suffering, this is the cessation of suffering, this is the way that leads to the cessation of suffering.' From him that considers thus his fetters fall away."

One thing only the Buddha was certain lay at the end of the road of suffering, and that was freedom and perfect peace. Whether it was the freedom and peace of annihilation or whether it was the freedom and peace of a positive existence, he did not state clearly. In fact, his answer to such questions usually was a list of the Great Indeterminates, chief of which are the following:

(1 and 2). Whether the world in its real substance is eternal or not.

(3 and 4). Whether the world is infinite or not.

(5 and 6). Whether the soul is the same as the body or different from it.

(7 and 8). Whether a man exists in any way or not after death.

"The jungle, the desert, the puppet-show, the writhing, the entanglements of such speculations is accompanied by sorrow, wrangling resentment, the fever of excitement. It conduces

D

neither to detachment of heart nor to freedom from lusts, nor to tranquillity, nor to peace, nor to wisdom, nor to the insight of the higher stages of the path, nor to Nirvāna."

Thus while it is true in general that the Buddha seemed to base his teachings on certain philosophical presuppositions, the chief of which we have given above, it seems equally true that he had not thought himself through to a clear position on even those points which his main teachings seem to imply; or if he did think himself through, he did not follow up his conclusions very consistently or positively.

3. *Karma* [10] *and Self.* — Now while the Buddha was not positive as to the continuation of the Enlightened One (the Arhat) beyond this life, and while he apparently denied the reality of the self and placed such problems among the Great Indeterminates, he nevertheless did assert positively that for the unenlightened man there was a "something" which continued beyond death. This "something" was a man's Karma. In fact, his very plan of salvation was primarily a way by which Karma should be destroyed, or exhausted, so that it would not again build up an individual being and cause suffering.

But what is meant by Karma and how does it differ from the self? This is a question to which no really satisfactory answer can be given, and illustrates what we said above, namely, that the Buddha did not think his position clear through, or at least that he did not explain just what it was.

The doctrine of Karma, as we said above, is one that was common to India long before the days of the Buddha. It was closely associated with that other great doctrine of Indian thought, the doctrine of the Transmigration of the soul. Gautama apparently denied the latter but not the former. He held to a transmigration from one existence to another so that a man's present misfortunes may be the effect of the sins committed in a former existence, but the identity of the present man with the man of the former existence was not a personal identity, but only a Karma identity. That is, the soul, or the self, does not pass from one body to another, as was held by most of the thinkers of Gautama's day, but only Karma passed over.   There is no memory or consciousness of a self; there is only Karma that endures.   Therefore if one is to understand the Buddha's position one must understand the meaning of the baffling conception expressed by the word Karma.

The word Karma expresses in general the doctrine of the universal reign of the law of Cause and Effect.   Of all doctrines none is more axiomatic than this causal-nexus axiom, and so the Buddha, like every true Indian of his day, accepted it with all its accustomed rigor.   Though he refused to go back step by step through the causal-nexus to the First Great Cause, he nevertheless held with others that everything that exists has a cause, and every effect in turn becomes the cause of future effects.   That is the meaning of the most famous of all Buddhist stanzas which one finds engraved on thousands of votive gifts to Buddhist shrines in India, and which reads:

"Of all the phenomena sprung from a cause
The Buddha the cause hath told,
And he tells, too, how each shall come to its end,
Such alone is the word of the Sage."

Now this causal-nexus axiom when applied to the human individual means nothing else than that a man is at any one moment just what his deeds and desires of the past have made him; and in the future he will become just what his deeds and desires of the past and the present are making him.   The words of the poet have for the Buddhist a literal meaning when he says:

"Our deeds follow us from afar,
And what we have been makes us what we are."

Good deeds will produce a good result; and evil deeds, an evil result; or to use the Indian mode of thought, a man's good Karma will tend to make a good individual, and his evil Karma will tend to make an evil individual.   The resultant is the combination of the two.   Now at death the individual falls apart into the component elements of individuality, namely, the five Aggregates,[11] Skandhas (bodiliness, sensation, perception, predisposition and consciousness), but the Karma, or the Tendency-energy, of the present life remains; and in the future it will collect other Skandhas which will function as an individual in harmony with the Karma, or Tendency-energy, which creates them. There is, then, no memory or consciousness which passes over from one birth to another, but there is this mysterious energy which is other than the body and the functioning of the empirical ego that does pass over from one individual to another, or rather, that builds up a new individual again when the old individual is dissolved in death.

From this it seems clear that the Buddha did not believe in the existence of the soul in the sense in which the ordinary philosophers of his day believed it. And further it seems clear that he did not believe in the existence of the spiritual self in the sense in which we moderns believe when we hold in our doctrine of personal immortality that beyond death there is a continuation of memory and a consciousness of real identity. That mysterious Tendency-energy known as Karma is, then, neither the mere energy resulting from the physical forces that make up the human body; nor is it, in the second place, simply the sum total of the functioning of the five Skandhas, seeing that it is the energy which collects the new Skandhas of the new individual in each successive stage of incarnation. And in the third place, it cannot be said to be like the spiritual self of the modern psychologist, but rather does it seem to be like that mysterious energy which we know in us as Will, especially like the Blind Will, or the Will-to-be of Schopenhauer's [12] system. It is this "blind will-to-be" which is the real cause of all becoming, and as long as it persists it will continue to create for itself new bodies and individuals after the old are dissolved through death. The empirical individual, which is but a composite of the five Skandhas and the seat of all sorrow and pain, ceases to exist when this combination is dissolved at death, but Karma, or that Will-energy, continues and creates the conditions of a new empirical individuality and so continues the life of suffering.

Nearer than this we cannot define what is meant by this baffling conception of Karma and rebirths, and by the Buddha's conception of the empirical ego.

4. *The Buddha's Mode of Salvation.* — Whatever, then, Karma may mean or may not mean, the aim and purpose of the Buddha's way of salvation is to break the Karma-chain so that it will not continue and form another individual and so prolong the life of suffering. The true Arhat is one whose Karma has been completely exhausted and so is assured of deliverance from the Wheel of Life. "Looking for the maker (Karma) of this tabernacle I shall have to run through a course of many births, so long as I do not find; and painful is birth again and again. But now, maker of the tabernacle, thou hast been seen; thou shalt not make up this tabernacle again. All thy rafters are broken, thy ridgepole is sundered, thy mind approaching Nirvāna has attained to extinction of all desires." This is one of the best authenticated passages of early Buddhism and seems to bear out what we have said, namely, that what the Buddha aimed at above everything else was to find deliverance from individual existence.

Another passage which illustrates the way the Buddha expressed himself on this central doctrine reads as follows: "As a flame blown out by the wind goes out and cannot be reckoned as existing; so a sage delivered from name and body disappears and cannot be reckoned as existing." And when his disciple asks him, "But has he only disappeared, or does he not exist, or is he only free from sickness?" the Buddha replies, "For him there is no form and that by which they say he is, exists for him no longer." Whether this may mean that the sage does exist in a higher form though free from the forms of the present life, is a question not easily answered. One thing, however, is certain, namely, that the Buddha did mean that the sage was not to be born again into this life, and this was for him the important consideration; that is what constituted the salvation he offered.

He, then, who would win this salvation let him walk in the Middle Way, the Noble Eightfold Path; for at the end of this path he shall surely find deliverance. He will become a true Arhat who can face the future in perfect peace, for he knows that henceforth there is for him no bondage. This blessed assurance gives the only joy worth having; it alone can satisfy man's desire. The Arhat feels no need of the gods, for he is infinitely superior to them. They are still bound to the Wheel of Life even though they may be on the top side now. The future will certainly bring them to the bottom again, and then they will be no better off than other beings. The Arhat, on the other hand, is neither on the top side nor on the bottom of the Wheel of Life; he is totally free from it.

Now from all that has been said thus far of the kernel of the Buddha's teachings it is clear that he placed the emphasis quite differently from where it was placed by the religious teachers of his day or from where it is usually placed. He agreed with the thought of his day that salvation is primarily "an escape from the evils of existence," and also with much of the thought of his day in the belief that, after all, man must save himself. But he held these two doctrines with a rigor with which few held them; and because of this he differed rather widely both from the thought of his own age and the thought of many minds in all ages in that he left practically no room for the God-idea or for a real future life of the individual — two cardinal doctrines of practically all religions.

It is not true that the Buddha was an out-and-out atheist, as is frequently asserted. Of course, if by an atheist is meant one who does not accept the Christian conception of God or the theistic conception in general, then he was an atheist. And it is also true that he had very little to say either about the Brahman of the philosophers of his day or of the gods of the popular pantheon. But it is not true that he denied either the existence of the former or the relative existence of the latter. The most that can be said is that he regarded the speculations about the Absolute as a waste of time, *i.e.*

he seemed to be an agnostic rather than an out-and-out atheist. And the gods of the common people he regarded as not being worthy of either the fear or the reverence given them. As we said, he did not exactly deny their existence, but rather held that they, too, belonged to the world of change and decay; so that no permanent help could come from them. How could these gods really help mankind? seeing that they could not deliver themselves from the "dread cycle of existence" to which they were still bound. Greater than the gods was he who like himself had attained enlightenment. And the God of Brahmin speculation was too far removed from the real needs of humanity to be of any true help. In view of the impotency of the popular gods and the unknowability of the Brahman, man must work out his own salvation with patience and persistency. Thus, though theoretically the Buddha cannot be regarded as an atheist, practically he lived as one who was without God and with hope only in himself.

It is only natural that the average Indian did not understand the Buddha's conception of Karma or his explanation of the cause of suffering. And it also seems that his early disciples did not all follow to its logical conclusion his general attitude towards the God-idea or the future-life-idea. Since he placed these questions among the Great Indeterminates he could not have been very positive in his teachings on these points, and so it is safe to say that at least the ordinary Buddhist never gave up entirely his trust in the gods nor his hope of a happy future life. Even among the thinkers in the early Buddhist community it would seem that salvation was regarded as more than a mere "escape from the dread cycle of existence," but to this was also added the thought that it was at the same time a happy future existence of real content. The word Nirvāna may mean the peace of annihilation, but it is not the only expression used by the early Buddhists. To be sure, when the Buddhist speaks from the standpoint of the ethical life and the struggle with the lower passions, salvation is conceived of as the "great emancipation," "the end of craving," "the going out,"

or "extinction"; but there are other expressions which have
a positive content. Thus the state of the Arhat is spoken
of as a "state of purity," "the supreme," "the transcendent,"
"the uncreate," "the tranquil," "the unchanging," "the
unshaken," "the imperishable." Such expressions as these
are a little too positive in content to stand for total annihilation. Therefore it would seem that while the Buddha was
himself not especially interested in what lay at the end of
the Noble Eightfold Path except that it meant to him deliverance from the bondage of individual existence, his followers put more content into this conception of salvation.

But whether the general run of disciples followed the
Buddha in these great questions or not, they could understand his practical ethical teachings, which, after all, was
the main purpose of his religion. The Middle Way,[13] the
Noble Eightfold Path, was a true way of deliverance from
the lower passions and the coarser sins; and to the extent
that India walked in this way to that extent it was a better
India.

The weakness of Gautama's religion is therefore not so
much in what he taught positively, but rather in thinking
that religion is possible without having some positive ideas
as to the great problems of God, the soul and its eternal
destiny. It is not enough to offer mankind a deliverance
from a present evil; the heart craves also a present and
future good, and fellowship with a power that makes these
certain. To be sure, practical ethical teachings and deliverance from the lower passions are more profitable than much
idle speculation about metaphysical problems, as was engaged in by Gautama's contemporaries, and this is why his
religion gained such a speedy hold on India; but, after all,
the heart needs more and demands some answer to these
great problems. These questions will not down, and while
it may be impossible to give perfectly satisfactory answers
to them, the teacher of religion who declines to make an
answer, as the Buddha seems to have done as a rule, will
find that either his system will soon fade away or that his
followers will try to answer these questions for themselves.

This latter fate is what befell Gautama's religion. Even in the Buddha's own lifetime it would seem, as we said, that the average disciple never gave up entirely his allegiance to the popular gods nor his hope of a happier future life. And in the course of the centuries, as we shall see in succeeding chapters, the Buddhist philosophers themselves not only gave answers to these deepest questions of the human heart, but frequently in a way that was quite contrary to the conceptions which the Buddha seems to have held, or at least contrary to what some of his positive teachings seem to imply. All the gods and spirits of the Indian pantheon (and later the gods of the Chinese and Japanese pantheon) came back into Buddhism with a glory they hardly had in pre-Buddhistic days. And the future life for the individual was painted in the most positive and lurid colors which the imagination could picture.

But we are going ahead of our subject, for this belongs to succeeding chapters. We must now resume the narrative of Gautama's life after he became the Buddha, and relate what success he had in bringing his message of salvation outlined above to the people of India.

C. *The Success of the Buddha's Ministry*

Tradition has it that while Gautama was engaged in his quest of truth and just when he had obtained enlightenment he was harassed with attacks from Māra, the Buddhist tempter, but he did not yield to these temptations. To be sure, he gave up, as we have said, the life of self-mortification, which to some appeared as a return to the lusts of the flesh, but he only gave up one of the extremes of life without falling into the other extreme. He rigidly adhered to the Middle Path of moderation. The great temptation therefore did not lie along this line, though many Buddhist texts have also much to say of how the Buddha overcame these grosser temptations. After the hour of illumination had dawned upon him the subtle temptation came to him that the great truth which he had discovered was too profound for this stupid world and that he had better forthwith enter into Nirvāna, taking the secret with him. But the World-Honored-One also overcame this temptation; and instead of selfishly keeping the secret to himself, he began his great work of instructing the people of India in the secrets of the Four Great Truths and the Noble Eightfold Path.

The Buddha's first disciples, it would seem, were the five mendicants who had been his companions in the forests of Uruvelā, but who had forsaken him when he left the way of austerities for the Middle Way of moderation. Naturally they were prejudiced against him after their experience, but so wonderful was his way of salvation that they entered it gladly as soon as he proclaimed it unto them. Beginning with these five, his disciples soon became numerous. They came from all classes, for the Buddha's religion was not a protest against India's caste system, as has been held by some. It was rather above caste and welcomed men from every station in life. To be sure, he attacked the Brahmin priests of his day, but largely because he felt that their false conceit about Vedic learning and ritual observances not only did not save man, but became a real hindrance to salvation. They were blind leaders of the blind and needed to be taught as much as those whom they tried to lead. Let them abandon their false learning and enter the one Way which is for all castes because it is above caste. Apparently a good many Brahmins did leave their own rank and entered the community of the Enlightened One. Some converts came over from rival sects [14] which were just then coming into life. Some came from the general class of Wanderers and Hermits of whom we spoke above and who belonged to no particular sect or system. The majority of the disciples, however, came from the people in general who were as sheep without a shepherd, lost in the desert of the lower passions and sin.

Just what constituted discipleship may be hard to say; but it would seem that rather early in Buddhist history the Triple Confession was set up as the door of entrance to the order, namely, the confession, "I take refuge in the Buddha, I take refuge in the Doctrine, I take refuge in the Order." Naturally, as was the custom of the day, there were certain simple rules to regulate the daily conduct of those who joined the order. The yellow robe, the shaven head and the begging bowl seem early to have been the outward badge of the monk, though the common believer did not go that far in his outward change of life. Beyond subscribing to the above-mentioned triple confession the common believer probably subscribed to nothing further than the first five of the ten Buddhist commandments which are a prohibition of: (1) the destruction of life, (2) theft, (3) unchastity, (4) falsehood, and (5) the use of intoxicating drinks. Naturally the monks had to observe beyond these the remaining of the ten commandments, which are a prohibition of: (6) eating at forbidden hours, (7) frequenting worldly amusements or spectacles, (8) using perfumes and ornaments, (9) sleeping on a raised couch, and (10) receiving gifts of money. In the course of time these simple rules were elaborated and developed into a rather rigorous code of discipline, though it would seem that this was not done at the Buddha's behest. In fact, it was over contentions as to what constituted the proper discipline that the Buddhist church, even before the death of the Buddha, began to develop the seeds which soon grew up into numerous schisms.

Of the Buddha's mode of life and activity during his long ministry of forty-five years we know very little definitely. It would seem that nine months of the year he spent in wandering up and down the kingdoms of Magadha and Kosala (the modern Bihar and Oudh), proclaiming his way of salvation to whomsoever would listen. The remaining three months, *i.e.* the rainy season, he spent with his disciples in one or the other of his favorite places such as Rajagriha in Veluvana or Sravāstī in Jetavana, instructing them in the fuller meaning of his doctrines. The latter place seems to have been a particularly favorite spot, as may be seen from the fact that many sutras begin with the formula, "Thus I have heard; once dwelt the Master at Sravāstī in Jetavana, the Park of Anāthapindika." This beautiful spot, like other similar places, was a gift of some admiring wealthy believer and proves indirectly what a hold the Buddha had on the upper classes of society.

These gathering places became the centers from which went forth the Buddhist disciples in ever growing numbers. They went forth not in companies, nor even in pairs as did the disciples of Christ, but singly in order that the teaching might be spread the more rapidly. In the course of time these temporary abodes became permanent places of residence and formed the beginning of that chain of Buddhist monasteries which stretches from Ceylon in the south through central and eastern Asia to the Hokkaidō in northeastern Japan.

Apparently early in the Buddha's ministry, he gained the sympathy of the ruling classes, and King Bimbisara of Magadha in particular seems to have been his patron. But it was not only because he gained the ear of the ruling classes that the Buddha's religion spread so rapidly and without much opposition; rather does it seem that a remarkable spirit of tolerance prevailed in the India of that distant day, so that the Buddha and his disciples could go where they pleased and talk with whomsoever they met. Of course there was some opposition from the Brahmins and the heretical sects which arose simultaneously with Buddhism, but it was the kind of opposition that helps rather than hinders a new teaching.

The most serious obstacle to the new faith came not from without, but from within; the real enemies were those of his own spiritual household. Some sources have it that even as early as the ninth year of his ministry there were quarrels and divisions among his disciples. While it is difficult to distinguish between legend and real history in the early Buddhist records, it would seem that the Buddha had among his inner circle of disciples not only his St. John (Ananda) but also his Judas Iscariot (Devadatta). Devadatta was ambitious to become the head of the order after the Master's death. When he was denied the request to be made the head, he sought to destroy his master by entering into a plot with Ajātasatru, the son of King Bimbisara, who dethroned and imprisoned his own father. But while the latter succeeded in his unholy ambition, Devadatta's success was not so immediate or complete. It would seem, however, that while he did not become the head of the Buddhist order as a whole, he succeeded in gaining a considerable following, and so caused the first serious schism in the Buddhist ranks. As late as the seventh century A.D. there were monks who followed the discipline set up by Devadatta, though some sources say that the rebellion was only of short duration.

Another difficulty that confronted the Buddha was the woman problem. What attitude should the new religion take toward the weaker sex? Buddhism, we said, was above caste, but the sex problem seems to have been more troublesome. As a young man of twenty-nine Siddhārtha, before he became the Buddha, had forsaken his wife and child, for family life was too much a life of earthly fetters for one who wished to walk in the path of holiness. It would seem, however, that afterwards the Buddha returned to his home, not to assume the family relationships, but to proclaim his way of salvation to his wife and child and to his father and other relatives. We also read of women from all classes who heard his message gladly. And how could the Buddha deny salvation to woman when he professed to proclaim a way of salvation for all sentient beings?

But while the new religion was to be a way of salvation for all, it did not mean that all were equally near the kingdom. And woman, just because she is woman, was regarded by the Buddha as being at least one step further removed than man. When the question arose as to whether she was to be admitted to the Buddhist order on equal terms with men, he hesitated and only with great reluctance did he finally yield the point. The following supposed conversation between him and his beloved disciple Ananda illustrates his attitude.

"How shall we behave toward a woman?" asks Ananda. "Avoid the sight of her," replies the Buddha. "But if we see her, Sir, what shall we do then?" "Not speak to her, Ananda." "And if she speaks to us, Sir, what then?" "Then be wary, Ananda."

Another passage equally characteristic reads, "O monks, look not upon a woman. If you meet a woman do not look at her and be careful not to speak with her. If you do speak with her say to yourself, 'I am a monk, I must live in this corrupt world like an uncontaminated lotus blossom.' An elderly woman regard as your mother, one a little older than yourself, as an elder sister, and a younger woman as your younger sister." Naturally in going from house to house with his begging bowl, the monk frequently came in contact with women, and so the regulations were rather strict. The monk was to cover his face with his outer garment and with downcast eyes was to receive what was offered him and then take his departure, uttering a blessing but without looking at the fair giver. The scriptures are full of records of temptations overcome, but, alas, also of failures.

While Buddhist nuns have never been as numerous as the monks or played as prominent a part in the history of this religion, it is nevertheless true that woman has had a big share in spreading the teachings of the Buddha, especially through her deeds of mercy and labors of love. In fact, woman has done a good deal more for Buddhism than Buddhism has done for woman; especially does this seem to be the case when compared with what Christianity has done for her. The attitude of the Buddha toward woman was, of course, a very natural attitude for an Indian of that day to take, and it simply shows that he was, after all, very much a product of his own age and environment. The Buddhist apologist may say that it was an accommodation of his teachings to meet the needs of the times, and there is an element of truth in this, but the succeeding centuries in all Buddhist lands have proved beyond a shadow of a doubt that the religion which came to save all sentient beings and which undoubtedly has done much to exalt gentleness and kindness towards all creatures, has done comparatively little for woman as woman.

The Buddha ended his long ministry of about forty-five years, ripe in age and experience. He had been spending the rainy season near Vaisali when he became seriously ill. He recovered somewhat and went on his way to Kusināgarā. Along the way he stopped to dine with a disciple who gave him fat pork which is said to have brought on the end soon after reaching Kusināgarā. Ananda, his favorite disciple, was at his side and wept bitterly when he saw the last hour approaching. The dying Buddha comforted him with these words: "Let it suffice, O Ananda, grieve not, neither mourn. Have I not told you that man must endure the separation from all that is dear and pleasant. How is it possible, O Ananda, that that which is born, which becomes, which is compounded and subject to change, that this does not end? It must be so. You, O Ananda, have long served the Perfect One with love and care, with benefit and good, without deceit and incessantly, with heart, mouth and hands. You have done good, O Ananda; be diligent, soon you will be free from evil." And again he said, "It may be, O Ananda, that you harbor the thought the doctrine has lost its master, and that there is no longer any master. You should not look at the matter in this way. The Law and the Discipline which I have taught and proclaimed, these are your master after my departure." He then made certain arrangements for the future, asked the monks three times whether any of them had any doubts in regard to the teachings, and when all kept silent he said, "O Disciples: I speak to you. Everything that becomes is transient. Work diligently for your salvation." With these words on his lips he passed away.

The funeral ceremonies are said to have continued for seven days; on the eighth day the remains were cremated and the ashes were divided among the various rulers and nobles who had become adherents of the new faith. A portion was given to the S'akyan clan, who buried the sacred remains and erected on the spot a stūpa. It is probably this stūpa which was discovered in 1898 by W. C. Peppé at Piprava in Tarai. This, when opened, was found to contain an urn inclosing various objects of crystal and gold. Below this urn was found a large sandstone sarcophagus brought evidently from some distance. Within the sarcophagus was an urn with an inscription in the Magadhi language written in the old Brahmi script which reads as follows:

"This vessel containing the relics of the exalted Buddha of the tribe of the S'akyans is the reverent gift of the brothers and sisters with the children and women."

Besides this urn the sarcophagus contained another urn and two vases, all of which were half-filled with ornaments of gold, silver, diamonds, crystals of various shapes such as stars, flowers, men, women, birds, elephants, etc., also gold plates with images of lions and the mystical Svastika.

This discovery gives the early Buddhist records and traditions an atmosphere of historical reality which, perhaps, they did not have before; and while we are still a long way from knowing the full facts of the Buddha's life, no one can safely deny any longer the historicity of the personality of Gautama Buddha.

If after what we have said about the kernel of early Buddhism the reader wonders how it was possible that such a doctrine could win such a speedy popularity and success, we might remark that the Buddha was himself often better than his logic; and, after all, it was the practical side of his teachings that appealed to the people of India. As a later Buddhist philosopher put it, "The doctrine in its logical fullness was a teaching only for the wise, not for fools," but practically the Buddha preached the importance of conquering the evil passions, overcoming the five hindrances of sensuality, ill-will, torpor of mind or body, worry, and wavering. "To have faith and good works, to renounce the pomp and vanities of life, to show kindness to every living thing, to seek salvation, to understand and so finally to leave no second self behind to suffer again" in this life of suffering — these were the things which appealed to India, and especially to those who were surfeited with the things of life and were world-weary. And even if salvation and Nirvāna did mean total annihilation to some, we should never forget that life to many in India has never had the fascination and interest that it has for the Westerner, and the highest bliss to many could only be the bliss of non-existence. It is not merely ceasing to exist in this present bodily life, for then suicide would be the remedy, but ceasing from being bound to the Wheel of Life, "the dread cycle of birth, suffering, and death" on and on without an end. It may be difficult for the Westerner, with his love and passion for life and self-expression, to understand this point of view, but in India with its hot climate, its poverty and suffering, the pessimistic mood which looks upon life as a great evil rather than an achievable good, seems natural. In fact, no matter what system of philosophy or religion holds the field in India, this pessimistic mood seems to run through all of them, and while the Buddha worked some practical reforms and on the whole stood for a loftier ethical life than the systems of his day, in the last analysis his system, too, was of one piece with the others. He, too, saw life as incurably evil and held that the only way of escape from this evil was to cut as much as possible the bonds which tie man to life. Even the bonds of love which tie a husband to his wife and a father to his child had to be cut if freedom is to be gained. So while the Western mind of to-day may marvel at the quick success of Gautama's religion in India, it is not strange when understood in the light of its time and environment.

The Buddha's religion was undoubtedly the best of its day. It delivered men from the fears and superstitions of a gross polytheism and demonology and taught kindness and the way of moderation to all. But even better than his religion was the founder himself. Strange as it may seem, he who apparently denied the existence of a true personality was one of the greatest personalities the world has seen. The unbiased student will have no hesitation in recognizing his essential sincerity in facing life's deepest problems. Such sincerity, linked with real ability, was bound to make a great impression upon the life of India. The Buddha

E

must therefore be classed among the great men of the world, and the religion which he founded five hundred years before Christ is to this day one of the living world-religions with which Christianity has to reckon.

Of its progress in India and its spread into the surrounding countries as well as its change from its primitive form into Mahāyāna Buddhism we shall deal in our next chapter.

CHAPTER II

DEVELOPMENT OF PRIMITIVE BUDDHISM INTO MAHĀYĀNA BUDDHISM

IN the preceding chapter we tried to give very briefly the circumstances under which Buddhism arose in India as well as a concise statement of what may be regarded as the essence of Gautama's teachings. We showed how Buddhism was a tremendous reduction of Brahmanism. Much of the metaphysical speculations about the Brahman, the One All, and the relation of the individual to it was brushed aside as vain mental gymnastics, for such problems, the Buddha held, were beyond the powers of the human mind. And many of the beliefs regarding spirits, gods, and demons innumerable which filled the world of the common people he denounced as mere ignorance and superstition. So far did he go in his opposition to the views generally held by the masses that in some of his sayings he went to the extreme position of apparently denying the reality of the human self and therefore the possibility of a future personal existence. And his attitude towards speculations on metaphysical problems, especially the problem as to the underlying core of all reality, led him to a position which for all practical purposes was one of atheism, or at least an agnostic position, so that he had little or nothing to say about God.

This is the negative side of the Buddha's teachings. The positive side clusters around the Four Noble Truths and the Middle Way or the Noble Eightfold Path. The essence of the teachings in short is this: Life is essentially pain and sorrow. Pain and sorrow have their roots in ignorance and our passionate cravings and desires. The tap-root, as it were, of all our desires and cravings is the desire for self-

expression; yea, the blossom and fruit on the tree of ignorance is the belief in the reality of the (empirical) self. Now
it is possible to escape from this life of sorrow and pain —
not by being saved into an eternal heaven by the gods, or
by an almighty God, but by a slow process of (self-)culture
and discipline until one attains enlightenment, in which one
sees that all the things of our life are mere shadows and
illusions and that our very self (at least the empirical self)
has no real existence. This state of enlightenment is attained
through obedience to the Middle Way, the Noble Eightfold Path of Right Views, Right Aspirations, Right Speech,
Right Conduct, Right Mode of Livelihood, Right Effort,
Right Mindfulness, and Right Rapture.

We also said that while these teachings about the non-
reality of the self and the practical denial of the existence
of God were the logical conclusion of Gautama's main position and the truth as held by the Buddhist philosopher,
they were never held in that extreme form by the general
run of Buddhist believers, and these never gave up entirely
the belief in the existence of God, or the gods, and the belief in the reality of the self and a future personal existence.

Now in this chapter we wish to trace very briefly the
spread of Buddhism into the neighboring countries and its
development into what is known as Mahāyāna Buddhism,
which, as we shall see as we go on, is often radically different from Gautama's teachings in its attitude to even the
cardinal elements of religion.

A. *The Buddhism of Asoka's Day*

When the founder of Buddhism died, about the year 480
B.C., the new religion had already won for itself a real place
in India's life. It was apparently popular with all classes
of society, and the Buddha was in favor with high and low,
even kings and noblemen delighting to do him honor and
helping further his cause. Just how far the new religion
spread during the lifetime of its founder it would be difficult to say. It would seem, however, that the region between the Ganges and the Himālayas, with Patna and Allaha-

bad as the eastern and western limits, is the general field of its early activities.

It must not, however, be supposed that all was plain sailing in the early Buddhist community. Not only were the Brahmins beginning to show active opposition to the new faith, but there were also fightings within the Buddhist ranks. We have already spoken of Devadatta's rebellion during the lifetime of the Buddha. Immediately after the founder's death we hear of the monk Subhadra addressing the grieving disciples with the rebellious words: "Brethren, quit your wailing and mourning. We are fortunate in being free of the great ascetic. He worried us with his saying, 'this is proper and that is not proper.' Now we shall do what we please and whatever does not suit us we shall not do." These words show that the seeds of discord had long been sown and that they would soon spring up and bear fruit. It is not surprising, therefore, to read that when, soon after the founder's death, the first great council [1] of the Buddha's disciples was held at Rajagriha, at which a part of the early canon was fixed (probably a part of the Vinaya and Sūtra pitakas), there were many monks (500 according to one tradition), headed by Purāna, who did not accept the findings of the official body and so held a council of their own. And at a second great council, held at Vaisālī about one hundred years after the first council, we find that Buddhism is already beginning to be hopelessly divided, there being some eighteen or twenty different schools.

With these divisions in the ranks of Buddhism it is not strange that the new religion found it difficult to cope with Brahmanism, which under the stimulus provided by the heretical teachings of the day was showing signs of new life. Then in addition to this a great calamity from the outside befell the home of Buddhism. Northern and central India was overrun by the armies of Alexander the Great; and with war and rumors of war Buddhism found itself more and more circumscribed. Obviously a religion which made all self-expression wrong and regarded even the killing of an insect as an accumulation of evil Karma, would not be very well fitted to help resist the foreign invader. It is true that Alexander's hold on India was not strong and did not last long, for after his death Chandragupta, founder of the Mauryan dynasty, established a strong kingdom of his own, one which also included the kingdom of Magadha, the geographical center of early Buddhism. The significance for Buddhism of the founding of the new kingdom under Chandragupta was the fact that Chandragupta's grandson, King Asoka (*i.e.* Asoka Priyadarsin, to be distinguished from the King Asoka who lived about a century earlier, known as Kalasoka or the Black Asoka), was a great patron of Buddhism. He is sometimes called the Constantine of Buddhism.

During Asoka's reign, which extended probably over the middle decades of the third century B.C., Buddhism may be said to have been changed from a local cult to a real world-religion. Asoka had waded through blood to his throne, and then he spent the remainder of his life in spreading a religion of retirement, mercy, and peace. Fortunately for the historian King Asoka carved his imperial edicts upon pillars of stone which are being found to-day all over what was once his extensive kingdom. On at least three different stones and in different parts of India were found the names of five Greek kings written in two different alphabets. These five kings are: Antiochus Theos, who reigned at Antioch from B.C. 262–247; Ptolemy Philadelphus, who reigned at Alexandria from B.C. 285–247; Antigonus Gonatas of Macedon, who reigned from B.C. 287–239; Magas of Cyrene, B.C. 308–258; and Alexander of Epirus, B.C. 272–219. From these inscriptions on Asoka's stone pillars we can fix fairly accurately the date of this royal patron of Buddhism, and his date becomes one of the very few guideposts for a study of the beginnings of this religion. Now during the eighteenth year of Asoka's reign (probably about the year 245 B.C.) he called a great religious council at Pātaliputra. The object of this council was apparently to purify the Buddhist order. Many abuses and great laxity had crept in. In fact, it would seem that for seven years the ordinary confessional had been entirely neglected by the monks, and many called themselves Buddhists who knew little or nothing of the master's teachings. Tradition has it that 60,000 monks were excommunicated as heretics and their representatives were not admitted to this great council, which is usually regarded as the Third Great Council. One thousand monks versed in the doctrine and true to the discipline as handed down constituted the official body. The leader of this third great council was Maudgaliputra, and it was he who at this time is supposed to have composed the famous Kathā-Vatthu which in the Pali version is preserved to this day and which probably gives us the most authentic statement of what orthodox Buddhists in the third century B.C. held to be the true teachings of the founder of their religion. It also gives us a glimpse of what were the main digressions from the orthodox position.

This third great council was of great historic consequences for Buddhism, for the zeal which sought to correct the laxity among the monks was apparently of real vitality and led to a great missionary propaganda. Under the protection of its royal patron the religion of Gautama reached out into the neighboring countries. Asoka claimed that he made Buddhism known not only throughout India but also that he sent missionaries to Cashmere, Kubalistan, the Græco-Bactrian kingdom, Burma, and Ceylon. Particularly successful was his mission to Ceylon; for when later on Buddhism was driven from India proper and Northern Buddhism had developed into something quite different from the religion of the founder, Ceylon Buddhism kept fairly true to the original type. And it is in the Ceylon Chronicles that we find Asoka's claims more or less confirmed. They record that Asoka sent missionaries, not only to Ceylon, but also to Cashmere and the Greek realms. An echo of this mission to the Greek realms may be seen in the statement of Epiphanius, according to which the librarian of King Ptolemy at Alexandria was anxious to translate certain Indian books. At any rate it is safe to say that during Asoka's reign Buddhism spread northward into what at one time was a part of the "Greek realms" of Alexander and his immediate successors.

The glimpse which we get of the Buddhism of Asoka's day — and this is the important thing for our present purpose — would indicate that while Buddhism had undergone some changes since the days of its founder, it had not yet developed into what we now know as Mahāyāna Buddhism. It was, however, beginning to show tendencies along those lines.

We have already stated above that by the time of the great council of Vaisālī eighteen or twenty different schools had developed. These were, of course, minor differences; but in the course of time the more radical of these schools became the core of the liberal wing of Buddhism which developed into Mahāyāna Buddhism; the more conservative wing corresponding roughly to what is meant to-day by the term Hīnayāna Buddhism. The tendencies in Asoka's day towards these two great wings may be seen most clearly from the differences in regard to three main points.

In the first place it seems clear that the old soul-theories rejected by the Buddha and his early followers were getting a stronger hold from year to year. If they did not come back into Buddhism in their exact old forms, the more liberal Buddhists were at least ready to make a compromise with the demands of non-Buddhistic thought that the soul is a permanent reality. In the second place, Gautama, who had robbed the gods of their glory by teaching that they, too, were subject to the law of change and decay, was himself being glorified as God, or at least as the revelation of the Divine. Gradually the legends centering around his birth and ministry increased in their miraculous elements (see Jātaka stories) until Gautama the man was disappearing entirely, and we have a superhuman being far removed from the Gautama of history. Then, in the third place, the ideal of salvation which the Buddha had held out as the highest, namely, Arhatship, which meant primarily enlightenment for self, was giving way in the liberal wing to the more altruistic ideal of the Bodhisattva state, *i.e.* enlightenment for the benefit of others. The Bodhisattva is willing to be born again and again into this world of sin and suffering in order that through his many incarnations of good works he might help others.

It will be seen that these three great changes are closely connected with one another, and that any one of them really implies the other two. For example, the change from Gautama the Great Teacher, or Super-man, to the divine Buddha implied that the historical personality known as Siddhārtha, or Gautama, had preëxistence. Such goodness and wisdom as were his were far "too perfect to have been wrought out or developed in a single lifetime." Through ages upon ages he had exercised himself in the perfection of wisdom and all virtues and therefore there must have been a real continuity of personality. And especially as the Buddha was said to have been willing to be born again and again for the good of humanity (this is the ideal of the true Bodhisattva) does it seem clear that he must have had a real personal identity from incarnation to incarnation, *i.e.* an identity other than the old-fashioned Karma identity.

We do not mean to say that in Asoka's day any one of these three characteristics of Mahāyāna Buddhism as distinguished from Hīnayāna Buddhism was fully developed, but even at that early date these tendencies were beginning to manifest themselves. And the third great council of Buddhism convened by King Asoka may be regarded as marking the real parting of the ways; one great school remaining more or less true to original Buddhism, and the other diverging gradually until in many respects, even in things fundamental, it often ran quite counter to the way laid down by Gautama.[2]

B. *The Rise of Mahāyāna Buddhism*

The period following Asoka's day and down to the first century B.C. is practically a closed book to the historian. It would seem, however, that Asoka's empire, in spite of its apparent greatness, soon fell to pieces. And with its ruin Buddhism fell on hard days again. The royal patron was gone, and Hinduism rejuvenated had its revenge and began to force Buddhism to the wall. Fortunately the wall was not insurmountable and the misfortunes at home led to prosperity abroad. To the northwest of India, among the Parthians, Yuetchi, and the outer branches of the S'akyans, Buddhism apparently found a welcome, and it is largely in this region that we must look for the further development of that expanded and altered form of Buddhism which later on became the religion of central and northeastern Asia and which to this day largely claims the allegiance of Japan.

What were the factors which worked the profound change from the religion of the founder and of King Asoka's day to the Buddhism which won the hearts of central and northeastern Asia during the first six or seven centuries of our era, remains still a dark problem. Let us indicate a few of these profound changes.

We have already pointed out that, even in Asoka's day, i.e. in the third century B.C., there were evidences of great changes coming over Buddhism. Those tendencies became stronger as time went on and they in turn brought about other changes. Thus we have not only a tendency to deify Gautama, but in such scriptures as the Saddharma-Pundarīka and the Paradise sūtras Gautama as a human being seems to have disappeared altogether and is replaced by the Eternal Buddha, or Buddhas. The historical Buddhas are many, each age or cycle having its own, but all these Buddhas are but manifestations of the Eternal Buddha, or Buddhas. Some scriptures speak of five historical Buddhas who preceded Gautama Buddha, others give long lists of names, and still others, without attempting to give their names, say that the Buddhas are millions and trillions; yea, equal in number to the grains of sand on the banks of the sacred Ganges. "The blessed Buddhas equal in number the sand of the Ganga."

Another great change is the change in the conception of the future life. If Gautama placed the subject of the future life of the Arhat among the great Indeterminates, the author, or authors, of the Paradise sūtras were of nothing more

certain than the future life of the saved. Not only did
Buddhists teach positively a doctrine of a future life; they
actually filled it with all the pleasures of sense which the
imagination of man can conjure up. To quote but one of
many descriptions of the Buddhist heaven: "In the land
of Highest Happiness there are waters in eight lakes; the
water in every lake consists of seven jewels which are soft
and yielding. Deriving its source from the King of Jewels
that fulfills every wish, the water is divided into fourteen
streams; every stream has the colour of seven jewels; its
channel is built of gold, the bed of which consists of the
sand of variegated diamonds. . . . From the King of Jewels
that fulfils every wish, stream forth the golden-coloured
rays excessively beautiful, the radiance of which transforms
itself into birds possessing the colours of a hundred jewels,
which sing out harmonious notes sweet and delicious, ever
praising the remembrance of Buddha, the remembrance
of the Law, and the remembrance of the Church." (Ami-
tāyur-Dhyāna-sūtra, sec. 13.) And so one may read page
after page of extravagant description of the beauties of
Paradise inhabited by myriads of Buddhas. Surely a great
change has come over Buddhist conceptions of the future
life. The very things which Gautama had denounced as
mere shadows and illusions were set forth in glorious array
to allure the heart of man and thus lead him to Paradise.
No longer was salvation a mere "escape" from the present
evils of existence, but rather the enjoyment of a future good.

The ideal as to what constitutes true enlightenment also
changed. In primitive Buddhism, as we have seen, the
highest ideal was that of the Arhat, one who seeks enlightenment chiefly for himself and is rather indifferent to the welfare of other beings. But in such Mahāyāna scriptures as
the Saddharma-Pundarīka the ideal of the Arhat is not
only augmented by that of the Bodhisattva who seeks
salvation also for others, but the Arhat ideal is actually
condemned, and the condemnation is put into the mouth
of Gautama himself. Perhaps this difference between the
Arhat and the Bodhisattva has received too great an em-

phasis by Mahāyāna Buddhists, for it is not quite true that the Arhat seeks salvation only for himself. His seeking salvation for himself was at least an example unto others, and to that extent his efforts were for the good of all. It is true, however, that the older ideal of enlightenment implied that every man must be his own savior, whereas in Mahāyāna Buddhism the Bodhisattva through his own virtues helped save others. That is, his own merit is some-how transferred to others who put their trust in him. This is especially true of the Bodhisattva Dharmakara who finally became the Buddha Amitābha to whose Western Paradise go all those who in simple faith call upon his great name.

This change of ideal as to what constitutes the highest type of enlightenment and true Buddhahood also implied a radical change as to the way of salvation. Gautama had taught that man is bound by the Karma chain to such a degree that every one must work out his own salvation through a long process of self-discipline. No one can really help another; not even the gods, for if there are gods they too are subject to the law of Karma and are bound to the Wheel of Life with its endless revolutions. But in certain books of Mahāyāna Buddhism man is not left to his own strength. He becomes an object of grace, especially the grace of the great Buddha Amitābha who saves by his might all those who believe in him and call upon his name. Amitābha has made the great vow to help all who desire help. "In obtaining Buddhahood I shall not enter into perfect enlightenment until all creatures of the Ten Regions (Universe) who wish sincerely to be born into my country or who practice tenfold meditations, shall have been born there." "My mercy towards all ye heaven- and earth-born creatures is deeper than the love of parents towards their children." And if it is not the Buddha Amitābha who saves man then it is Vairochana or some other great Buddha. In the Sad-dharma-Pundarīka we read these almost Christian words: "Now are the Three Worlds [3] (the phenomenal world) mine, and all beings in the same are indeed my children. But great and many are their afflictions, and it is I alone who can save them." Thus there is established in Mahāyāna Buddhism the great principle of salvation through the strength of another; and, as we shall see later, salvation through a vicarious savior and through faith in the grace of some Buddha, or the eternal Buddha — all of which seems radically different from the teachings of Gautama.

A final great change which we must mention here as coming over Buddhism is the love for speculation on metaphysical problems. We said in the preceding chapter that Gautama considered the speculations of the Brahmin priests about the Brahman as an idle waste of time, and that he rather hesitated to express himself on metaphysical questions even when pressed by his disciples, but put such problems in his list of the Great Indeterminates. But in the literature of Mahāyāna Buddhism one is almost nauseated with the barren heights of speculations in which the authors love to indulge. In spite of the protest of the founder against such things, his religion has become par excellence a religion which is couched in a metaphysical mold. Even the earlier Hīnayāna books contain much idle speculation on the problems of metaphysics, and to that extent are also a great change from what seems to have been Gautama's attitude towards such problems.

Thus while the common ethical teachings as contained in the Noble Eightfold Path, the Ten Commandments and the elaboration of these in various systems of Monk's Rules, may not have changed so seriously as the years went by, the great fundamental doctrines of religion — the God-idea, the doctrine of a future life, the conception as to the real nature of human life, and the way of salvation — all these seem to have undergone rather radical changes. For a fuller discussion of the main doctrines of Mahāyāna Buddhism, especially the Japanese form of it, the reader is referred to the succeeding chapters of this book, especially Chapter V.

Now the question which we asked above and which we now shall try to answer very briefly is as to what were the main factors which brought about this great change from primitive Buddhism to Mahāyāna Buddhism.

Some scholars see in this great change the influence of Western thought, particularly Christian thought. It is, of course, quite possible that when Buddhism spread into the countries northwest of India, it came into contact with and was influenced by the religions of the West; just as it is reasonable to suppose that especially such heresies in Christianity as the Gnostic heresy were in part at least the result of the impact of Buddhism upon Christianity. At any rate, it seems safe to assume that there was a good deal of intercourse between the East and the West after the time of Alexander the Great, if not before. The careful historian will be slow to say what was possible and what not in this matter of intercourse between the nations in ancient times.

The student of Indian archæology is finding many traces of Western influence; especially is this true of northwestern India. There are a good many relics of pure Greek art dating probably from the first and second centuries B.C.; and still more numerous are the relics which show a blending of Greek and Indian art. Then, further, the results of recent discoveries in the lands northwest of India would go to show that the great religions of the world seem to have come into contact with one another on their march into China. Buddhism, *e.g.*, can be traced in Bactria as early as the second century B.C. Zoroastrianism, of course, had flourished in these regions for many years, and fragments of Zoroastrian scriptures were found recently in Turkestan. The Mithras cult, in particular, during the first and second century A.D., would seem to have had a strong hold not only on the Roman Empire, as Cumont has shown, but also in the lands east of its origin. Then by the third century A.D. Manichæism had come into existence and Mani himself visited both Turkestan and India. The German expedition to Turkestan found fragments of his writings which until then had been regarded as lost. The religion of the O. T. had probably made itself felt in those lands from the time of the Babylonian Captivity, and Christianity itself most likely reached these lands before the end of the first century. And we know positively that by the first half of the seventh century Nestorian Christianity was planted in the midst of Buddhism as far east as Sin-an-fu, China. From all this it will be seen that the lands north-west of India must have been the scene of the mingling of various religious streams, and it seems only natural that no religion could pass through these lands without undergoing some modifications.

But after all this has been taken into account, we are still inclined to hold that the great change from primitive Buddhism to Mahāyāna Buddhism was brought about by influences nearer home. Not that we would deny the influence from the West, but that the chief factor, after all, was Indian in its origin. The real revenge which Hinduism had on Buddhism was not that it ultimately drove it out of India proper, but rather that it forced upon Buddhism step by step a great deal of its own philosophy about those very things against which Gautama had protested so much. And, perhaps, that is why Buddhism finally died out in India proper — it had ceased to justify its existence since it became essentially one with rejuvenated Hinduism. Nothing is more striking than the similarities between the Vedanta philosophy and the speculations of Mahāyāna Buddhism; the one is as characteristically metaphysical in its mold as the other. Perhaps nothing shows the influence of Hinduism on Mahāyāna Buddhism more clearly than the Buddhist cosmology, with its realms upon realms of beings ranging all the way from the lowest hell to the highest heaven, practically all of which was taken bodily from Hinduism. And what is still more striking to the student of Chinese Buddhism is the fact that the Confucian opponents of the new religion were apparently more akin (not historically, of course) to the view of the founder of Buddhism than was Chinese Buddhism itself; for especially after the fourth century A.D. a continual stream of Indian thought poured into China, and this stream brought not so much the Buddhism of Gautama as the wealth and rubbish of Hinduism which gradually swamped the purer Buddhism.

It is only natural that Buddhism gradually took on much from Hinduism and became equally speculative as a system of philosophy and all-inclusive as a religion of the masses. In fighting Hinduism it was forced to use the weapons of its opponent and this led to its becoming like that which it opposed. We have here simply another case of what happened with early Christianity. The Apostle Paul, it will be remembered, regarded the philosophies of his day as vain speculations and some of the Apostolic Fathers looked askance at the wisdom of the Greeks and felt that in the revelation of Christ they had the sum total of all that was worth knowing. But we know what happened with the Ante-Nicene and Post-Nicene Fathers — in their attempt to meet the current philosophies they cast Christianity itself into a metaphysical mold and spent much time and energy on those very things which earlier Christians had denounced as vain philosophy. And this we say is what happened to the religion of Gautama in its opposition to Brahmin speculations. It gradually took on those very things which at first it had opposed.

But to be more specific: The names which are held by Mahāyāna Buddhists in special esteem are those of Asvaghosha, Nāgārjuna, and the two brothers Asanga and Vasubandhu. Practically all Chinese and Japanese sects, though they trace in one way or another all branches of Buddhism back to Gautama as the ultimate source, nevertheless look upon Asvaghosha as the specific founder of Mahāyāna Buddhism and upon Nāgārjuna as playing a prominent part in founding many of the leading sects. Asanga and Vasubandhu exercised a great influence in Mahāyāna Buddhism through their numerous writings, and the former in particular seems to have been a great factor in furthering that syncretistic movement through which Buddhism was enabled to absorb the most heterogeneous elements.

Who were these men and when and where did they live? The answer to these questions is largely the crux of the whole problem as to the real sources of Mahāyāna Buddhism; particularly is this true of the answer to the question about Asvaghosha.

To begin with, it would seem that there were several Asvaghoshas, so that the writings which appear under this name may have been the products of different minds and written at different times and places. The date of Asvaghosha (or the dates of these Asvaghoshas) is uncertain because the date of the Indo-Scythian king with whom tradition connects him is still a matter of dispute, being placed all the way from the beginning of the first century B.C. to the beginning of the third century A.D. Most accounts, however, agree that there was an Asvaghosha who was a Brahmin by birth and who wandered up and down India seeking for knowledge until he finally settled at Benares, where he became famous as a great scholar and clever reasoner. He was a light in Brahmanism until he was converted to Buddhism, and as a Buddhist monk he became known far and wide for his sanctity.

It was during his life as a Buddhist monk at Benares, tradition says, that the Indo-Scythian king Kanishka appeared before the walls of this Buddhist center; perhaps about the year 90 A.D. The king agreed to spare the city if it would turn over to him Gautama's begging bowl and the great sage Asvaghosha. The ruler of Benares, it is said, was loath to surrender these two great treasures and was bent on rather sacrificing the city than these, when the sage Asvaghosha reproached him with these words, "The teaching of Buddha is for the salvation of all living beings and it is a mistake to think that it is only for the benefit of one country." The king thereupon complied with the demands of the besieging king, and Asvaghosha was taken to the north, where he spent his life in spreading Buddhism. By northern Buddhists Kanishka is held in high honor much the same way as Asoka is by southern Buddhists. He, too, exerted himself for the extension of the religion and convened the fourth (third according to northern Buddhists) great council of Buddhism, at which

F

it is claimed the religion was purified and the canon was more clearly defined.

Asvaghosha's "Life of Buddha" (Buddha-Karita) and especially his "Awakening of Faith" (Kishinron) have exerted a tremendous influence on Northern Buddhism, and the latter writing is regarded by many as the real foundation of Mahāyāna Buddhism. Now we said that practically all traditions agree that Asvaghosha was originally a Brahmin scholar converted later to Buddhism. What is more natural than that this converted Brahmin scholar should bring into Buddhism a great deal of his earlier training and especially that he should give back to Buddhism those very fundamentals of religion which the heart of man demands, namely, the belief in a Supreme Being and a future life for the individual? Not that Asvaghosha brought these as something new; for it would seem that the common man even in the Buddha's day had never given up his faith in some sort of a god and his faith in a future life. And we have also seen that even as early as Asoka's day Gautama was being raised to the place of a god. But the contribution which Asvaghosha made was that he gave these great beliefs a philosophical formulation and embodied them in the doctrines of the religion, and through his writings he handed them down to succeeding generations as the orthodox teachings of Buddhism.

Asvaghosha's work was ably supplemented by the work of that second great saint of Mahāyāna Buddhism, Nāgārjuna, who, too, was a Brahmin converted to Buddhism. He lived probably in the second century A.D. and, as we have said above, laid the foundations for a number of the leading sects of Chinese and Japanese Buddhism. Nāgārjuna was followed by Asanga and Vasubandhu, who lived in the fifth century; and these two scholars, like their great predecessors, were steeped in the thought of India and the speculations of Brahmanism. It is only natural that they should bring to their adopted religion much from the religion in which they had been trained. They added to the ever growing complexity of the Mahāyāna school until it contained in its capacious womb not only what was in original Buddhism, but also everything which the founder of Buddhism had opposed. Especially must Asanga be regarded as the master par excellence in matters of religious compromise. Through his influence Mahāyāna Buddhism, which was already rather all-inclusive, assumed more and more that compromising attitude towards other religions which has ever since been its strength and weakness. On the one hand it enabled Buddhism to adapt itself to any local condition it happened to meet. Not only were the leading Sivaite and Vishnuite gods of India admitted to the Buddhist Pantheon, but the gods of all nations found ready access, for it was simple to regard these as so many Buddhist Bodhisattvas or as the various manifestations of the Eternal Buddha, or Buddhas. Asanga did not stop with the enrichment of the Buddhist Pantheon, he is also credited with incorporating into the newer Buddhism a great deal of the mystic Tantric doctrine from the prevalent animism, which to this day plays a leading part in the Lamaism of Tibet and the Shingon sect of Japanese Buddhism. This latter move enabled Buddhism to make proselytes of many half civilized tribes who knew nothing of the Four Great Truths or the Noble Eightfold Path. The weakness of this compromising attitude lay in the fact that it filled the Buddhist household with all sorts of rubbish which is utterly unworthy of the religion proclaimed by Gautama. In its triumphant march across Asia Buddhism gathered up into itself everything that came into its way. Victory through compromise becomes the ruling principle, and this has remained the chief characteristic of Mahāyāna Buddhism to this day It is justified by the Buddhist scholar on the ground that truth must accommodate itself to the varied needs of humanity. But of this guiding principle of Mahāyāna Buddhism we shall speak more fully in a later chapter.

From what we have said, then, it seems rather clear that Mahāyāna Buddhism has its sources primarily in Indian thought, though we do not wish to deny that it has received some influences from the West. The point we wish to make is that there is little in the fundamentals of Mahāyāna Buddhism which cannot be accounted for by a natural evolution and a mingling of Buddhism with Brahmanism and other Indian streams, modified further by the native beliefs and practices of the northern peoples among whom Mahāyāna Buddhism had its fuller development. The student of comparative religions has long since learned that similarities between different religions does not necessarily prove interdependence; and so if we find in Mahāyāna Buddhism much which reminds one of Western thought and Christianity, it does not necessarily follow that there has been a historical connection or that one has borrowed from the other. Our medieval missionaries to China, Huc and Garbe, saw in the striking similarities between Catholicism and Mahāyāna Buddhism a clear piece of the devil's work who had thus made a cheap counterfeit of Christianity in order to deceive the very elect. We smile at this theory to-day but it is not much more absurd than the theory of some of our modern students who see in all parallelisms of religions a necessary historical connection and interdependence.

There is, however, one great point in Mahāyāna Buddhism which seems to be more than a mere parallelism and which bears on the face of it traces of influence other than Indian. We refer to the doctrine of salvation through the strength and grace of another. In India the doctrine of Karma was all but universal, and this doctrine, as we saw in the last chapter, was the causal-nexus principle applied with rigor to the psychic life of the individual. Man is what his thoughts and deeds of the past have made him, and his future is conditioned by the present. "Whatsoever a man soweth that shall he also reap," and no one can sow or reap for another — either good or bad. This is the doctrine of early Buddhism as well as that of all other Indian systems of thought. The first glimpse, it would seem, which we get in Buddhism of the opposite great principle, namely, the principle which recognizes the fact that one life can help another and that one can be saved through the strength of another, is the story in one of the three Paradise sutras

(Amitayūr-Dhyāna-sūtra) about the Buddha's conversation with Vaidehī, the queen of Bimbisara. The story is in substance as follows:

The queen had suffered hardships at the hand of her own son, and in her distress she turned to the Buddha for consolation. She asked him why it was that she must suffer such things at the hands of her son. The Buddha replied in the manner consonant with the Indian doctrine of Karma, namely, that the queen was simply suffering for her own sins — sins committed either in her present life or in some previous existence. Then in her despair the queen cried out and said, "Is there no escape from this dreadful chain of Karma?" "Not in India," replied the Buddha, "but there is a Western Buddha Field where one does not have to atone for all one's sins." Whether this is a true story or not, it remains true that it is an old story and that the doctrine of the forgiveness of sin was known rather early in Buddhism, but known as belonging to the Western Buddha Field.

If the Buddha himself uttered these words it is possible, as Professor Lloyd has suggested, that he knew something about the religion of the O. T. through the prophets of the Exile. If it is a later story, then it is possible that this doctrine entered Buddhism after the conquest of Alexander the Great. And if we put it as late as the first century A.D. (for which there is good reason), then it may be connected with Christian influences. If it is neither Jewish nor Christian in origin there still remains the possibility of its coming from the near West, namely from Persia, particularly from the Mithras cult. We realize, of course, that the doctrine of salvation by divine grace is found also in the popular Vishnu and Siva schools of Hinduism, but whether it was in these before it entered Buddhism, and if so, whether it was Indian in origin, remains still a problem.

Whatever were the origins of this doctrine of divine grace, it would seem safe to say that it did not reach any degree of real vitality in Buddhism until after the formation of the great Pure Land sects in China and Japan which make this their central teaching, proclaiming as they do the possibility of salvation for all sinners who rely upon the strength of Amitābha. But these sects regard as their greatest teacher a man by the name of Shan-tao (Japanese, Zendō) whom we know to have been contemporary with the Nestorian missionaries of the seventh century at Sin-an-fu, China. Thus it would seem that if this doctrine did not come originally from Christianity, it was strengthened by the influences of Nestorian Christianity and made a real live doctrine in Mahāyāna Buddhism. We shall speak of this again in a later chapter.

C. *The Spread of Buddhism through China*

Eitel claims that Buddhist missionaries accompanied the caravans of traders into China as early as the days of King Asoka, *i.e.* in the middle of the third century B.C. Others claim that the first century B.C. saw the first Buddhist efforts in that land, but even that seems quite doubtful. It is, however, safe to say that Buddhism did reach China during the first century A.D. We are told that in the year 61 A.D. the Emperor Ming-ti had a dream. Several nights in succession he had a vision of a man standing before him in golden raiment, holding in his hands a bow and arrows and pointing to the West. The emperor was much moved by the vision, and so sent eighteen men to the West to seek for the True Man whom he had seen in his dream. The messengers, we are told, got as far as the land of the Getæ bordering on India when they met two monks coming through the mountain pass, leading a white horse laden with scriptures and images. The messengers returned to the court with these two monks, where the strangers were well received and given lodgment in a monastery which exists to this day, namely, the celebrated Pomash, White Horse Monastery. The two monks died a few years later and the only memorial they left behind, it would seem, was the famous scripture of the Forty-Two Sections, which has remained to this day one of the most popular writings of Chinese and Japanese Buddhism.

There are scholars who have suggested that these two monks were not Buddhists at all, but Christians, namely, disciples of St. Thomas in India or from the lands north of India and west of China. The legend that St. Thomas reached India is not altogether without foundation; and further is it true that the Jews of the Diaspora seem to have had as their easternmost settlement a colony at Kaifong-fu in Honan, China, at this time. (This colony of Jews has survived to our day and is only now disappearing.) Thus it was quite possible that the Emperor Ming-ti should have known something about the True Man who had appeared in Palestine. But, of course, the mere possibility of such an acquaintance is a very slender thread on which to hang any claim that Christianity reached China as early as the seventh decade of the Christian era. And the further claim that the sūtra of the Forty-Two Sections has Christian elements is equally weak, as all advanced religions have a great many things in common, so that similarity, as we said before, does not prove dependence.

Whatever these monks were, their influence seems to have been very little as far as establishing either Buddhism or Christianity in China. Between A.D. 76–88 a number of Buddhist books were brought into China from Turkestan, but their influence is also very difficult to trace. Not until 147 A.D. did Buddhism make a real beginning in that land. The Buddhism which won China at first did not come directly from India proper, but largely from the new home of Buddhism among the Scythians and Parthians. (After the fourth century the connection between India and China seems to have been more direct, Indians coming to China in great numbers and Chinese pilgrims visiting the birth-place of their new religion.) Asvaghosha and Nāgārjuna had already done their great work in giving Buddhism a new turn. And their work had been advanced by others, so that ideas which they held only in germ had reached full fruition. For example, as we saw above, these two great scholars seemed to have faith in a Supreme Being whom they knew as Amitābha, but they knew him, as it were, only from afar. On the other hand, the great missionaries to the Chinese, Anshikao (Prince of the Parthians), who gave up his royal position to become a Buddhist missionary, and Lokaraksha, were devout preachers of this great doctrine of Mahāyāna Buddhism. And it was they who seem to have brought the chief scripture of the Amitābha faith, namely, the Larger Sukhāvatī-Vyūha, to China in 147 A.D.

The progress of Buddhism in China was not very rapid at first. The first century and a half or more was a period of importation and translation of scriptures. In fact, China seems to have been flooded with books; so that the Emperor Hweiti in 306 A.D., wishing to free himself of this foreign importation, ordered a great many books to be burned, and for many years the Chinese were forbidden by imperial edict to become Buddhist monks. But after 335 A.D. matters took a turn for the better. The people were allowed to take monastic vows, and many began to give the new religion serious attention. The thing that, perhaps, more than any other won the Chinese to Buddhism was the latter's attitude towards the deep-rooted ancestor worship. Buddhism did not openly antagonize ancestor worship; in fact, it enriched it by a distinct contribution, for it offered the Chinese a way of raising the dead to the exalted position of Buddhas. Ancestors should not only be revered, but they should be worshipped as Buddhas. Then of course Buddhism also satisfied the religious longings better than Confucianism was doing. Especially did the Amitābha faith meet a great need in a land where religion was entirely too much a matter of mere human relationships. Buddhism went, of course, to the other extreme; but even so it filled a great need in the heart of the Chinese people, and from the fourth century on became very popular.

Naturally when Buddhism began to be really rooted in the hearts of the people they became interested in the origins of their adopted religion and in the home of its founder. Many began to turn their steps towards India. The first of these of whom any record is left was the celebrated Fahhian who started for India in 399 A.D. and returned in the

year 414 A.D. From his writings we get the best picture
we have of India for that period. He found Buddhism
in a flourishing condition in the countries northwest of
India, but when he reached the cradle of Buddhism he
found things in a state of decay. The historical Buddha
and the scenes of his activity seem to have been lost sight of;
and Buddhists were no longer concerned with him as a man,
but only with the deified Buddha. Fah-hian's studies on
the field of Buddhism's beginnings soon showed him that the
Buddhism which had been introduced into China differed
rather widely from the Buddhism of India proper. This
would indicate that by this time, *i.e.* at the beginning of
the fifth century A.D., the main features of Mahāyāna Buddhism had been developed and that the seat of its development
was not in India proper, but rather in the regions lying north
and northwest of India; though, as we have said above,
Indian elements were the predominant ones in this development.

Under the Ts'in dynasty in 401 A.D. Kumārajīva was
brought from Tibet as a prisoner to Sin-an-fu, China. His
great work was the translation of numerous books — many
of them of purely Indian origin. From these translations
and studies it became increasingly evident that the Buddhism imported into China by the great Anshikao and Lokaraksha in 147 A.D. was not the pure Buddhism of the
founder. This discovery gave rise to great discussions and
divisions in the ranks of Buddhism and thus weakened the
new religion in its conflict with Confucianism and Taoism. But these discussions and divisions, in the long run,
led to further developments of the new religion and to the
formation of some of the great sects which later were trans-
planted to Japan, where they are active to this day.

It is from this time on that Chinese Buddhism began
to take up many of the elements of Confucianism, Taoism
and the minor local cults. From Confucianism Buddhism
adopted much which made its ethical teachings more practical
and suited to the tastes of the Chinese. And from Taoism
it gathered on the one hand some of its philosophical for-

mulæ to express its own concepts, converting *e.g.* the Law of the Buddha into the Laws or Way of the Universe, *i.e.* the Tao, or Way, of Taoism. On the other hand, Buddhism also took up many of the superstitions of Taoism and local cults as held by the ignorant masses. And, as we have said above, from this time on the connection with India and the countries south of China became close, so that all the wealth and rubbish of these countries kept pouring into China and helped swell the ever growing stream of Mahāyāna Buddhism.

The growing popularity of Buddhism in China during the fifth century led to a bitter religious controversy with the Confucianists and Literati, so that finally the king of the Wei dynasty in the north was induced to issue an edict calling for the destruction of Buddhist books and images. But by 451 A.D. a king of the same dynasty authorized the establishment of one Buddhist temple in every city of his dominion and forty to fifty inhabitants of each place were permitted to become monks or priests. This friendliness on the part of the rulers made China a safe place of refuge for the Buddhists of India, who were being persecuted by their Brahmin rivals. Thus one account has it that at the beginning of the sixth century the number of Indian refuges in China was more than 6000. This in turn helped raise the prestige of Buddhism, as may be seen from the statistics of that period, which give the number of Buddhist temples as upward of 13,000.

Of all the Buddhists who came to China from India during this period there is none whose coming was of such significance for Chinese Buddhism as that of Bodhidharma, the founder of the Contemplative school of Buddhism in China. Bodhidharma was the twenty-eighth patriarch of the Dhyāni school in India, claiming to be in real apostolic succession from Gautama down; and with him we may say the center of this type of Buddhism is shifted from India to China. Whatever may be said about the apostolic succession claim which this school makes, it is certainly true that even to this day it is in many respects nearer the original Buddhism than other Chinese or Japanese sects; especially is it nearer than the sects which make Amitābha the center of their faith. Bodhidharma was a remarkable man and left his impress on a great section of northern Buddhism. The Zen sect in Japan, of which we shall speak in succeeding chapters, is to this day one of the most vital forces in Japanese Buddhism and looks to him as its real founder. The following interview with the Chinese Emperor Liang Wuti, taken from Edkin's "Chinese Buddhism," illustrates what was the temper of the man and the characteristics of his true followers:

When Bodhidharma lived at Nanking the emperor came to him one day and said, "From my accession to the throne, I have been incessantly building temples, transcribing sacred books, and admitting new monks to take the vows. How much merit may I be supposed to have accumulated?" The reply was, "None." The emperor: "And why no merit?" The patriarch: "All this is but the insignificant effect of an imperfect cause not complete in itself. It is the shadow that follows the substance, and is without real existence." The emperor: "Then what is true merit?" The patriarch: "It consists in purity and enlightenment, depth and completeness, and in being wrapped in thought while surrounded by vacancy and stillness. Merit such as this cannot be sought by worldly means." The emperor: "Which is the most important of the holy doctrines?" The patriarch: "Where all is emptiness, nothing can be called 'holy' (sheng)." The emperor: "Who is he that thus replies to me?" The patriarch: "I do not know."

Some time after this interview the emperor became a Buddhist monk, much to the disgust of the Confucianists.

According to the "History of the Wei Dynasty," says Edkins, the number of Buddhist monks and priests about this time reached 2,000,000 and the number of temples was 30,000. This seems to be an exaggeration, but it shows that Buddhism was exceedingly popular. The statistics given in connection with the accounts of the great persecutions of Buddhists during the eighth, ninth and tenth centuries show that Buddhism kept increasing at the expense of its rivals. In 714 A.D., *e.g.*, we are told that 12,000 monks and nuns were compelled to return to secular life, and the edict against Buddhists issued by Emperor Wu-tsung in 845 A.D. is said to have led to the destruction of 4,600 monasteries and 40,000 smaller edifices, and more than 260,000 monks and nuns were compelled to return to common employments, the temple property being confiscated and the copper of images and bells being converted into coins. Again in the first half of the tenth century we hear of persecutions which closed 30,000 temples. But none of these and similar oppressions, many of which were purely local, sufficed to check Buddhism in China; for, after all, it satisfied the spiritual needs of the people better than Confucianism and Taoism could do, and so the Buddhists, though frequently oppressed and persecuted, always found their way back to favor and prosperity.

We may say, however, that in these oppressions and persecutions we have an indication of China's chief objection to the religion of the Buddha. We said above that Buddhism did not openly antagonize ancestor worship and that it even enriched it by converting ancestors into Buddhas who are truly worthy to be revered and worshiped. But, after all, the highest life-ideal to the Buddhist is that of the monk or nun who withdraws from active life and so becomes an economic loss, and by their vows of celibacy they cut the very nerve of ancestor worship. The Chinese are too practical and matter-of-fact people to accept the monk and the nun as the highest type of manhood and womanhood, and especially too deeply devoted to the ancestor cult to accept Buddhism without serious questions; for the sin above all other sins in the eyes of a faithful son of China is the sin of having no children. Ancestor worship demands an unbroken line of descendants, and if there are no children by legal marriage "either adoption of a son or polygamy becomes an ethical necessity." And so however much Buddhism may flatter the Chinese by converting ancestors into Buddhas or however much it may satisfy other religious needs, this ideal of celibacy and the lack of emphasis upon the practical problems of life are contrary to the most deep-rooted characteristics of Chinese life and customs.

From China as a center Buddhism spread in several directions, mainly, however, in its Mahāyāna form. During the seventh century it reached Tibet and there developed into what is now known as Lamaism. Lamaism, during the time of the great Mongolian conqueror, Kublai Khan, became the religion of Mongolia and also flowed back again into China proper, thus adding one more current to the ever swelling stream of Northern Buddhism. Before this, however, namely, during the latter part of the fourth century, Buddhism had reached Korea. At this time, there was really no Korea as we know it at present, but it was divided into the three small independent kingdoms of Koma (Ko-gur-yu), Kudara (Pakche), and Shiragi (Silla), with some small buffer states between the latter two. In 372 A.D. a priest from Sin-an-fu, China, reached Koma. An Indian priest, Masananda by name, came to Kudara from eastern China in 384 A.D. And Shiragi received its first Buddhist missionary from Koma in 424 A.D. We know very little of the nature of Korean Buddhism of this early day. It would seem, however, that the new religion early won its way among the upper classes and enjoyed the protection of the royal families; for it was the king of Kudara, King Seimei, who in the year 552 A.D. sent Buddhism across the narrow channel which separates Korea from Japan when he sent his Buddhist mission to the emperor of Japan.

With these few scattering remarks we must leave Chinese Buddhism. The point we are to remember, however, is that Chinese Buddhism from the very beginning differed rather widely from the religion of Gautama, and that during its long history in that country and in its conflict with Confucianism, Taoism and minor local cults, and later through the direct influx of Indian thought into China, Buddhism took up more and more elements which were radically different from primitive Buddhism. In short, in China Buddhism became a conglomerate system of beliefs and practices which makes it practically impossible to say just what Chinese Buddhism is. We shall say more on this point when we come to an exposition of Japanese Buddhism in our next chapters, for in many respects Chinese Buddhism is better preserved in Japanese Buddhism than in the existing Chinese sects [5] themselves.

CHAPTER III

Developments of Buddhism in Japan

A. *Introduction of Buddhism into Japan*

In the last chapter we tried to show briefly the development of primitive Buddhism into Mahāyāna Buddhism. We saw that Buddhism in its spread from India northward and in its triumphant march across China and Korea underwent some radical changes, not only in minor points, but in the very fundamentals of religion. And thus when Buddhism reached Japan in the middle of the sixth century A.D. it was no longer the pure religion of the founder. It was not the Buddhism of the Pali scriptures and the religion which western scholars usually describe when they speak of Buddhism, but it was that expanded and much modified religion which we know as Mahāyāna Buddhism. A part of the original Indian stream and a great many later streams from Hinduism reached Japan through China; so that Japanese Buddhism does go back to India, but the stream had been enlarged by many tributaries from the local cults and religions of other countries, and these were so well mingled with one another that it is impossible to say just what was Buddhist and what was not.

Now in this chapter we shall trace the flow of this great stream of many waters across Japanese life and we shall see as we go on that in Japan, too, it was fed by other streams — principally by that mighty current of the native Shintō which modified Buddhism so seriously after its union with it in the beginning of the ninth century that the resultant stream was known for many centuries as Ryōbu-Shintō, Two-sided Shintō.

As we saw at the close of the last chapter, Buddhism reached Korea from China during the last half of the fourth century A.D. and from Korea it crossed the narrow channel which separates the peninsula from the island empire of Japan. Japan and Korea had known each other for many years. The Japanese claim that as early as 32 B.C. the little province of Mimana or Kara sought the protection of Japan against the oppressions of the kingdom of Shiragi, and for several centuries it remained a sort of dependency of the emperor of Japan. Then in the year 202 A.D. the great Japanese heroine, Empress Jingō, made her famous expedition to Korea and apparently reduced the kingdom of Shiragi to a dependency of Japan. Empress Jingō's son and successor, Ōjin Tennō, deified later as the God of War, is supposed to have continued the suzerainty over southern Korea, and during his reign there was probably a real vital connection between the two countries. This is a point on which some of our modern imperialistic Japanese love to dwell, and in connection with the annexation of Korea it was used as an argument by some to justify Japan in taking the step.

Japan's hold on Korea was, however, never very firm, and, as we have said, by the time Buddhism reached Korea in the fourth century the peninsula was occupied by three small independent kingdoms. And this was also the political situation about one hundred and fifty years later, when, in 552[1] A.D., King Seimei of Kudara sent a gold and copper image of Buddha (probably an image of the Buddha Amitābha and not of Gautama), Buddhist books, and a letter in which he praised the great merit of Buddhism to the emperor of Japan. As a matter of fact this was but one of many missions sent by this king. It would seem that the three Korean kingdoms were always more or less at war with one another, and it is quite likely that the king of Kudara was moved by political considerations rather than religious when he recommended his religion to the Japanese court. To gain the friendship of this island empire would be a real advantage in his conflicts with his rivals; and all the more did this seem necessary, for the Chinese monarch was showing himself quite unfriendly to Buddhism at this time and in consequence not over-friendly to the Buddhist king of Kudara. Whatever were the motives that lay back of this official Buddhist mission from Kudara, we know that it was sent and that it met with success.

It is an interesting story how these Buddhist beginnings were received. The emperor of Japan was apparently greatly pleased with these gifts, for it must be remembered that images and books were exceedingly rare among the simple Japanese of that early day. He said to the messengers, "I have never heard such sublime teachings, yet I myself dare not decide whether to accept this doctrine or not." The matter was submitted to the counsel of his vassals and one Soga no Iname replied, "Western countries all believe this doctrine and why should not we?" But two other ministers of a more conservative disposition said in substance, "We have our own gods, and if we now change and worship the gods of other nations we are in danger of bringing the wrath of our gods upon our heads." The image was turned over to Soga with the instruction that he was to worship the new god and give the new religion a test; for like the Athenians of old the Japanese did not dare run the risk of leaving any god without an altar even though they already had myriads of their own. Soga accordingly converted his own house into a temple, set up the new image and began the new cult.

But soon after this introduction of the new god a terrible pestilence afflicted the land and the conservative party were not slow in discovering in this the wrath of their native gods. Soga's temple was burned to the ground, and the Buddhist image was thrown into a canal of Naniwa (Osaka). The Buddhist god was, however, to get his innings and show what he could do. A great conflagration suddenly destroyed the great hall of the Imperial residence, and, of course, this could have but one meaning. Furthermore the pestilence seems to have only increased in violence and threatened to extinguish the nation. Some claim that the image was therefore speedily fished up from the sea and reverently

G

placed in a new house of worship. At any rate it seems true that, under the leadership of Soga Mumako, son of Soga no Iname, Buddhism began to take root in Japan.

Thus we see how trifling and chance occurrences may play a great part in momentous issues. Not that these were the only or even the main determining factors, for in the long run the success of Buddhism in Japan was due to its real superiority over the native Shintō faith.

Before we proceed with a narrative of the development of Buddhism in Japan from these small beginnings, it may be well to pause a moment and give very briefly what the native Shintō was and what were the conditions of Japan in general at this time; for the successful entrance of a religion into a country depends more or less upon the religious, social, political and intellectual condition of the people to be won to the new faith.

The population at this time consisted possibly of about two million people — hunters, fishermen and farmers, divided up into many different clans. The center of population was in the Ōsaka-Kyōto region, and the dominant tribe whose head was the Mikado exercised authority over a considerable portion of the main island, though the outlying portions,[2] especially in the north, were still in the hands of the aboriginal Ainus. The people, though very simple in their manner of life, were intellectually well gifted and later proved to be endowed with extraordinary æsthetic ability. Their religion was Shintō[3] — The Way of the Gods. This religion was and is in some of its phases even to-day an animistic and polytheistic Nature Worship with a strong admixture of Ancestor Worship.[4] The forces of nature are personified and anthropomorphized, while the heroes and ancestors, especially those of the royal family, are deified.[5] The soul of Shintō is reverence and implicit obedience to the Mikado; and religion and patriotism are made one. Yamato Damashii,[6] The Spirit of Japan, is largely the product of this religion, and it has played a great part in the conquest, unification and civilization of the entire country. Japan is regarded by Shintō as the sacred land of the gods; and every mountain, river, rock, tree and cloud is the abode of some deity. But Shintō was really too childish in many of its conceptions and did not satisfy the deeper needs of the human mind and heart. The rising tide of Japanese civilization, quickened as it was by the introduction of new ideas from the continent, made Shintō more and more inadequate, and Japan was on the whole ready for the new and more elaborate faith of Buddhism.

So much for a summary of conditions which prevailed in Japan when Buddhism was first introduced. It was therefore comparatively easy for the new religion to get a firm hold, especially upon the more progressive element. Its success was, however, not due simply to its superiority as a religion, but even more to the fact that it was the vehicle of a higher civilization, namely, the Chinese civilization from whose fountains Japan has ever drunk deeply even up to almost the present day. We have a modern parallel in what is happening in Korea today. The success of Christianity in that land is due in some measure at least to the fact that it is the vehicle of western civilization and not simply because it is a superior religion.

Soon after the incidents connected with the introduction of Buddhism related above, the ruler of Japan, more anxious for the concrete things of Korean and Chinese civilizations than for the new religion, sent a message to the king of Kudara in which he asked the king to send no more Buddhist priests and images, but to supply him with physicians, apothecaries, soothsayers, almanac makers and artisans of one sort and another. The priests, books and images, however, continued to come together with the things specially asked for. This influx of so many new things had very much the same effect that the influx of western things has had in our own day; it caused a temporary upheaval and led to much internal strife and war. But it was not long till Buddhism had won for itself a place in the heart of members of the ruling family and thus secured protection. Empress Suiko (593–628 A.D.) became an ardent Buddhist, giving over the affairs of state to the Crown Prince Mumayado (better known as Shōtoku Taishi), so that she might have more time for advancing the new faith. More important than this was the fact that the Crown Prince himself embraced the new religion and administered the affairs of state in such a way that every thing tended towards the spread of Buddhism. In the so-called constitution of Seventeen Articles promulgated by him, he expressly ordered his people to pay all due respect to the new religion. He "bent all his energies to import from Korea, scholars, priests, architects, wood carvers, bronze founders, clay modelers, masons, gilders, tile makers, and weavers; in short, all skilled artisans whose work was involved in creating and installing a great Buddhist temple such as were already known in the peninsula kingdom." In fact, it is held by some scholars that the prince was no mean artist himself and that the famous Hōryūji near Nara erected under his direction has among its art treasures some created by his own hands. It is therefore not at all strange that by the end of Empress Suiko's reign (628 A.D.) there were already 46 temples in existence, and 816 priests and 569 nuns had been consecrated. Not only did Buddhist missionaries pour in from Korea and China, but Japanese were beginning to go in greater and greater numbers to the continent to study at the great centers of religion and culture and then come back with new learning and enthusiasm for the Buddhist faith.

The influence upon Japanese civilization of this close contact with the higher continental civilization can hardly be overstated. In a comparatively short time this simple island people had taken over the fruit of centuries of Chinese culture and made it their own. In fact, the assimilation of western culture in our own day which has astonished the world is no more wonderful than what happened in the history of this people during the seventh century. With the founding of the great monastery of Hōryūji early in the seventh century began that marvelous development of the fine arts which in a few decades issued in the production of world masterpieces, for art critics claim that the famous

Shaka trinity with its marvelous lacework screen created at this time has never been surpassed as a work in bronze by any people in any age. Not only did Japan quickly learn what China and Korea had to teach, but the pupil went beyond his teacher in many respects, so that if one would see the highest development of Asiatic art one has to turn to Japan for specimens.[7] In the political world, too, Japan was quick to learn from the continental neighbors. The great reform, beginning in 645 A.D. and continuing through the rest of the century, known as the Taikwa Reforms, changed the ruler of Japan from what was little better than a tribal chief into a real monarch of an empire.[8] We might say in a word that the impact of Chinese culture fostered largely by Buddhists changed, at least in the upper classes, a simple, unlettered people into a people of culture and refinement.

B. *Rise of the Nara Sects*

It is a rather significant fact that Buddhism was firmly rooted in Japan before any sectarian differences were introduced. For a period of about seventy years wise missionaries were content with teaching the general tenets of their faith. Perhaps this was due to the fact that the people of Japan were really not intellectually prepared to appreciate the fine points of the sectarian speculations, and were more interested in the external trappings of religion and the simpler teachings contained in the moral maxims and precepts more or less common to all the sects. Finally, however, the sectarian differences made their appearance early in the seventh century.

Curiously enough the first sect to be introduced was the highly metaphysical Sanron Sect (Mādhyamika school founded originally by Nāgārjuna). It was brought in from China in the year 625 by Ekwan. Its headquarters was the famous Hōryūji near Nara mentioned above. The Sanron sect belongs to what is called the Provisional [9] Mahāyāna school. Starting with the Hīnayāna position of the non-reality of the ego, it carries the principle of negation to the point at which it denies the reality of all phenomenal existence; and the noumenal world, it holds, can only be defined in negative terms.

Synchronous with the establishment of the Sanron was that of the Jōjitsu Sect (Satya-siddhi-sastra Sect). This sect never gained a real independent existence, but was propagated in conjunction with the Sanron. It belongs to the Hīnayāna school and represents in its doctrines a rather strong subjective idealism.

The third sect to find its way into Japan was the Hossō (Dharma-lakshana Sect, *i.e.*, the Yoga school). It was brought over from China by Dōsho probably about the middle of the seventh century, though some would put it as early as 625. The Hossō, like the Sanron, belongs to the Provisional Mahāyāna school. This is the sect which in the person of Gyōgi Bosatsu, during the eighth century, initiated that syncretistic movement by which the claims of the native Shintō and the new religion were reconciled. Of this we shall speak later.

The Kusha Sect (Abhidharma-kosa-sastra Sect) was the fourth to be established in Japan, being introduced in 658 by two Japanese priests who had studied in China, namely, Chitsu and Chitatsu. This sect is usually regarded as the best representative of the Hīnayāna school of Buddhism. The center of its teachings is an elaborate psychological analysis through which it seeks to account for the complex of the phenomenal world and yet at the same time denies the reality of the ego.

About three quarters of a century elapsed before the fifth Chinese sect was introduced. This was the Kegon (Avatamsaka-sūtra Sect) brought over in 736. The Kegon was the first sect of the true Mahāyāna school which later was to be the type [10] of Buddhism which really won Japan. Though this sect has now practically disappeared, it has exerted a great influence upon other sects through its chief scripture, the Kegonkyō (Avatamsaka-sūtra), which has ever been popular with Buddhist scholars as one of the chief sources of Mahāyāna philosophy.

Last of these older sects to reach Japan was the Ritsu

(Vinaya Sect), introduced in 754, though it would seem that its doctrines, or rather its classifications of the moral laws and precepts contained in the Vinaya scriptures, were among the first teachings to be introduced into Japan. In fact, it was probably these practical moral teachings rather than the philosophical speculations of the other scets which helped win Japan so speedily to the religion of the Buddha. The Ritsu belongs to the Hīnayāna school. It, too, like the other Hīnayāna sects, has disappeared, but its teachings have been more or less absorbed by the existing Mahāyāna sects, and in that way still exert an influence.

Now these six sects are frequently spoken of as the Six Sects of Nara to distinguish them from the later Kyoto and Kamakura sects. They are called Nara sects because it was in and around Nara and during the Nara Epoch (710–794) that they attained their highest development. The marvelous progress made by Japan during the seventh century, of which we have spoken above, was continued during the eighth. In fact we may say that the eighth century marks one of the great culminations of Japanese history. Many of the great things of old Japan came into being at this time. Thus, e.g. Nara, which was made the capital of the realm in 710, was the first real city Japan had up till that time. And it was no mean city even when compared with the great cities of other lands, its population, it is claimed by some, reaching upward of 500,000. Here, or in the immediate vicinity, were to be found many a noble Buddhist edifice filled with treasures of art, some of which have come down to our own times to be the wonder of connoisseurs. It was in the Nara epoch, namely in 749, that the enormous Nara Daibutsu, the world's largest bronze statue, was cast. It is 53 feet in height and into its creation entered 500 Japanese pounds (about 666 lb.) of gold, 16,827 pounds of tin, 1,954 pounds of mercury and 986,180 pounds of copper and some lead. The famous Tōdaiji Bell, over 13 feet high and weighing 40 tons,[11] belongs to this century. Early in the Nara Epoch were published Japan's oldest histories,[12] namely, the Kojiki in 712 and the Nihongi in 720. Aston calls this age the "Golden Age of Poetry," for during this period were written the Manyōshū, or "Collection of Myriad Leaves," containing more than 4000 pieces, mostly short poems (Tanka) but also some longer ones (Nagauta).

All this splendor of culture and civilization was largely the work, either directly or indirectly, of Buddhism and shows to what power and influence the new religion had attained by this time. It must not, however, be supposed that the common people of the land had been won over completely to the new faith. This outward splendor and magnificence made, of course, a very strong appeal to the imagination; but, after all, there was deep down in the heart of the average man still a strong loyalty to the old things of the native cults, and he was therefore ever ready to blame the gods of the new religion for the adverse things which befell him or the nation from time to time. It was so even during the Nara Epoch. A great epidemic of smallpox afflicted the realm. Introduced from Korea into the southern island of Kyūshū, it spread northward until in 735 it began to devastate even the aristocratic circles in the capital itself. Offerings were made at the various temples by priests and their royal patrons, but all seemed to be of no avail. It was at this time that the Emperor Shōmu contemplated the erection of the great Nara Daibutsu. However, before he dared to show his confidence in the Buddhas in such an open manner he had to find a way by which to appease the native deities and their devotees. Accordingly, he sent the illustrious Gyōgi Bosatsu, a grandson of a Korean immigrant, to the Ise shrines to inquire of the Sun Goddess what she thought of the emperor's project. Gyōgi remained at the shrine for a week and then he returned to Nara with a favorable answer, viz. that the Sun Goddess had declared herself as identical with the Buddha to whose honor the statue was to be erected. A few nights later the emperor himself is said to have had a dream in which the Sun Goddess said to him, "The Sun is Biroshana." (Biroshana is the Japanese transliteration for Vairochana). This marks the beginning of that syncretistic movement so successfully carried out during the ninth century by Dengyō Daishi and especially by Kōbō Daishi which resulted in reconciling the claims of the two religions in the hearts of the people. It should, however, be added that it also resulted in perverting things, and so in the long run really did more harm than good, as every unprincipled compromise must do.

The influence of Buddhism during the Nara period was great, not only in the spheres mentioned above, but it extended perhaps even more into the field of politics and state affairs. This is only natural, for it must be remembered that Buddhism gained its first and chief hold on the upper and ruling classes rather than upon the common people. Frequently this influence was for the good, as might be expected from the fact that it was the men who had studied in China, or under Chinese priests in Japan, that were best acquainted with politics and matters of government as conducted on the continent.[13] This superior knowledge gave these men a natural place as advisers to the court and other officials. But the temptations which this influence gave to the disciple of Buddha was more than could be endured, and it was not long therefore till the monks and priests became more interested in the "things that are Cæsar's" than in their true mission. In fact things reached such a state that during the reign of Empress Shōtoku (765–770) a Buddhist monk, Dōkyō, had managed to make himself the most powerful subject in the land and was even planning to place himself upon the imperial throne. In this, however, he did not succeed, and while the ambitious clergy continued to meddle in such things, the time was fast approaching when not only the guilty were to suffer for their sins, but the whole Buddhist world which had centered around the old capital of Nara, yea Nara itself, was soon to wane in importance and yield its place to another.

C. *The Kyōto Sects*

In the year 782 Emperor Kwammu succeeded to the throne. He must have been a man of daring and originality, for it

was he who cut the Gordian knot of the political tangle of
his day by simply abandoning Nara to the Buddhists and
their schemes and setting up his capital first at Nagaoka and
then at a place he significantly called Heian (Peace),
namely, the present Kyōto. This took place between 784–
793, and here at Kyōto the capital of the empire remained for
almost 1100 years, namely down to 1868, when the late
Emperor Meiji removed his seat of government to Tōkyō.
Kyōto soon overshadowed Nara and became indeed one of
the world's greatest centers of culture. The decline of Nara
had apparently a disastrous effect upon the Buddhist sects
entrenched there, for it must be remembered that a Japanese,
true to the fundamental principle of his native Shintō, is
first a patriot and then a man of religion. When the two
conflict, religion is apt to be the loser. To this day this seems
to be a characteristic of the average Japanese. Religion is
presented by its advocates as something good for the welfare
of the state, and by those who oppose it, it is opposed on the
grounds that it is injurious to the state. The greatest
obstacle which Christianity has met in Japan is the claim on
the part of its enemies that it undermines the state. Even
a scholar in Japan is very slow to follow where truth would
lead him if it should seem to conflict with the sacred traditions of the nation.

Now this running away from the meddling of the Nara
sects did not mean that Emperor Kwammu had turned his
back on Buddhism as a religion. He simply wanted the monks
to keep their proper place and to leave for Cæsar the things
that are Cæsar's. But to make sure that he was getting
the right type of religious leaders he sent a promising young
man directly to China to bring back a purer religion which
would minister in things spiritual and leave the affairs of
state in his own hands. This young man was Saichō,
better known as Dengyō Daishi, the founder of the powerful
Tendai sect in Japan. He was followed a few months later
by the equally famous Kukai, known best by his posthumous
title Kōbō Daishi, the founder of the other powerful sect of
this period, namely, the Shingon Sect. These two, Dengyō

Daishi and Kōbō Daishi, are the great names in Japanese
Buddhism of the ninth century; and the two sects which
they founded have occupied a prominent place in Japanese
history down to the present day.

1. *Dengyō Daishi and Tendai.* — The Tendai sect may
be characterized as the harmonizing, comprehensive sect.
That is, Tendai tries to hold to all the contradictions of
the voluminous Mahāyāna and Hinayāna scriptures as
being the direct teachings of the founder of Buddhism.
It was Chi K'ai, the founder of the Tendai (Chinese,
T'ien-t'ai) Sect in China who worked out an elaborate
harmonizing [14] scheme by which he tried to show how every
Buddhist scripture has its own peculiar place and is the
direct or indirect product of S'akyamuni's mind. Humanity
has varied needs and these needs must be met in different
ways. Thus every scripture has its truth, each giving its own
peculiar angle of vision. This irenic attitude was taken by
Chi K'ai in the face of contending sects, each of which
seemed to proclaim a different system. There were *e.g.* in
China at that time the old Abhidharma sects which tried to
define all truth with an Aristotelian precision of detail. On
the other hand the Pure Land sects were teaching that all
attempts of salvation through knowledge of detailed truth
was vain and that there was only one way, namely, the way
of Faith in the Grace of Amitābha. And still another
group of sects were the contemplative sects which held that
neither book learning nor a pious trust in Amitābha saved
a man, but that quiet meditation and abstract contemplation was the only true way. Now in the face of these contending schools the comprehensive Tendai Sect arose and it
included *all* ways, rejecting none. Thus a Tendai disciple
may find salvation through philosophic wisdom, or, rejecting
the great mass of doctrines contained in the voluminous
scriptures, he may select merely the comfortable doctrine
of salvation through faith in Amitābha's great name. Or,
again, he may reject all book learning and all simple faith
and work out his own salvation through silent meditation
and abstract contemplation, as do the contemplative sects.

The broad-minded Tendai philosopher, however, would try to hold to the truth in every way, though as a matter of fact very few ever attained this supposedly lofty ideal. After all, there was developed what we might call an orthodox Tendai system which did reject some things and included others as characteristically Tendai teachings. Thus while theoretically Tendai accepted all scriptures as of equal value, Tendai teachers looked upon the Saddharma-Pundarīka-sūtra with peculiar reverence. This sūtra together with the Mahāprajna-pāramitā-sūtra contain, after all, the loftiest teachings of S'akyamuni; and while the teachings of other scriptures are not false they must be regarded as incomplete and only provisional. As we have said in the preceding chapter, the Saddharma-Pundarīka breathes a Buddhism quite different from the Buddhism of S'akyamuni. S'akyamuni himself is regarded as but one of the manifestations of the Eternal Buddha, or Buddhas. The identification of the historical manifestation with the Eternal Buddha is the great revelation of this scripture. To know this and to trust in this knowledge far outweighs all merit which man can heap up by practicing the Buddhist virtues and perfections through countless incarnations. Inasmuch, then, as Tendai lays peculiar stress on these scriptures it does have its peculiar doctrines, but it does not thereby exclude absolutely other doctrines even if they should seem to be contradictory.[15]

Now this all-inclusive system was brought to Japan by Dengyō Daishi early in the ninth century. But the Japanese Tendai Sect underwent certain changes and differs considerably from the parent sect in China. This is due to the fact that not only Dengyō Daishi, but also other learned Japanese priests, such as Jikaku Daishi who studied in China, drank not only from the fountains of wisdom which flowed from the sacred mountains of T'ien-t'ai, but also from the deep wells of truth guarded by other Chinese sects. Another factor which was operative was that deep-rooted Japanese characteristic which is quick to adopt anything new but always only after some slight modifications and a mingling with something from other sources. Japanese Tendai claims to be eclectic rather than all-inclusive. That is, it does not simply take everything contained in other schools, but it rather chooses what it regards the best of all schools. But, of course, an eclectic process may be carried so far that it ceases to be eclectic and becomes simply an absorption of things good, bad and indifferent. And that is what seems to have gradually taken place in Japanese Tendai. It is practically impossible to say for what it really stands. Thus, *e.g.* some Tendai temples you will find littered up with images of Buddhas and Bodhisattvas innumerable. They impress one as religious junk shops. Other temples may have only a trinity of Buddhas, and still others seem to honor but one Buddha. In the temples which sprang from the famous Miidera, Amida (Amitābha) seems to be the sole object of worship. Thus the Amida teaching was held in Japan long before the real Amida sects came into existence. Again in one and the same temple, one believer may preface his meditations and prayers by the formula, "Namu Amida Butsu," "I adore Thee Thou Buddha of Eternal Life and Light" and another believer may use the equally popular form of, "Namu-Myōhō Renge-kyō," "I worship Thee Thou Scripture of the Wonderful Lotus"; the former being to-day the special prayer of the Amida sects, and the latter the "vain repetition" of the Nichiren Sect.

Now the Tendai harmonist may believe that he can reconcile the varied beliefs and practices of his own sect by saying that they are but different angles of the same truth; to the Western mind, however, it is difficult to see how such a harmony is anything more than an empty formula. And to the practical Japanese mind it also has appeared so, and that is the chief reason why the Tendai Sect not only split into several sub-sects but also why from it went out many great reformers who could not endure the contradictions. Thus, as we shall see later, from the Tendai Sect came forth the founders of the great Amida sects of Japan, the Zen sects and the Nichiren Sect. In these independent sects these conflicting doctrines found their freest development, and these sects in the course of time gradually overshadowed the great Tendai Sect itself.

2. *Kōbō Daishi and Shingon.* — As we stated above, at the time Dengyō Daishi introduced the Tendai Sect Kōbō Daishi laid the foundations for the beginnings of the Shingon Sect. The latter, like the former, studied at the various centers of learning in China. He remained abroad several years and seems to have come into contact with various influences — Buddhist and others. When he returned to Japan he brought with him many scriptures from the Chinese canon, and these he studied assiduously. He soon began to preach his new teachings, the core of which was that man can even in this present life attain Buddhahood since he is essentially one with the Eternal Buddha. His teaching was naturally challenged by the priests of the older Nara sects, but tradition has it that in his disputations with them he usually gained a miraculous victory on account of which he was held in high esteem by emperor and people. Especially did he gain the gratitude of Japan when once, after a long drought, the heavens responded to his prayers offered at the request of his Imperial patron. Kōbō was not only a man of prayer but also a man exceptionally gifted in other lines. He is credited by some with the invention of one form of the simple Kana script, and his linguistic ability may be seen in the fact that the Emperor Saga often summoned him to the palace that he might hear his beautiful language. As an educator of the common people he may be said to have been a pioneer, for he it was who founded the Sōgei Shuchiin which was the first institution in which the general public had access to education and which was the forerunner of those temple schools which were often the chief centers of light during the dark ages in Japan. The culture of the silkworm, from which industry Japan to this day draws its greatest revenue, was apparently greatly promoted by him. As a sculpturer he must have been a marvel, for there are many places in central Japan which boast of relics of his work in stone.

But while popular with emperor and people, Kōbō Daishi preferred solitude, and after much searching for a quiet spot he finally found Mt. Kōya, where with the emperor's permission he built a temple. Later when his Imperial admirer gave him the temple Tōji in Kyōto he settled there and made it the center of his sect. But when old age approached and he saw the end coming he fled to his quiet retreat on Mt. Kōya, where he died in 835 in fasting and silent meditation. There he is buried, and the pious followers of this great teacher believe that he is sitting in his tomb waiting for Maitreya (Miroku), the Buddha of the Future, to come and convert the world. When Maitreya comes Kōbō will come forth from his tomb and join in the glory of victory.

If Dengyō Daishi's teachings may be described as a comprehensive system, Kōbō Daishi's system is characterized by the words Mystery and Magic. In many respects the Shingon Sect is furthest removed from the teachings of S'akyamuni. Strange to say, it, too, holds the Saddharma-Pundarīka in highest regard, and its great Buddha is the Eternal Buddha Vairochana of whom S'akyamuni is but one of many manifestations. Where the Tendai holds to a theory of successive stages in the Buddha's teachings, Shingon divides the doctrines into exoteric and esoteric teachings, and calls its own peculiar doctrines, The Secret Teachings (Himitsukyō). The great secret is the revealed secret that man can even now attain Buddhahood because he is essentially one with the Eternal Buddha. There are, in general, two ladders by which this pinnacle of all truth may be reached; one is the intellectual ladder and the other the moral ladder, each of which has ten rungs. The intellectual ladder leads upwards, rung after rung, from the lowest being to the highest being, from the finite to the Absolute. The moral ladder is the Buddhist decalogue with its elaborations in the various monk rules which have been handed down from century to century.

In Shingon we have "a world of ideas" (Kongōkai, literally, Diamond World) which is unchangeable and everlasting, having existence only in universal thought. Parallel to this "world of ideas," as a sort of material counterpart, is the world of phenomena. The center of both worlds is the great Buddha Vairochana. In the "world of ideas" the central sun Vairochana (Dainichi, literally, Great Sun) tends to draw all bodies to itself, and when one has reached the highest enlightenment one sees that the thought of Vairochana really includes all thoughts, for Vairochana is the All. In the world of the material counterpart, however, the movement is in the opposite direction, *i.e.* the movement is outward and from Vairochana emanate other Buddhas. From these other Buddhas emanate Bodhisattvas; from the Bodhisattvas, in turn, issue other and lesser beings, and so the emanation process goes on till the whole phenomenal world is evolved. The source of all existence, then, is the Eternal Buddha. All other beings have only relative existence. They are not void but neither are they permanent as such. Vairochana as the center of "the world of ideas" is conceived of after the analogy of a planetary system, Vairochana being the sun and Akshobhya, Amitābha, Ratnasambhava and S'akyamuni being four great planets, each of which has lesser beings as satellites. Vairochana as the center of the world of phenomena is conceived of as the heart of an eight-leaf lotus flower, the eight petals being Amitābha, Avalokitesvara, Dioyagosha, Maitreya, Ratna Shvaya, Samantabhadra, Muktapushpa and Manjusrī.

Thus as we have said, Vairochana is on the one hand the source of all life and of all beings, and on the other hand he represents the sum total of all truth. Since man is but a fragment of the sum total of all Being his knowledge is fragmentary; but the great and saving revelation of Shingon doctrine is the great secret that man, just because he is an emanation from Vairochana, is really one with him. Man's apparent separateness is not real; deeper than this is the fact of his oneness in essence with the Great All.

This doctrine of the essential oneness of man with the great Eternal Buddha Vairochana differs very little from the pantheistic philosophy underlying the teachings of most Buddhist sects. The difference comes with the method by which this truth is to be reached. We said that Shingon holds that parallel to "the world of ideas" is the world of phenomena, the former being the underlying cause of the latter. From this it follows that ideas are the source of things, and thus if one has the correct ideas one can control things. This is the real meaning of the name Shingon, True Word. The True Word which becomes the Magic Word will become an efficient cause of the desired phenomenon. The one, then, who knows the Magic Word is able to achieve results by simply thinking or speaking the thought expressed by such words. Thus, as we said above, Shingon is characterized by the words Mystery and Magic, and Shingon priests are past masters in all mystery as to magic words and signs made with the fingers and the hands. These occult powers may be used for the benefit of the living or the dead. Especially are the dead to be delivered from the sufferings of hell and lower realms of existence by reciting the correct magical formulæ or making the required signs with the hands and fingers.

Both in its theory of emanations and in its wealth of magic and mystery Shingon seems rather far removed from the teachings of original Buddhism and also from other forms of later Buddhism. Some scholars have sought to find historical connections with other religions and philosophies, and particularly has it been pointed out that there is much affinity with Manichæism. It is doubtful whether it can be shown that Shingon has historical connections with Manichæism,[16] nor does it seem necessary to go very far for the source for these peculiarities of the sect. We have already seen in the last chapter that in the fifth century Asanga had thrown open the flood-gates to all the "magic and mystery" connected with the animism of India and the lands west and north of India. This stream was increased in volume later on by a powerful current which had passed through Tibet and then joined the Chinese Buddhist stream again. But whatever was its source, it is clear that this

H

prominent aspect of the Shingon Sect is in flat contradiction to the teachings of S'akyamuni, who branded such things as superstition and folly and the real enemy of the ethics of the Middle Path.[17]

We said that Kōbō Daishi was a great benefactor of Japan, and his piety and good works must have done much to recommend his religion to his people. The thing, however, which had more to do with making his religion acceptable to the people of Japan than anything else he did was his clever compromise with the native Shintō. We have already stated above how during the preceding century Gyōgi Bosatsu had begun the movement of religious syncretism by the clever answer he brought back from the Ise shrines, viz., that the Sun Goddess had declared herself to be identical with the Buddha Roshana or Birochana (Vairochana) to whose honor Emperor Shōmu erected the great Nara Daibutsu. How far Gyōgi carried his scheme is hard to say, but as he was one of the greatest artists of his day it is quite likely that with his marvelous creations in bronze and wood he made the union of Shintō and Buddhist deities very real to the people of his day. But, after all, it was Kōbō Daishi who must be given the honor of being the one who really succeeded through his Ryōbu Shintō in making the two religions but two sides of the same thing. The Sun Goddess, Amaterasu, was made identical with Vairochana, the great Buddha of Shingon (Vairochana is usually called Dainichi, Great Sun), and the lesser Buddhist deities were identified with the lesser Shintō gods, or the latter were declared to be just so many manifestations of the Eternal Buddha. The Shingon theory of emanations lent itself unusually well to this syncretistic movement, for it was easy thus to account for the essential oneness of the Buddhist and Shintō pantheons. One and all of the many gods of both religions were but emanations or radiations of the Central Sun which Buddhists knew as Vairochana and Shintōists as Amaterasu. Since the Central Sun is one and the same in both systems the emanations must be essentially alike, no matter what different names they might have.

This movement, of course, resulted in bringing into Japanese Buddhism many elements which were quite foreign to original Buddhism, and carried still further the tendencies which manifested themselves as early as the third century B.C., namely, the tendency to overcome alien beliefs by compromise and absorption. From the deification of its founder, Buddhism went on step by step to the admission of gods upon gods, the greatest of whom being the Buddhas Amitābha and Vairochana, both of whom were symbolized by the sun. And when these had been declared to be identical with the Sun Goddess, Amaterasu, the next steps in this religious syncretism were comparatively easy to take. Even the Shintō War God, Hachiman, was not refused entrance into this new religion which in the mind of its founder was to have been above all else a religion of peace and one which subdues the passions which lead to strife and war. It is not strange, then, that Japanese Buddhism has always been and is to this day — at least as far as the uneducated masses are concerned — a polytheistic and idolatrous religion. And Kōbō Daishi, the saint par excellence of early Japanese Buddhism, who succeeded in making his religion popular with the people, may be regarded in a true sense as a perverter of Buddhism.

This clever compromise made not only Kōbō's sect popular but also the Tendai Sect, for Dengyō Daishi, too, had worked out a scheme by which he harmonized the claims of Shintō and Buddhism. All over the land temples were built in which both the old Shintō deities and Buddhist saints and Bodhisattvas were worshipped. The two new sects grew with leaps and bounds, so that they soon overshadowed the old Nara sects. Mt. Hiei was gradually being covered with monastery after monastery, and soon branch temples of the famous Enryakuji were being built in other parts of the land. The same was true of Mt. Kōya and the Shingon sect.

Just as in the Nara period so in the Heian period Buddhism was closely identified with the ruling classes. Kyōto became the capital of magnificence and splendor that it was largely because the Buddhist monks who went back and forth between China and Japan kept the latter country in close contact with the superior civilization of the former. The light of culture and refinement which radiated from Japan's new capital in ever widening circles till it reached even the more remote places of the empire was strongly tinged with Buddhist colors. What Chamberlain says so well of Japanese Buddhism as a whole is especially true of the Heian epoch when he writes: "All education was for centuries in Buddhist hands, as was the care of the poor and sick; Buddhism introduced art, introduced medicine, molded the folk-lore of the country, created its dramatic poetry, deeply influenced politics and every sphere of social and intellectual activity. In a word, Buddhism was the teacher under whose instruction the Japanese nation grew up." A few instances from the time of Emperor Shirakawa (1072–1086) may indicate how extensive must have been its influence by that time. It is said that *e.g.* the Buddhist injunction against taking life was so strictly enforced that "eight thousand fishing nets were seized and burned; no gifts of fish were to be offered to the court; hunting and hawking were rigidly prescribed, and the hawks set at liberty." This same emperor spent immense sums of money upon Buddhist temples and equipments. "Besides 5470 scrolls or hanging pictures painted and presented to various fanes, Shirakawa was responsible for the erection of one huge idol 32 feet in height, 127 half that size, of 3150 life-size, and of 2930 three-feet images. Then of seven-storied pagodas the tale was twenty-one, and of miniature pagodas as many as 44,630." And what he did so lavishly others imitated to a considerable extent; so that all central Japan was literally studded with Buddhist structures of one sort or another.

From this the reader should not infer that all was well with the Buddhism of the Heian period. Though it did much to advance civilization in Japan in many ways, it must be admitted that there was not a corresponding advance in the moral and spiritual life of the people. In fact, towards the end of the tenth century the great centers of religion themselves began to be hotbeds of vice and intrigue rather than seats of learning and virtue. The age itself, of course, was partially responsible for this, for it was beginning to be an age of political disturbances and military conquest as a result of a complex of causes for which no one in particular was responsible. But, after all, the Buddhist leaders must be blamed for not doing their duty as spiritual guides. In truth, they sank to the level of their surroundings and in many cases became the blind leaders of the blind. "By the end of the eleventh century," writes Murdoch, "any one of these great fanes (*i.e.* Enryakuji, Miidera and Kōfukuji) could readily place several thousand men in the field at very short notice. Each of them had become a huge Cave of Adullam, — a refuge for every sturdy knave with a soul above earning a livelihood by the commonplace drudgery of honest work. Each of them had in truth assumed the aspect of a great fortress garrisoned by a turbulent rabble of armed ruffians. And each of them had degenerated into a hotbed of vice, where the most important precepts of the moral code were openly and wantonly flouted. . . . And yet in spite of the foulness of their lives, the prestige of the priests had never stood higher, while the resources of the monasteries had never been greater; and year by year they were adding to their wealth." The ex-Emperor Shirakawa well expressed the situation in a witticism when he remarked that although he was the ruler of Japan there were three things in the Empire beyond his control, — "the freaks of the river Kamo (which often inundated and devastated the capital), the fall of the dice, and the turbulence of the priests."

Thus we see the irony of history; the very Buddhism which Emperor Kwammu had fostered in his new capital of Peace to counteract the influence of the old Nara sects, in the end turned out to be a greater nuisance and meddler in the affairs of state than the older rival ever dared to be. Not infrequently did these occupants of Hieizan set at defiance both the entreaties and threats of the imperial court itself. Truly Buddhism had wandered far from the path of quiet meditation and peace in which its founder had sought to lead his followers.

D. *The Sects of the Great Awakening*

But as out of decadent Catholicism sprang the great Protestant Reformation, so out of this prosperous and degenerate Heian Buddhism came the great religious awakening in Japan during the twelfth and thirteenth centuries.

What might be regarded as a voice in the wilderness was that of a half-witted wandering priest called Kūya who according to some was really an Imperial prince, a son of Emperor Daigo. He went dancing from place to place, repeating incessantly the Nembutsu (the prayer, Namu Amida Butsu) by which he hoped to direct the attention of the people to the spiritual side of life which had been so utterly buried in the confusion and tumult of the age. He did not, however, confine his activity to preaching and praying, but gave expression to his faith in a real concrete way; for he built bridges, improved roads, repaired temples, dug wells in barren lands, tunneled mountains and labored with his hands unceasingly — all with the purpose of turning men's minds to the better and higher things of life. It is difficult to say whether Kūya's preachings did more than arouse a passing curiosity.

A man who indirectly exercised a great influence on the generation of religious reformers which was to appear later was Genshin. While still a youth of tender years he dreamed that a priest gave him a small mirror and asked him to polish it. He did not understand the significance of the dream until later when he entered, at the age of thirteen, a Tendai monastery on Mt. Hiei, where under the great priest and scholar Jie he was led into the deep truths of Tendai doctrines. At the early age of fifteen he began his lectures on the sacred scriptures and was greatly admired by the emperor who gave him many beautiful garments as a token of his esteem. Young Genshin was much elated over this recognition and sent these gifts to his mother. But his mother was not so pleased as he expected her to be and sent him the following reprimand: "The idea of your leaving home was that you might enter the path of true enlightenment and not to gain any profit or make a name for yourself. Do not be led astray by these things. I thought you would be a bridge to connect this world with the next, but I am sad to find that you are only a monk of this world." These words were sufficient, and the young Genshin turned his back on worldly ambitions and gave himself to a diligent search for the truth. He wrote to his mother in reply to her rebuke, "I regarded books as bridges that lead across this life (*i.e.* learning as a way of success in life), but now happily I have entered the Way of Truth through them." It is said that when his mother was on her deathbed Genshin spent the last hours at her side leading her into the joy of the faith and trust which he had found, namely, the faith in the name of the great Buddha Amida.

The books which Genshin wrote attracted attention not only in Japan but even learned priests in China were deeply impressed by his learning and marveled that Japan should have men of such profound insight and piety. And the Chinese emperor, when he learned of Genshin's death, built a special pagoda in which he had an image of Genshin placed. Genshin was not the founder of a new sect nor did he inaugurate any great reform in the decadent Buddhism of his own day. He remained a priest of the Tendai Sect though he is regarded as one of the great church fathers of the Amida sects which arose soon after his day. This is due to the fact that by his writings he helped lay the foundation for the reforms and new sects of the Kamakura period. His three small volumes on Paradise, the Intermediate States and Hell have exerted a great influence and should be of special interest to Western readers, especially to students of Dante. His description of the eight Buddhist hells, each with its sixteen compartments, affords particular interest to one familiar with Dante's Inferno. Genshin probably received most of his ideas on this subject from Indian sources, and one cannot help but wonder whether

Dante may not have drawn from the same. Genshin, of course, wrote several centuries before Dante's day.

1. *Ryōnin and the First Amida Sect.* — Genshin was followed by Ryōnin (1072–1132) who, too, was a student at the Tendai monasteries. Ryōnin also studied the doctrines of the Shingon sect, but he felt that in all his studies he was not really entering the way of true enlightenment. Not only did he himself fail in his search but he saw that this was the experience of other monks. All of them were so busy with their much learning that they did not really take time to find the heart of truth. He therefore retired to a quiet spot and spent his time in reading and repeating the prayer "Namu Amida Butsu," "I adore Thee Thou Buddha of Eternal Life and Light." It is said that he repeated this prayer sometimes as often as 60,000 times in one day, thus concentrating his mind and heart on Amida. One day when he was thus absorbed in prayer and deep meditation Amida appeared to him in a vision and said: "Great is the merit of Nembutsu (*i.e.* repeating the prayer, Namu Amida Butsu). If by your own prayers you teach others to pray the Nembutsu, their prayers will become your merit and in this way there will be mutual benefit. This is entering Paradise through the power of another." This thought impressed Ryōnin very much and so he formed the Yūdzū Nembutsu Sect (Society of Mutual Benefit through Nembutsu). He went to Kyōto with a roll-book and enrolled the Emperor Toba and many courtiers and officials. Afterwards he wandered from province to province enlisting people in his new sect.

The Yūdzū Nembutsu Sect is the oldest of the four Amida sects in Japan and the first outward expression of that great religious development which took place during the twelfth and thirteenth centuries. It is the first distinctively Japanese sect; the Six Nara sects and the Tendai and Shingon sects having been introduced from China. But while it is the oldest of the Amida sects and as a sect the first Japanese product, it must not be regarded as the beginning of the Amida teaching in Japan nor as even a fair representative of this great division of Japanese Buddhism. The truer representatives of this type of Buddhism are the Jōdo Sect introduced from China but greatly modified in Japan, and its main offshoot, namely, the great Shin Sect of which we shall speak presently. But before we come to these we wish to make a few remarks about the beginnings of the Amida doctrines in Japan.

The idea that one can be born into Amida's Western Paradise by praying sincerely the prayer "Namu Amida Butsu" is a very ancient one in Japan. To begin with, it would seem that the image sent by the king of Kudara to the emperor of Japan in the year 552, when Buddhism was officially introduced, was an image of the Buddha Amida, and so the Amida faith may be said to date from the very beginning of Japanese Buddhism. This may be stretching a point and so we lay no stress upon it. It does seem true, however, that Shōtoku Taishi, the first great royal patron of Japanese Buddhism, expressed longings for the Western Paradise, and during the reigns of Kōgyoku and Kōtoku (642–654), Enon is said to have lectured on the Paradise scriptures in the palace. Gyōgi Bosatsu, the Father of religious syncretism in Japan, preached salvation through the name of Amida; and Chikō of the old Sanron Sect drew pictures of the Western Paradise and wrote an essay on Paradise. Coming down to the end of the Nara period, i.e. at the end of the eighth century, we find pictures of Amida and his Western Paradise in most of the head temples of every province. Besides this it seems to have been the custom at this time to copy on the forty-ninth day after a death occurred the Shosan Jōdokyō (a hymn on birth into Paradise), and on the first anniversary it was the custom to erect an image of Amida six feet in height. All of this goes to show that the Amida doctrines were more or less known at this time. After this Dengyō Daishi, the founder of the Tendai Sect in Japan, gave Amidaism a prominent place in his comprehensive system, and another great Tendai priest, Jikaku Daishi, carrying out Dengyō's wish, built a special hall in which he placed an image of Amida. We have already stated above that the Tendai temples which were connected with the famous Miidera give Amida the highest place of honor. The half-witted priest Kūya, as we have said, went everywhere repeating the Nembutsu, and the learned Genshin laid a more lasting foundation for this doctrine in his writings. But Amidaism as a separate sect did not come into existence in Japan until Ryōnin founded his society of Mutual Benefit through Nembutsu, *i.e.* the Yūdzū Nembutsu Sect.

2. *Hōnen and the Jōdo Sect.* — Ryōnin's conception of Amida's way of salvation was, however, a very inadequate one. He laid too much stress on the idea of merit of the believer, *i.e.* the merit of repeating the Nembutsu. This was really too much of "a vain repetition of the heathen" to satisfy thoroughly the deeper religious sense of the people of Japan. The great teacher of Amida Buddhism was yet to come. This was Genku, better known as Hōnen Shōnin. When Ryōnin died in 1132 Hōnen was a baby boy of two. It was an age of civil wars,[19] — wars in which not only the Samurai took part, but also the monks of Hieizan, Miidera, Kōfukuji and the other great monastic centers of the time. One day the father of Seishimaru (Genku's name as a boy) was mortally wounded in the conflict, and the little lad, reared in the atmosphere of war, attempted to kill his father's enemy. The father praised his son for his loyalty and courage, but in his dying words he said: "I now die through this misfortune, but you must not take vengeance on my enemy. My death is only the reward of my former life. If you avenge my death you will in turn be subject to the vengeance of your enemy's descendants. All living beings fear death. As I suffer from my wounds, other men suffer; and as I cling to life, shall not others cling to life equally? Henceforth pray only for salvation for yourself and your fellowmen. Cast away all vengeance and malice and seek to attain enlightenment."

These words made a profound impression on the boy, and soon after this incident he entered a monastery of the Tendai Sect on Hieizan. He was a diligent student and penetrated far into the various doctrines of not only the Tendai Sect but of all the sects. But in all his seekings he found no peace for his soul. Like Luther more than three centuries later, Genku longed for a deeper assurance of salvation and a more vital religious life than was offered at the centers of learning on the slopes of Hieizan. One day, as if by chance, he hit upon Genshin's "Ōjōyōshū" (Collected Essays on Entering Paradise). A little later he became acquainted with the writings of Zendō Daishi, from which he drank deeply; for here he learned that man's salvation does not depend upon his own strength so much as upon the grace of Amida. Even the lowest sinner may find a way of escape from this life of misery and suffering into a life of happiness and peace if only he has learned to pray in faith to the great Buddha Amida who has prepared for those who believe in him his Western Paradise. When Genku read these great words of hope, he flung away then and there the ordinary way of salvation which Japanese Buddhism had usually been proclaiming, namely, the way of salvation through one's own wisdom and virtue;[20] and he became the prophet of the new way, the way of faith in the mercy of Amida. He became the founder in Japan of the great Jōdo, Pure Land or Paradise Sect (1175) which has as its chief tenets a semi-theistic conception of God, a doctrine of a personal future life and salvation for all men who believe in the grace of Amida. This way of salvation, it holds, was worked out for man by the vicarious sufferings of the (divine) man Hōzō Bosatsu.

With the founding of Hōnen's sect, Amida Buddhism may be said to have been thoroughly established in Japan. The influence of Hōnen's teachings soon became far-reaching. People from all classes of society — from the nobility and the royal family down to the lowest peasants — entered the new sect. Priests of other sects, one after another, began to give their allegiance to this new school and helped spread the way of salvation through faith in Amida. Among Hōnen's followers were a great many men of real ability and this naturally gave prestige to the Jōdo Sect. But strong men are often "strong-minded" men and that frequently becomes a seed of discord. It was not long therefore before the new sect began to divide into several branches or factions, all of which seem to have had a remarkable vitality and so hastened to spread the influence of the sect. The differences were usually very minor and not sufficient to make any serious break.

3. *Shinran and the Shin Sect.* — There was, however, one disciple, Hōnen's greatest disciple, namely, Shinran Shōnin, who thought that his master had not gone far enough in his exposition of the Amida doctrine, and so felt compelled finally in 1224 to establish an independent sect. This sect is the powerful Jōdo Shinshū, The True Pure Land Sect, usually spoken of by the shorter term, Shin Sect.

When Hōnen founded the Jōdo Sect in 1175, Shinran was two years old. He was of noble birth; being a descendant on his father's side of the great Fujiwara family, and on his mother's side, of the illustrious Minamoto family. As a lad of four he lost his father, and in his eighth year his mother also died. Acquainted early with the vicissitudes of life, neither his social standing nor the luxury of his condition could at all satisfy his heart. His mind became more and more set upon deeper things and at the age of nine he became a pupil of Jichin, the abbot of Shōrenin monastery on Hieizan. He is said to have composed the following beautiful line when he took this step: "The heart that thinks there is a to-morrow is as transient as the cherry blossom, for is there not the midnight wind?" He spent a good many years on Hieizan studying the deep things of Tendai philosophy. He also visited Nara and there learned what he could from the scholars of the older sects, among whom there were a great many men of real ability at this time. So profound was his learning that he was popularly known as "The Genius of Hieizan" and "The Famous Priest of the Future." He was made abbot of one of the monasteries on the mountain and was in a fair way of becoming a high priest of the Tendai Sect and of being placed at the head of the Sansenbo, the 3000 monastic buildings which studded Hieizan, thus over-shadowing with his dignity the whole mountain and the neighboring capital of Kyōto. But like the founder of Buddhism, Shinran, having given up all worldly ambition when he first entered the way of enlightenment, was not to yield to the temptation of occupying a conspicuous place as a high priest. He rather gave himself the more diligently to the search after truth and to prayer.

One day Shinran happened to hear Hōnen preach on the way of salvation through faith in Amida's great name. After the sermon he called on Hōnen in his study and after an earnest inquiry as to the fuller meaning of this teaching he then and there gave up the old way of salvation through the Law (Shōdomon) and accepted the doctrine of salvation through faith in Amida (Jōdomon). This was at the age of twenty-nine. Two years later, influenced by a vision of the Goddess [21] of Mercy (Kwannon) and urged on by his master Hōnen, he married Princess Tamahi, the daughter of Prince Fujiwara Kanezane, thus setting an example to the Buddhist world of a new type of priesthood. By this step he broke down the barrier between priest and layman, seeking to demonstrate to the people of Japan that religion should not make a man live an abnormal life and break up the most sacred institution of humanity, namely, the family. Shinran also ate meat and other food forbidden to the priesthood, and in his dress he conformed to the style of ordinary citizens of the land. In short, he lived as a man among men, for he felt that religion has to do with the ordinary things of life and should enable the ordinary man to live this life in the best way possible.

It is not strange that he was attacked fiercely by the priests of the other sects, for his innovations were every whit as extraordinary as any thing Luther ever thought of. He was accordingly banished in 1219 to the province of Hitachi, but he looked upon this exile as an opportunity rather than a hardship. "If I do not go to my place of banishment," said he, "how can I convert the people of those remote parts? This, too, is a blessing flowing from the master's teachings." After six years the ban was removed, but he was in no hurry to get back to Kyōto and civilization. He took a roundabout way through the outlying provinces, preaching the new way and building temples as he went. After an absence of twenty-eight years he finally reached Kyōto, rich in his experience and confident in his gospel of salvation through Amida's Name. The remaining years of his life he spent in writing and preaching. People came even from the distant places to sit at his feet and learn from this great teacher how to walk in the way of Amida's grace. He died at the ripe age of eighty-nine, true to the end to his determination not to know anything but Amida and salvation in his Western Paradise. "Vain thoughts flee at the prayer Namu Amida Butsu. Both the mouth which utters these words and the heart which believes them are in Paradise." "When you see the change which befalls all men, arouse your heart to rely upon Amida." (Shinran.)

At no point in the history of Buddhism would a comparison with the founder of Buddhism and his teachings be so interesting and instructive as just at this point. If the reader bears in mind what was said in Chapter I about the kernel of S'akyamuni's teachings, the contrast between that and the teachings of Shinran and his sect will be striking. It is impossible to give here in detail the doctrines of the Shin Sect and the reader is referred to the author's translation of "A Catechism of the Shin Sect," but we must give at least an outline of the main tenets of this remarkable form of Buddhism.

As we stated above, Shinran taught salvation through faith in the Name of the Buddha Amida and rejected the old way of salvation through one's own wisdom and virtue. Just what does this mean? Briefly stated it means the following:

There may have been a time back in the "golden age" of the human race, said Shinran, when it was possible for man to save himself through his own strength, but in "these latter days" this is quite out of the question; for man is entirely too corrupt and lost in ignorance and sin for this task. There is for him now only one way of salvation, namely, the way of simple faith and trust in the great mercy of Amida. But who or what is Amida?

Not trying to give the history of the Amida faith we shall give simply what is believed about this Buddha Amida. Amida Butsu (Buddha Amitābha), before he became a Buddha and while he was still the Bosatsu Hōzō (Bodhisattva Dharmakara) many æons ago, made a great vow [23] in which he vowed that he would not enter the full bliss of Buddhahood until he had worked out a way of salvation for all men, including even the lowest sinners. He remained true to his vow and after many incarnations of self-sacrificing lives he finally succeeded in heaping up so much merit that he became the great Amida Butsu, the Buddha of Eternal Life and Light who offers every man entrance, or rather birth, into his Pure Land of Bliss. There is but one thing which man must do in order to win this birth into Paradise, and that is to accept the gift that is offered in a spirit of simple faith and trust. The believer is told to call upon the name of Amida in the prayer Namu Amida Butsu which probably means, "I adore Thee," or "Have mercy upon me, Thou Buddha of Eternal Life and Light." He who does this shall be saved. Some go even so far as to say that the faith itself which enables the believer to utter this prayer effectively is also a gift of Amida. The works of the Law, *i.e.* the good works of a man's daily life, which most Buddhists regard as a heaping up of merit or good Karma, are of no avail, according to the followers of Shinran. Faith in Amida's great Name and that alone can save. Good works are not excluded, but they are regarded as only expressions of the believer's gratitude to Amida for his gift of salvation. That is, good works are not the cause of a man's salvation, but they are the effect of his having been saved through faith.

The teachings of the Shin Sect in regard to the way of salvation do not only differ widely from the teachings of the founder of Buddhism and those of the older Japanese sects but also somewhat from the teachings of other Amida sects. The Yūdzū Nembutsu Sect, of which we spoke above, also preached salvation through Amida's name; but, after all, salvation had to be earned by a faithful repetition of the Nembutsu. That is, the believer made merit, or heaped up a good Karma, by repeating his simple prayer over and over again. Then the great Jōdo Sect, of which the Shin sect is really an offshoot, also continued to lay a good deal of stress on making merit. While Amida's grace was held to be sufficient to save, still the believer was warned to be strict in his observance of certain rules of conduct and was made to feel that, after all, good works had a great deal to do with one's salvation. The follower of Shinran, on the other hand, is taught to rest in perfect peace of heart and to trust solely in Amida. He should not even worry about his moral condition or have any anxiety as to his growth in character. "Whether we are saved because our sins have been blotted out or not we do not know; it is as Amida has ordained. We have nothing to do with it; we have but to believe." And Rennyō, one of the great lights in the Shin Sect, says, "The important thing according to the founder's (*i.e.* Shinran's) teachings is nothing else than this heart of faith. He who does not know this is to be regarded as an outsider; he who knows what faith is has the true marks of a follower of Shinran."

Now this way of salvation proclaimed by Shinran, and to a certain extent also by other Amidaists, obviously signifies a rather radical departure from the fundamentals of S'akyamuni's religion. In the first place it would seem that Amidaism, at least in the minds of some of its adherents, not only makes room for a real God-idea, but this idea seems to come very near a theistic conception. In Chapter V, under the general heading of "The God-idea" and the section on "Theistic Buddhism," we shall discuss this point more fully, but here we simply wish to point out the fact that in these Amida sects the conception of Amida is very much the same as the conception of God in theistic systems. It is significant that the Buddha S'akyamuni almost disappears in the Shin Sect and is regarded simply as the teacher of the gospel of Amida. He is revered as a great man and the founder of Buddhism, but he is not usually held up as an object of worship. If he is worshipped at all it is only because he is regarded as an incarnation or partial manifestation of Amida; never as the highest Buddha as such. As we have just said, we shall treat of this subject more fully later and show that Amida Buddhism is not a real monotheism, but for the present we may treat it as pointing in the direction of a truer conception of the divine than is found in the other schools of Buddhism.

Another fact about these Amida sects and the Shin Sect in particular is that salvation means the salvation of the individual into a future life where there seems to be a real continuity and identity of the individual and not a mere Karma continuity and identity. The Shin Sect teaches that at death the believer really enters Amida's Western Paradise, and to many this hope of a future life of happiness seems to have been a real source of joy and peace. There are even cases on record where men have committed suicide in order to hasten their departure from this world and enter Amida's Paradise. Others have lived in such a joyful anticipation of this that this world was turned into a Paradise for them; in fact, Shinran rather emphasized the thought that salvation begins in this life.

A third point of difference is in the conception of sin which one finds in the teachings of the Shin Sect. Man is regarded as totally depraved and beyond the possibility of saving himself. Sin is not regarded as mere outward evil or misfortune, as it is so often in Buddhist thought, but rather as a condition of the heart which may cause outward evil and misfortune. The one thing necessary, then, is to have a change of heart, and this change of heart comes through faith and not through an effort on the part of man to cleanse his heart through his own wisdom or strength. When Amida is received through faith he controls the heart and so uproots all sin. "When we firmly believe in this vow (*i.e.* Amida's vow to save all living beings) and do not doubt it for a moment, Amida graciously governs our heart. Our evil heart at once becomes united with the good heart of the Nyōrai (*i.e.* Amida)." (Shinran.)

Thus in some of the great fundamentals of religion, namely, the God-idea, the doctrine of the future life, the

I

conception of sin, and especially in the conception of the way of salvation, Amida Buddhism in Japan seems to differ rather widely from the rest of Buddhism and the teachings of the founder S'akyamuni; particularly is this true of the great Shin Sect founded by Shinran Shōnin.

A further difference, which though it may not be a fundamental of religion is nevertheless of great importance, is the attitude towards the duties of men as citizens of this world. Where other sects divide the teachings of Buddhism into esoteric and exoteric, or into higher and lower truths, the Shin Sect divides its teachings into doctrines which relate to salvation into a future life and doctrines which relate to a man's duties as a citizen of this world. Buddhism has always been exceedingly other-worldly, and from the very beginning it has held up the life of retirement from the world, the ascetic life of the monk or nun lived in some secluded spot, as the highest type. All through the long centuries the chief function of the average Buddhist priest seems to have been to officiate at funerals and to take charge in one way and another of those who have passed into the great beyond. The Shin Sect, too, is other-worldly; in fact, it has the clearest doctrine of a future life, but it also has a good deal to say about a man's duty as a citizen of this world. We saw above that Shinran himself married and lived the normal life of an ordinary citizen of Japan. This was not a mere accident, but it grew out of a profound conviction that a man of religion should be a model citizen. Household rather than temple or monastery religion was the thing the world needed.

This emphasis on the every-day duties of life really grew out of two things. One was the conviction that salvation has its beginning in this world, *i.e.* the believer is even now united with Amida and so can live in the world without being in bondage to the sins of the world. "How happy the thought," says Hōnen, "that though we are still here in the flesh we are numbered among the holy ones of Paradise." The other reason is the fact that in Japanese Buddhism in general and in the Shin Sect in particular there is much less emphasis put upon the evils of our present existence than in Indian Buddhism. This world, S'akyamuni had said, is a world of suffering and sorrow and therefore its hold on us should rigorously be reduced to the lowest terms possible. The Japanese mind has never accepted this doctrine fully, and the Shin Sect, which is the purest Japanese product of all Japanese sects, has been least influenced by it. It is more natural for the Japanese mind to look upon life and the things of life as good, for Japan is above all else "the land of the gods," and Japanese are the offspring of "the sons of heaven." Thus the religious life cannot be so very distinct from the normal life of a man as a citizen of Japan, and any teacher who can show how religious faith and practical conduct may be harmonized is bound to have a great following. Shinran did have a great following and his sect is to-day the strongest of all sects of Japanese Buddhism. In fact, it has a vitality which is rather unique among the old religions of the orient. Unhampered by any elaborate metaphysical system, it seems to be able to adjust itself to the great changes — political, economic and social — which have come over modern Japan, and to continue its hold upon the people of this generation while most of the other sects seem to be on the decline. If Buddhism has any future in Japan it will be the Buddhism of the Amida sects in general and the Shin Sect in particular.

With these few remarks we must leave for the present this most interesting of all Japanese Buddhist sects and pass on to an account of the other great sects.

4. *Introduction of the Zen Sect.* — Between the founding of the Jōdo and the Shin sects there was introduced from south China one of the main branches of the Dhyāna school, namely, the Rinzai branch of the Zen Sect. The Dhyāna school of Buddhism reached China from India in the year 520 A.D. when Bodhidharma came to China as a missionary. Bodhidharma (Japanese, Daruma) is regarded as the twenty-eighth patriarch, being in direct "apostolic succession" from S'akyamuni. With his removal to China the center of the school passed from India, and so he is also looked

upon as the first Chinese patriarch. At this time China was being flooded with Indian books and the bewildered Buddhist did not know to what book or books he was to turn for the correct teaching. Bodhidharma came with the message that the true teaching of the master was not contained in any one book nor even in all the books put together, for truth is too great and deep to be expressed in any written or spoken word. Truth is in the heart itself and it must be transmitted from heart to heart by a sort of spiritual telegraphy; or even better, the heart must teach itself through silent meditation. The chief characteristic, therefore, of the Zen Sect is silent meditation and abstract contemplation. The true follower seeks thus to penetrate into the inner recesses of reality, into what might be called "the white silence of Truth." It is said of Bodhidharma that he sat seven years staring at a blank wall and that when he was asked questions as to religion and himself he kept silent. And of another Zen philosopher it is said that when he fell into the hands of bandits and they tried to intimidate him by thrusting a sword at his face he did not so much as bat an eye but sat unmoved. No wonder that the ruffians were themselves terrorized and fled leaving this holy man in peace.

Now this method of approach to the truth and salvation as a resultant of the knowledge thus gained was known in Japan from the early days of Buddhism on, being introduced by the high priest Dōsho who established the old Hossō Sect in this land. After him Dōsen, Dengyō, Jikaku and other prominent leaders in religion practiced and preached the Zen way of salvation. By the twelfth century there were a great many, especially men of deep natures, who were acquainted with this quiet way of approach to the truth, but still the followers of Zen had never organized themselves into a separate sect but continued to remain in the existing sects, especially in the all-inclusive Tendai Sect. Finally, however, late in the twelfth century appeared Eisai. Like other great leaders of his day he, too, studied Buddhism at the famous monasteries on Hieizan belonging to the Tendai

Sect. He also became a student of the "Secret doctrines" of the Shingon Sect, but finding no satisfaction in this he returned to Hieizan and for eight years studied profoundly the voluminous canon of Mahāyāna Buddhism. An opportunity presenting itself he carried out a long cherished wish and sailed for China where he studied for a while at the headquarters of the Tendai Sect. Here he secured thirty volumes of rare books and with these he returned to Japan, hoping thus to find the object of his earnest quest. A few years later, however, he felt again constrained to go to China and there at the Tendai center he was initiated into the true teachings of the Zen Sect. When he started for home his teacher bestowed upon him, as a special mark of his achievements, the Great Mantle, the symbol of his having mastered the truth as known by the Zen school. The Zen Sect dates its origin in Japan from about the time of Eisai's second return from China, *i.e.* about 1191. In 1201 the reigning shōgun invited him to establish himself at the Kenninji in Kyōto, and later at the Kenkōji in Kamakura, which city became the center for the sect. And having its center in this military capital of Japan is one reason why the Zen Sect has always had and why it has to this day a great many military men among its adherents.

Not many years after the founding of the Rinzai branch of the Zen Sect a sister branch of this contemplative school, namely, the Sōtō branch, was established by Dōgen, or Shōyō Daishi, with headquarters in the province of Echizen. The chief difference between the Sōtō and the Rinzai branches of the Zen Sect is that the former puts more weight upon book learning as a subsidiary aid to silent meditation on the truth.

It is the claim of the Zen Sect that it represents most truly the spirit and teaching of the founder of Buddhism. This claim seems substantiated by the facts in the case. Not only does the historic connection with early Indian Buddhism seem more direct than in the case of other sects, but its emphasis on meditation and self-discipline seems nearer to the practice and teachings of S'akyamuni. To be sure,

Zen philosophy does not give the Four Great Truths and the Noble Eightfold Path the same importance as S'akyamuni probably did, but still it insists, as he had done, on the doctrine that man must save himself through his own strength and must not depend for help upon God, or the gods. In fact the Zen Sect makes little or no room for the God-idea, or for the idea of the real permanency of the individual in a future life. It has nothing to say about an Eternal Buddha, though it does recognize an ultimate reality transcending the power of the human mind to grasp, which reality S'akyamuni himself, as we saw, did not deny. While S'akyamuni laid his chief emphasis upon the idea of "escaping from the evils of this life," the Zen teachings of Japan lay the emphasis on the escape from the limitations of the present and empirical self into the glorious liberty of the union with the Greater Self; without stating, however, what that Greater Self is or what the nature of such a salvation might mean.

The practice of Zen, or Zazen, is a kind of mystical self-intoxication by which the believer seeks to rise above the world of sense with all its limitations and differences into the freedom and harmony of the Reality which lies beyond and in which there are no differences and jarring contrasts. Naturally not all who practice Zazen pass exactly through the same experience. With some it is entering into a feeling of oneness of all reality, so that the consciousness of the self and all individual existence fades into nothingness and only a "holy vacancy" remains. With others it may go no further than a heightened sense of the oneness of all reality, so that no matter what loss may come to the individual, there can be no permanent loss since the self is regarded as being really one with the Greater Self, or the Universal Self. But in any case, the believer who has entered this ecstatic state feels himself no longer bound by the ordinary laws of our every-day experience. "He has ceased to think of good or evil, released himself from a relative idea of wise and common beings, given up any discussion or consideration of ignorance and intelligence, and delivered his mind from an idea of the boundary between Buddhas and sentient beings. He gives up doing all works and abandons perceiving all objects, does nothing at all, and abstains his six organs of sense from performing their respective functions."

All our ordinary knowledge, *i.e.* the knowledge of the sense-world in which we make differences between things, is regarded as illusion. Even our moral distinctions have no value and must be treated as the product of the unenlightened mind.[25] "The ancients say: 'When illusion vanishes, quietude will appear; when quietude appears, knowledge will arise; when knowledge arises, truth will make its appearance.' If you want to put an end to such illusive thoughts, you should abstain from thinking of good or evil, and without perceiving objects or performing works, you should not think with the mind and do anything with the body. This is the first precaution to be taken. When illusive objects vanish, the illusive mind will consequently vanish. If the illusive mind vanishes, the entity that never changes will appear.[26] It always knows things distinctly. It is not an object of quietude, nor an object of activity."

In order to attain this state of mind which is void of all sense objects and in which Reality Itself will appear, the student of Zazen is given minute directions as to how and where he is to sit in his silent meditations. We can do no better than quote rather at length from a translation of the works of the founder of Sōjiji, one of the two head-monasteries of the Sōtō Sect, from which the above excerpts are also taken.

"As for the place of meditation, a quiet place is good; the cushion you use must be thick; you should prevent wind and smoke from coming in, and rain and dew from moistening you; you should take good care of the place where you sit, and always keep it clean. . . . The place of sitting should not be too bright in the daytime, nor too dark at night, it should be warm in winter and cool in summer. . . .

"While you sit, you should abandon the ideas of heat, will and consciousness, put an end to the thoughts of recollection, perception and contemplation; you should not intend to become a Buddha and care for right or wrong; and valuing time highly, you should be so urgent in the practice of Dhyāna as though you were trying to rescue your head from fire. . . . Shih-hsiang taught his disciples to become like dead trees, and Ju-ching of Tai-pai used to warn his disciples against dozing. For the Dhyāna man there is no need of burning incense, worshipping, invocating the Buddha-name, making confession, reciting Sūtras, or performing daily services; he has only to sit on in meditation and thereby he will attain enlightenment.

". . . There are two ways of sitting: full cross-legged sitting, and half cross-legged sitting. According to the former way, you must put the right foot on the left thigh, and the left foot on the right thigh. Your clothes must be loosely tied and well arranged. Put the right hand with the palm upturned on the left foot and the left hand on the right palm. The thumbs of both hands stand supporting each the point of the other, kept closely to the body. The points of the thumb must be kept just in front of the navel. Keeping the body upright and sitting erectly, you should not incline or bend the body to right or to left, nor should you lean your body forwards or backwards. Your ears and shoulders, nose and navel should be kept respectively in perpendicular lines. Your tongue must be stuck to the upper gum. Breathing must be made through the nostrils. Lips and teeth must be stuck to each other. The eyes must be opened moderately, neither too widely nor too narrowly. Thus making proper arrangements of the body, you should inhale and exhale a few times through the opened mouth. Next, settling your body, you should move your body from side to side, each time decreasing the degree of the motion, and finally coming to a firm upright sitting, when you should consider unconsiderableness. How could unconsiderableness be considered? It is considerationless, which is an important means of Dhyāna sitting, by means of which you must forthwith destroy evil passions and obtain full enlightenment.

"When you want to rise from sitting, first of all you must put both the upturned hands on the knees and move the body from side to side seven or eight times, each time increasing the degree of the motion and breathing out of the opened mouth. Putting your extended arms on the ground, stand up easily and walk slowly along the left side of the room, ever turning to the right."

As one reads these detailed instructions given to those who would practice Zazen, one cannot but be struck with the contradiction involved in the means of achieving this goal of abstract contemplation and the goal itself. The one is the most careful — almost puerile — regard for the details of the sense world, while the goal is a state of mind in which the sense world has no existence. The follower of Zazen may say that this regard for the detailed arrangement of the body is only provisional and these things vanish with the illusive mind when once the believer has entered the state of perfect quietude and truth. Quite so; only then it should not be necessary for one who has reached such a state to return again to an ordinary state of consciousness in which the details and differences of the sense world seem so very real. That is, the student of Zazen should not be given any rules as to how to arise from his posture of sitting in meditation; for why should he wish to arise and return to the sense world if he has really entered a state in which Truth has appeared and in which he knows that the objects of our every-day consciousness are illusive? Obviously the world of sense is too real to be disposed of in this way for any length of time, and the problems of truth and reality must be approached in another way than by a mystical self-intoxication lasting under favorable conditions for only a few hours at best. That the "quiet mind" is the most favorable condition in which Reality may be apprehended, no one would question; but it cannot be apprehended simply by a process of elimination and evacuation of the content of our ordinary conscious states. This can only end in an abstraction and vacuity which may be a pleasant feeling to those who would escape for a little while from the "evil of existence" in this "incurably evil world," but it can hardly satisfy permanently the hearts of those who would overcome the evils of Life and enter a life of a Positive Good.

It seems a curious phenomenon that a sect which lays such an emphasis on the contemplative life and which holds out the "white silence of truth" as the highest goal should have always had among its followers a great many men of the military class. Even in modern industrial and bustling Japan it is the fashion of military men to practice "Zazen." Besides the reason already given above, namely, the fact that the Zen Sect made the military capital of Japan its center of activity,[27] there are two other reasons. One is that the Zen Sect has always shown itself very friendly to Confucian ethics and made it a part of its practical teachings. From the earliest times Confucianism has been a sort of religious philosophy for the military classes and never has it been regarded in Japan as antagonistic to Buddhism. The vagueness of the God-idea in Confucianism is exceedingly congenial to the Zen mind, and the definiteness of the Confucian ethics, especially the ethical teachings which deal with the relationship of lord and vassal, formed a good substitute for the ethics of the Noble Eightfold Path. At any rate, the former were not regarded as contrary to the latter. The other great reason for the popularity of Zen thought with military men is the fact that it lays a strong emphasis upon self-discipline and self-control, the primary qualification of any true soldier. Even the physical discipline of a true student of Zen is Spartan, and the mental discipline is often such that men become indifferent to all dangers and face death without a tremor. The capture of Port Arthur in the Russo-Japanese war was in part at least the fruit of Zen discipline. For a further presentation of Zen thought the reader is referred to Chapter V.

5. *Nichiren and the Nichiren Sect.* — There is one more great sect which arose during this remarkable period of Japan's religious history, namely, the Nichiren Sect founded by Nichiren Shōnin in 1253. Of all the founders of sects

in Japan or leaders in things religious, Nichiren is the most
picturesque and in many respects the most powerful personality.   He was born in 1222 in an unknown village of Awa
Province.   As a lad he became somewhat acquainted with
the teachings of the Shingon Sect, but later he went to Mt.
Hiei and studied under the great priests of the Tendai Sect.
For about ten years he gave himself to these studies and then
returned to his native province ready for his great campaign.
Like all great reformers, Nichiren did not start out to found
a new sect.   He began by denouncing what he regarded as a
real perversion of the master's teachings.   Such perversions
he found especially in the teachings of the sects which were
just then coming into great popularity, namely, the Jōdo,
the Shin and the Zen sects.   In his Rissho Ankoku Ron,
Nichiren's chief writing, he makes a vehement attack on
Hōnen, the founder of the Jōdo Sect, and upon all the followers of the Amida doctrine.   He laments that the teachings
of Dengyō Daishi and the older type of Buddhism were being
neglected and that the people had ears only for the writings
of Zendō and the Amida scriptures.   This bears testimony
to the wonderful success the Amida sects had soon after
their coming into existence.   The Zen sects, too, he could
not endure and opposed them as the invention of the devil.
Even his first love, the Shingon Sect, he denounced as "a
traitor to the country."

The reason Nichiren so bitterly opposed these other sects
was because he felt that they were dividing Buddhism, and
especially that the Amida sects were taking away the glory
of S'akyamuni and giving it to another, namely, Amida.
And on the other hand, with a divided religion Japan would
be a divided nation, and so both religion and state would
be destroyed.   That is why he cries in one of his impassionate
utterances, "Awake, men, awake! awake, and look around
you.   No man is born with two fathers or two mothers.
Look at the heavens above you: there are no two suns in
the sky.   Look at the earth at your feet: no two kings can
rule a country."   But this, he felt, was exactly what was
happening in Japan.   Politically the country was divided

into factions, some giving their allegiance to the emperor, at Kyōto, others to the shōgun or regent at Kamakura.[28] Spiritually some were true to what he thought was the real teaching of the founder and others were followers of Amida, Dainichi or some other Buddha. And as the former was the real outgrowth of the latter division, there was but one thing to do, namely, to uproot the sects which had proved themselves disloyal to the pure teachings of the founder.

Not only was the political and religious world divided and disintegrating, but because of this the nation was being destroyed, he felt. Evidence of this seemed abundant on every hand. In 1257, *e.g.*, a terrible earthquake shook things from their very foundations. This was followed the next year by an equally terrible hurricane; and as a result of these two calamities, famine and pestilence completed the work of destruction. And still further, there were signs that what was left by these natural calamities would fall a prey to a foreign invader, the Mongols who in 1264 had established themselves in Peking under Kublai Khan and were threatening to subdue the whole of eastern Asia, including the islands of the Sunrise Kingdom. To avoid this impending peril Japan must be a united nation both politically and spiritually.

That Nichiren was not a mere alarmist is shown by the events which followed in the political world. The predicted invasion of the Mongols actually materialized, and apparently the only reason it did not succeed beyond the occupation of a few minor islands and a narrow strip of coast line in Kyūshū was the timely appearance of a severe typhoon which caused the Mongol ships to share the fate of the great Spanish Armada. The proud Japanese, however, prefers to lay greater stress on the valor of his illustrious forefathers, who, he claims, were the only people of that age able to check the advancing hordes of the Mongols which at one time or another overran great portions of the two continents of Asia and Europe. Nichiren was equally right in his estimate of the religious situation. The new sects, especially the Amida sects, were doing much to dethrone the founder of Buddhism from his place of honor; for it is a fact that most Amidaists regard Gautama as simply the great teacher and not the Buddha to be worshiped. If he is worshiped at all it is only because he might be regarded as one of the historic manifestations of Amida. The Shingon was equally a departure though in quite a different way, as we have already shown above. Whether his attacks on the Zen Sect were justified on the same grounds is a question; for, as we have said above, the Zen is nearer the teachings of the founder in many ways than, perhaps, any other Japanese sect. But on the whole Nichiren was correct in raising an alarm and trying to bring his people back to the historical Buddha S'akyamuni if Japanese Buddhism was to follow the teaching of him whom they professed to follow.

But while Nichiren was zealous to restore Buddhism to its pristine purity it does not at all follow that he even knew what the pristine purity of Buddhism might mean. Both the spirit of his religion and the content of his doctrines prove that he knew really very little on this subject. As a student of the Tendai he became acquainted among other books 'with the Saddharma-Pundarīka-sūtra (Japanese, Hokkekyō) which he made the main foundation of his teachings. As we have already pointed out, this is a comparatively late writing and breathes a Buddhism quite different from the Buddhism of S'akyamuni. The great Buddha of that scripture is the Eternal Buddha of Original Enlightenment with whom S'akyamuni is identical, or of whom he is one of many manifestations. But the historical Buddha S'akyamuni had nothing to say of such a Buddha, and he certainly never claimed to be identical with or the manifestation of such a Buddha. Then further, Nichiren and his followers lay great emphasis on faith, faith in this sacred scripture which is regarded with a superstitious reverence. The prayer which is so constantly upon the lips of Nichiren's disciples, "Namu Myōhō Renge Kyō" (Hail, Thou Scripture of the Lotus of the True Law), seems of all "vain repetitions of the heathen" the most vain; especially is this true when judged from the standpoint of what S'akya-muni regarded as the kernel of his teachings.

Then Nichiren's bitter attack on other sects was also a great departure from the spirit of older Buddhism, which was nothing if not tolerant of views that differed. This tolerant attitude was especially characteristic of the Tendai Sect, from which Nichiren learned practically all that he knew about Buddhism. This characteristic of Nichiren was not altogether a bad one, for if there is anything that Buddhism needed it was a firmness which would enable it to hold to some definite things and reject others that were incompatible. But we simply wish to point out that Nichiren, in trying to give Buddhism some backbone, was infusing into it his own vigorous personality to whom distinctions were real and vital, and he was not restoring a characteristic of the older Buddhism. In his Rissho Ankoku Ron this comes clearly to light, for in this dialogue between the master of a house and a guest the latter frequently makes the point that the spirit of Buddhism is one which tolerates all views and persecutes none, and the master has great difficulty in proving from the sacred scriptures that heretics should be opposed. The truth of the matter is that Nichiren was anything but a reformer of Buddhism. He thought he was one, but in reality he was a man who gave Japanese Buddhism a new turn. This new turn was not in the doctrines he taught, for there is nothing new in the teachings of the Nichiren Sect, but in the spirit which he infused into the new sect which he founded. The very fact that it is the only Japanese sect which calls itself by the name of its founder shows that it was founded on Nichiren's spirit and personality rather than upon any new doctrine or upon any old Buddhist teaching restored to life. Nichiren has transmitted his positive spirit to his followers, though it must be admitted that the positiveness which made him a towering figure in Japanese life, in most of his followers assumes a fanatic character which is the enemy of all true progress and has made the sect, as one has put it, "the Ishmael of Buddhism."

Nichiren's bitter attacks upon the political and religious leaders of his day naturally led to counter attacks from his many enemies. By the priests of other sects he was accused of promulgating heresy, and his political enemies accused him of inciting rebellion. In 1261, he was arrested and brought before the regent's court at Kamakura. It is not strange that he was found guilty and that he was banished to the peninsula of Idzu. Three years later, however, he appeared again in the streets of Kamakura, more outspoken than ever. For a while he was safe, for the people believed that it was in response to his prayers that the heavens sent rain after a long drought. Like Elijah of old, he mocked the "false prophets" and came off victorious. But even so, it was impossible for a man of his temper to keep out of trouble, and we soon find him again before the regent's court. This time the charges were so serious that the court felt constrained to condemn him to death.[29] He was led to the sands on the Kamakura beach and the executioner's sword was about to strike the fatal blow when, as if by miracle, a messenger from the regent appeared upon the scene and saved his life. Nichiren was instead banished to distant Sado, where he remained till 1272, when he returned once more to resume his preachings and warnings. By this time, he had won so many followers that he was quite safe. The remaining ten years of his life he spent at Minobu and Ikegami, which two places are regarded to this day as the chief seats of the sect. At Ikegami Nichiren entered into rest from his strenuous life, and there is his tomb, which is still a sacred shrine to thousands. Every autumn his numerous followers gather there from all quarters to do him honor. But the thoughtful student, when he listens to the deafening noise of those drunken worshipers — drunken not with Nichiren's enthusiasm and inspiring message but with cheap *saké* — mourns the thought that one so earnest and on the whole so sane should have such unworthy followers. For it is true that while there are some educated people in the Nichiren Sect the rank and file come from the most ignorant and lowest classes; and the religion which they profess, instead of lifting them to a higher and purer life, seems only to rivet upon them more tightly the superstitions and follies of a darker age.

6. *The Ji Sect.* — Another sect which came into existence about this time and which we mention just in passing is the last of the four Amida sects, the Ji Sect founded by Ippen Shōnin. Some hold that it was first founded by Kūya and that Ippen is the second founder, but if it was founded as early as Kūya's day it made no place for itself before Ippen's day. It is of little consequence now as it has only about 500 temples in all Japan, but in its early history it promised to be of great influence and at one time had even an imperial prince for its head. Ippen Shōnin was remarkable for his zeal in trying to spread his message, going from one end of the land to the other to teach men the Easy Way, the Way of Faith in the Mercy of Amida. He seems to have transmitted this characteristic to his followers, for the sect has apparently always laid great stress upon itinerant preaching. One naturally wonders why such efforts have produced no greater results, unless it be that they are reaped by the more powerful Amida sects from which the Ji Sect really does not differ enough to warrant a separate existence.

*   *   *   *   *   *   *

All four of these great sects, the Jōdo, Zen, Shin and Nichiren came into existence within a period of about three quarters of a century, namely, between 1175–1253, and their beginnings undoubtedly represent the greatest outburst of religious life to be found in Japan's long history. The student who reads with an unbiased mind this movement and the lives of the great men who led the way, cannot fail to be impressed with the positive contribution made by Japan to at least one of the world's great religions. To know this period of Japanese history will cure any man of the superficial thought so often expressed by Westerners that the Japanese have borrowed everything they possess and that they are only imitators. The religion of these four great sects is as truly a real development of Indian and

Chinese Buddhism as is the Protestantism of Germany, England and America a development of medieval and early Christianity; the only difference is that it took place some three centuries earlier. The old Nara sects and the two Kyōto sects of the ninth century had their influence on Japan because they represented a higher civilization than that of Japan, but these four great sects of the Kamakura period gained their hold because they were the first real expression of Buddhism in terms of things Japanese, *i.e.* with them Buddhism may be said to have been thoroughly planted in Japanese life. It was planted not only in the life of the upper classes, as was largely the case with the older sects, but in the life of the people at large. It is only natural that these sects should become very popular, and while the old Tendai and Shingon sects continued to exercise a great influence they were relegated to a secondary place, especially in the new Kwantō [30] region, the center of the military rulers of Japan. Out of a total of 72,000 temples in existence to-day over 53,000 belong to the above-mentioned four great sects, and as we shall see later, they represent the dominant forces of Japanese Buddhism to-day.

Unfortunately this reformation of Japanese Buddhism in the twelfth and thirteenth centuries had in it also some of the evils of the Protestant Reformation. It had in it from the beginning the seeds of schism and divisions. We saw above that Nichiren was alarmed at the influence the new sects were having and that he sought to rally Buddhists around the one standard of loyalty to S'akyamuni and one earthly ruler; but as a matter of fact his efforts resulted in making further divisions and in bringing in a period of strife and hatred among the various sects. Not that Nichiren was responsible for all these fights and divisions but that he marks in himself the tendency of the age. Any account of these divisions, or even the barest outline of them, would try the patience of even an interested student. It is enough to say that the process went on and on, old schisms dying out and new ones taking their place, until to-day, Japan has over fifty Buddhist sects recognized by the government.

K

Of these there are thirty-six divisions and subdivisions within the four sects of the Kamakura period.

The differences between the main divisions of Japanese Buddhism, of which it is customary to make twelve, are often much greater than the differences between the great divisions of Christianity. On the other hand the differences between the subdivisions of a sect are often very minor. Thus, *e.g.*, the ten subdivisions of the Shin Sect are due not to any doctrinal differences but sometimes simply to the fact that some temple, harboring perhaps a royal or other important personage, became thereby too prominent to be regarded as a branch-temple and so was made independent and the center of a new subdivision. In other cases subdivisions were caused by the rise of some great priest who by his own personality impressed himself so powerfully upon his followers that they banded themselves together into a brotherhood without thereby intentionally cutting themselves loose from the parent body but which nevertheless in the course of time became independent. In still other cases, the divisions were due merely to geographical conditions, for in a mountainous country like Japan, before the advent of the railroad, travel and intercourse were exceedingly difficult. This fact had made the political divisions very real for centuries before the advent of Buddhism, and these political divisions in turn made the religious differences very natural and easy.

Thus Japanese Buddhism is quite accustomed to the idea of schisms and divisions, as indeed Buddhism in India and China was from the early days; but it must be added that the average Buddhist, especially the average Buddhist philosopher, sees in this nothing to be regretted, but only a sign of life. Even a Christian must admit that schisms are often a sign of life, though frequently a misdirected life. The Buddhist philosopher on the other hand would hold that because Truth is many sided and men's minds are so finite, it is the glory of a religion to have many divisions each of which brings out its own peculiar angle of the whole truth. So far do some philosophers carry this half truth that they do not hesitate to regard the most glaring contradictions as but the opposite sides of the same truth.[31] But of this characteristic of Buddhism we shall speak more fully in Chapter V, when we take up the Buddhist theory of knowledge, and so we leave it to pass on with the historical narrative.

E. *Political Strife and Religious Decline*

The wonderful religious outburst of the twelfth and thirteenth centuries was followed by a sad decline. For about one hundred years after the founding of the Kamakura shōgunate Japan enjoyed peace and a measure of prosperity. The Hōjō regents who supplanted the descendants of the great Yoritomo were on the whole strong and capable rulers, and under their administration the country was able to recover somewhat from the devastating wars which had preceded this period. But in the beginning of the fourteenth century things began to change for the worse again. In 1333 the Hōjō regents were overthrown, and upon this followed the long Wars of Succession when Japan had two rival lines of emperors, and for more than fifty years civil war and private wars were the order of the day. Finally in 1392 the Ashikagas succeeded in bringing the land once more under one central authority, but this did not mean much gain to the average citizen. As a matter of fact the peace under the Ashikaga shōguns was often less endurable than war, for the tax-gatherer was more to be dreaded than the soldier or the plague and famine which in those days usually followed in the wake of war. It is claimed that in one form or another the poor peasants had to pay about 70 per cent of the produce of their fields as taxes. The money thus extorted from the people was not used to repair the ravages of preceding wars but was squandered in extravagant and luxuriant living by the shōguns and their hangers-on. The third Ashikaga shōgun, Yoshimitsu, *e.g.*, spent enormous sums on magnificent palaces and private residences. One writer states that his "Flower Palace" cost about five million dollars; a single door costing as much as $150,000.

In this mad craze he was followed by the upper classes who could — and more often could not — afford it; so that the city of Kyōto had at this time between six and seven thousand such extravagant residences. Even when the land was stricken with a severe plague and famine, as it was, *e.g.*, in the time of the eighth Ashikaga shōgun, Yoshimasa, when in two months about 80,000 people perished, this extravagant style of living was kept up.

It is therefore not strange that in such days the heart for quiet and industrial living was taken out of the common people and that industry and the constructive forces of life lagged. Nor is it strange that finally Japan was so impoverished that when, *e.g.*, in 1500 the Emperor Tsuchimikado II. died it was forty-four days before enough money could be gotten together to defray the funeral expenses, while his successor, Nara II., had to wait twenty-one years before he had sufficient means to celebrate his coronation appropriately.

That this should be a period of religious decline goes without saying. Of course, in one way religion seemed to gain a firmer hold on the people just because of the adverse circumstances under which they lived. Especially those sects which held out to the common man the hope of a speedy entrance into paradise from this "vale of tears" found a rather congenial atmosphere in which to propagate their doctrines. In fact the pessimistic spirit of Buddhism as a whole, which was one born in a world-weary civilization and which regards life as incurably evil and everything as evanescent, fitted in remarkably well with the temper of the age. The very woes of the people became a source of prosperity to the unscrupulous priests, who were usually quite ready to exchange their "spiritual treasures" for deeds to broad acres and stately manors. The pleasure-loving Yoshimitsu and his successors were indeed ever ready to spend goodly sums upon temples and temple decorations. Yoshimitsu was specially generous towards the Zen Sect and gave liberal gifts to the five great fanes of Kamakura (Go-zan) and the five great fanes in Kyōto and its vicinity.

He went so far as to direct that each province should have its own great Zen monastery. The land owned by all the temples and monasteries was exempted from taxation, and many monasteries received funds from the special tax known as Dansen. And still further, certain ones received directly the custom duties and transit duties collected at the various barriers which were now being erected all over the land. Thus, *e.g.*, the great Kōfukuji of Nara received the customs of the port of Hyōgo.

With such favors extended to the Buddhist monks and priests it is only natural that outwardly at least religion was flourishing in this age of bloodshed and misery. But a religion which lives on the fears and tears of its adherents is not a healthy product; and as a matter of fact this period of the great Succession Wars and Ashikaga shōguns was not great in spiritual realities. Very few indeed were walking in the Noble Eightfold Path of the founder. Not only had the Buddhist layman wandered far from this path but the priests and monks seem to have gone even farther astray. Even the new sects which had been founded as a protest against the corruption of the old Kyōto sects had gone the way of all the rest. The great monasteries were great only as formidable camps of fighting monks, for the military monk was the order of the day. Some authorities claim that in the early part of the sixteenth century the Buddhist priests were on the whole the strongest political force in Japan. This is probably not an exaggeration, for it must be remembered that by this time all semblance of a central authority had vanished. The emperors were figure-heads and even the shōguns were mere puppets, and the various feudal chiefs were each a law unto himself. And often greater than the authority of these feudal chiefs was that of the rich monasteries with their extensive lands and their mountain fortresses. But, of course, the priests did not wield this authority as a unit nor in the interest of what might work for the good of the land. When they were not taking part in the general civil wars of the age on one side or the other, the various monasteries fought among themselves. Hieizan, Miidera and Kōfukuji had been in the habit of doing this for centuries, but now they were imitated by the new "centers of light." Particularly fierce was the feud between Jōdo and Nichiren sects. Even the followers of the great Shinran apparently believed in the power of the mailed fist as much as the rest, for we read that towards the close of this age a great monastery of this sect was able to resist successfully Nobunaga's besieging army of sixty thousand.

But it was not only that the religious leaders of this day had exchanged their spiritual weapons for steel swords and spears and that the foes they were fighting were their own brethren and not the hosts of sin and darkness, that marks the spiritual decline of the times. These "centers of light" were guilty of far more infamous deeds of darkness. We read, e.g., of the abbots of monasteries, after taking the customary vows of poverty and celibacy, spending their days in riotous living with lewd women. And the worst of it was that apparently nobody regarded this wrong or inconsistent. In the middle of the fifteenth century, when famine and plague stalked through the land and daily between seven and eight hundred peasants fell by the wayside, it was quite common to dispose of the daughters of poor families by selling them to brothels, while the boys were frequently sold to the priests, "who shaved their eyebrows, powdered their faces, dressed them in female garb and put them to the vilest of uses, for since the days of Yoshimitsu, who had set an evil example in this as in so many other matters, the practice of pederasty had become very common, especially in the monasteries, although it was by no means confined to them."

It would, however, not be correct to infer from what we have just said that Buddhism did not exert any influence for good during this period of bloodshed and misery. In fact there are many cases in which Buddhist priests intervened with the mercy of Buddha to stay the wrath of men. Buddhist monasteries were often like the cities of refuge in ancient Israel, and political criminals frequently were allowed to choose between the tonsure and the sword. It is true that the guilty occasionally escaped thus from well-deserved punishment, but more often the law from which they escaped was not the law of right but only that of might. Then here and there were individual priests of real power who exercised a great influence for good over the rulers of the day and so helped guide them through these periods of storm to days of peace. Perhaps the most conspicuous case of such an influence was that of the relation between Ashikaga Takauji and the famous Zen priest Soseki. Not only did such men give spiritual consolation to these leaders in their trying times but perhaps more often gave them real solid advice as to the affairs of state. Soseki especially seems to have tried to apply the truths of religion to the practical problems of life. He sought to show Takauji that mercy, patience and serving others were not only the expression of the Buddha heart but also the quickest and surest road to a reign of peace. "If one rises above the clouds, the moon can be seen without an obstruction," he once wrote to the founder of the Ashikaga shōgunate. Little did he realize how few would be able to do this during the two centuries which followed.

Then again, should it be said to the credit of Buddhism, that this period marks a wonderful development in pictorial art, *viz.*, the rise of the great Zen school of painters which has dominated the ideals of artists in one way or another down to almost the present day. Of course, such an influence may not have been very far reaching in that age, but the fact that this development of at least one of the fine arts was possible at all goes to show that, after all, there were individuals here and there who had time and taste for the higher aspects of life.

But after this has been said it must be confessed that the period of the Ashikaga shōguns was in general one of religious decay. Buddhism though outwardly strong was really bankrupt morally and spiritually. Here and there a man, *e.g.*, like Rennyō (1415–1499) of the Shin Sect appeared and tried to make Buddhism a real spiritual force in society, but the darkness of the age was against them. Rennyō, *e.g.*, was compelled to write out the doctrines of his sect in the simple Hiragana script, as not only the lower classes but also the middle and some of the upper classes were unable to read or understand anything written in Chinese characters in which all the Buddhist scriptures were published. It is true, some light continued to stream into Japan from China during these dark days, but it was rather faint, for the Neo-Confucianism which was to exert such a great influence during the Tokugawa shōgunate had not yet taken a firm hold, though a number of Zen scholars had been more or less under its influence from the end of the thirteenth century onward.

F. *Religion in the Tokugawa Period*

1. *Reconstruction Days and the Catholic Mission.* — The long period of strife and bloodshed of which we have just spoken was followed finally by the great peace of the Tokugawa shōgunate. By the middle of the sixteenth century the movement had begun which was gradually to bring about a unification of the empire and restore peace and prosperity to a much afflicted people. There are three great names around which the history of Japan centers during these reconstruction days, *viz.*, Nobunaga, Hideyoshi and Tokugawa Ieyasu. Of course, there were other great men who helped in the unification of the empire, but these three stand out like great peaks. We shall not stop to give even an outline of their lives, though it would not be out of place in even such a hurried review of the development of Buddhism, for while they were not men of religion they had a great deal to do with determining the religious development of the empire for several centuries. All three were men who rose from an obscure environment, and Hideyoshi,[32] the greatest of the trio, was the son of a simple peasant. A Japanese wit has well expressed their respective characteristics as follows: "If you do not sing," said Nobunaga to a nightingale, "I will wring your neck." "If you do not sing," said Hideyoshi, "I will make you." "If you do not sing,"

said the more diplomatic Ieyasu, "I will wait until you do." The nightingale finally did sing the song of peace and unity for Ieyasu, but each of the three had a big part in making it sing. Their work resulted in the great Tokugawa shōgun-ate, which ruled the land with such skill and firmness for about two centuries and a half that there was hardly so much as a dogfight on this blood-drenched soil.

It was just at the beginning of this reconstruction period that the Catholic mission under Xavier came to Japan in the year 1549. The mission landed from a Portuguese ship in the southern island of Kyūshū. The missionaries were well received, for in their train came the merchants and traders with guns and other implements of war so much appreciated by a warlike age. We are told that even the Buddhist priests received these Christian missionaries in a friendly spirit, for they regarded their religion as simply one more form of the comprehensive Mahāyāna teaching. And besides, they were not half so much concerned with rivals in things spiritual as in worldly power and prestige. It goes without saying that the Catholics were not willing to com-promise with the Buddhists, though they did not take an openly hostile attitude until they had first ingratiated them-selves with certain political factions to whom they looked for patronage and protection.

We find thus the missionary Froez, in the year 1568, seek-ing an interview with the great Nobunaga. At this con-ference, apparently, an understanding was reached by which the Catholics were to be utilized for fighting and crushing the Buddhist monasteries, which had incurred Nobunaga's enmity. We do not know the details of the arrangement, but it is a fact that Christianity in Japan at that time ad-vanced with leaps and bounds and that Nobunaga in 1571 exterminated the three thousand monasteries which studded Mt. Hiei. This wholesale destruction of the historic center and home of Buddhism was but the beginning of similar operations against the other monastery centers in the land. By the zealous Catholics Nobunaga was regarded as the "true scourge of God." Nobunaga, however, was not a Christian himself; he simply used the Jesuits to serve his purpose. His religion was his own ambition, for he built a great temple and placed in it a stone image of himself which he expected the people to worship. But as in the case of vain Herod of old, his self-exaltation was speedily followed by his downfall. The hand of the assassin, inspired by his trusted general Akechi Mitsuhide, brought his career to a sudden end.

Nobunaga was succeeded by his friend and lieutenant Toyotomi Hideyoshi. Hideyoshi was quick to conserve what Nobunaga had begun. He "made the nightingale sing," not so much by threatening "to wring its neck" as by less drastic measures, though he, too, resorted a good deal to the sword to carry out his program of harmonizing the nation. Hideyoshi, too, was not a friend of the Buddhists and continued the work of Nobunaga in reducing their military strength, though he showed some consideration for certain monasteries which he could use to an advantage. He had begun to suspect the Jesuits of political intrigues and in 1597, he suddenly dropped his mask of friendship and had twenty-six of them crucified on Martyr's Peak near Nagasaki. This did not mean that all Christians were put under the ban, for later on he entrusted the Christian general Konishi with a regiment of Christians to carry out a military expedition against Korea, though he took the precaution to send also some Buddhist troops with them, the idea being that the two groups would spy on each other and so neutralize their influence. Hideyoshi like Nobunaga made his own ambition his religion as may be seen from the fact that he erected a magnificent temple to the New War God which was to be none other than himself.

Hideyoshi was succeeded by Ieyasu, the last of the great triad. Nobunaga and Hideyoshi had done preparatory work for the unification of the empire, Ieyasu consummated and consolidated it. He had but one great battle to fight, namely, the famous battle of Sekigahara, and then he could wait till the "nightingale sang" its song of peace. And sing it did, for Ieyasu became the founder of the illustrious

Tokugawa shōgunate which gave peace and order to Japan for more than 250 years. The emperor at Kyōto was allowed the nominal rule of the empire but it is an open secret that the shōgun's word at Yedo (Tōkyō) was supreme, and when Commodore Perry opened the closed doors of Japan in 1853 it was with the shōgun that he dealt as the real ruler of the land. The relative power of emperor and shōgun may be best appreciated when it is remembered that the annual appropriation for the royal family and its dependents was only 150,000 koku of rice and this was not taken directly from the national revenue but was given by the shōgun out of his own fat income of 4,000,000 per year.

Ieyasu's attitude toward religion differed from that of his two predecessors in that he was himself a professing Buddhist and took a more or less active interest in religious reform. Whether he was really a religious man is another question. The truth of the matter seems to be that he was very liberal in his views and looked upon organized religion as a force that might help him in the affairs of state, for Ieyasu was above all else a shrewd statesman. That is why he was so intimate with the priest Tenkai who became his right hand man to control not only the Christians but also the Buddhists themselves. And that is also why he encouraged the revival of Confucianism in Japan, for he saw in the Confucian philosophy of state and its emphasis on the spirit of loyalty a desirable force to help him in his great work of national unification.

2. *The Closing of the Doors and the Suppression of Christianity.* — It may seem strange at first sight that a man so liberal minded should be the one who closed the doors of Japan to the outside world. The truth of the matter is that this policy which seems so narrow to us moderns was really in the interest of peace and order. The only mistake was that the doors were kept closed so long after the danger which Ieyasu sought to avoid had passed. It is safe to say that if his successors had been as open minded as he was they would have changed the policy long before they actually did. Ieyasu's reason for cutting Japan off from the outside

world was simply to enable him to consolidate his work of unification. He did not wish any disturbing element to come in from the outside and upset the peace that had been bought at such great cost. Too long had Japan bled from the wounds of discord. Now Christianity was undoubtedly a foreign element and in the form in which it had been propagated in Japan from the beginning it meddled entirely too much with the things that belong to Cæsar to be allowed with impunity. The Buddhists, of course, meddled even more than did the Christians but Buddhism had been the religion of the people for centuries and could not be opposed too much. It was enough to regulate it through the priests themselves. But Christianity was a new outside element and if it was not willing to be merged in the national religion of the land there was but one thing left, namely to exterminate it. An additional reason for this attitude towards Christianity was the fact that the Jesuits were the real agents of the pope at Rome and that all true disciples were called upon to regard the pope as not only the spiritual head but as also superior to earthly rulers in temporal matters. It is only natural that Ieyasu should see in the rising Catholic church in Japan the seed of future political troubles.

We find accordingly that step by step the regulations against Christianity became more and more severe until it was positively forbidden by law after 1611. Whereas under Nobunaga's régime the Catholics were used as an instrument to fight Buddhist monasteries, Ieyasu turned the tables and used the Buddhist monks to suppress Christianity. In every city and village of the land certain officials were set over well-defined districts, their sole duty being to spy out those suspected of being Christians. (It is an interesting fact that the second man to become a bishop in the Japan Methodist Church, Bishop Hiraiwa, is the son of such an official, the office having been hereditary in the family for several generations.)

The story of the suppression of Christianity in Japan has been told by others and we need not repeat it here. We simply state that after the first severe persecutions the majority of the thousands and tens of thousands of the nominal Christians who became such in the period of governmental patronage recanted and entered the Buddhist ranks. One of the requirements of the day was the registration of every Japanese citizen as an adherent of one of the Buddhist sects. This, we might remark in passing, accounts for the fact that to this day the great majority of the people regard themselves as Buddhists, though as individuals they may not care a fig for the religion or know the barest outline of Buddhist teachings. But not all these Catholic Christians recanted. Many of them died the martyr's death, and in spite of the closest watch on the part of the government for 250 years Christianity kept cropping up again and again. There are many people still living who saw the edict boards against Christianity along the highways of the empire; and the brass crosses worn smooth by the feet of those who thus proved that they were not Christians, may be seen in the museums of the nation. But when the edicts were finally taken down there were several thousand Christians in and around Nagasaki who had kept the faith. And in other parts of the land there are Christians in whose families precious Christian relics have been handed down in secret from generation to generation.

3. *Partial Revival of Buddhism.* — We have said above that the Buddhists were used as an instrument of the government to suppress Christianity. This does not mean, however, that Buddhism under the Tokugawa shōguns ever got back its former vitality or even its outward prestige.[33] The truth of the matter is that the blow which Nobunaga dealt to the famous Tendai monastery on Mt. Hiei proved almost fatal. And as Mt. Hiei was really the mother of all the great leaders who founded the leading sects this blow proved serious to Japanese Buddhism as a whole. All the more serious was it for the religion of Buddha when it is remembered that other great centers of the faith were equally disturbed during the stormy times that preceded the great calm.

After peace was restored and prosperity and culture began

to return, Buddhism, too, recovered somewhat from the shock. In almost every one of the leading sects appeared men of real ability and character. It is therefore customary among Buddhist writers to speak of the "Middle Reformers," *i.e.* the men who after the devastating wars of the Ashikaga period brought new prosperity to the various sects. Thus, *e.g.* the Tendai Sect, while crushed in and around Kyōto, began to show new activity in the Kwantō with Nikkō and Yedo as centers. In the Shingon Sect we see the New School party growing in power and influence. The Rinzai and Sōtō branches of the Zen Sect had suffered most severely from the wars, for as we have said, these sects had a great many military men as adherents, and the old law that he that takes the sword shall perish by the sword held good in Japan as truly as elsewhere. But when peace was restored these sects became quite flourishing, especially in outward things, for it was the fashion of the day among the various feudal lords who were usually military men to bestow much property upon Zen temples and monasteries. The Jōdo Sect seemed specially favored from time to time by the Tokugawa shōguns and it recovered much of its former glory, having among its strong temples such places as the famous Chionin of Kyōto and the Zōjōji of Tōkyō, and counting among its priests many men of real ability. And what is true of the Jōdo is equally true of the Shin Sect. Its great temples built in the modern period and some during the past few decades are numerous. The headquarters of the two Hongwanji branches in Kyōto are especially a credit as magnificent specimens of temple architecture. The Nichiren Sect, too, had its reformers and shared with others a certain degree of prosperity during the peaceful days of the Tokugawa period.

This day of renewals saw even the introduction of a new sect from China, namely, the Ōbaku branch of the Zen Sect founded in 1659 by a Chinese priest named Ingen and by Chinese refugees who came to Japan after the fall of the Ming dynasty. This sect has never attracted many adherents but it has exerted a great influence and counts among its few followers a number of the strongest men of Japan. The distinguishing feature of the sect is its use of modern Chinese for its scriptures whereas other sects still use the ancient Chinese, though in very recent years they have begun to use Japanese translations for the general public.

But after all this has been said about the renewal of Buddhism during the Tokugawa period it cannot be held that the religion of Buddha ever reached again the heights it had attained during the great period of religious awakening in the twelfth and thirteenth centuries. In spite of this outward prosperity and activity which led in some cases to the formation of new subdivisions, the period as a whole cannot be regarded as a great period for Buddhism as far as real spiritual influence and strength is concerned. The truth of the matter is that the springs of the spiritual life for this age were really outside of Buddhism, namely, in Confucianism.

4. *Neo-Confucianism.* — Confucian thought had influenced Japan from the earliest days — even before Buddhism was introduced during the sixth century. But while this is true it cannot be said that Confucianism before the Tokugawa age was ever the dominant life-current in this land. It was rather like a number of minor tributaries which fed the main stream; particularly was its influence felt in the realm of practical ethics. In fact, as we have said before, much of the ethical teachings of Japanese Buddhism is really only a restatement of Confucian ethics. That is, the strongest influence which Confucianism exerted on Japan before the Tokugawa age was exerted through Buddhism.

Now it is a peculiar coincident that at the very time when Buddhism in Japan burst forth into the four great sects of the Kamakura period, namely, the rise of the Jōdo, Zen, Shin and Nichiren sects, Confucianism in China was being reshaped in the Neo-Confucian schools of Shushi (Chinese, Chu Hi 1130–1200) and Ōyōmei (Chinese, Wang-Yang-Ming 1472–1528). The foundations for the Ōyōmei school were really laid by Riku-Shōsan (1042–1094), and so while Ōyōmei, who gave the school its permanent influence, belongs to a little later period we may say that these Neo-Confucian schools arose about the time of the great Buddhist awakening in Japan. It was this type of Confucianism which was to overshadow Buddhism during the Tokugawa period. Particularly was the Shushi school to become the dominant force in the official world of Japan, for it was made the authorized system of education by Ieyasu and became so firmly entrenched that any one opposing its teachings was regarded as a traitor to the state.

This reshaping of Confucianism in China into the Shushi and Ōyōmei schools was really more than a restatement of an old system; it was in fact a syncretism of Confucianism and Buddhism. Even as early as the days of Mencius and a little later Confucianism was being strongly influenced by Taoism. That is, Confucian scholars, while clinging to the practical ethics of the Five Relations, began to seek for a metaphysical and religious basis for their ethics. Then with the coming of the Zen philosophy in the sixth century A.D. and the general development of Mahāyāna Buddhism in China, the movement in Confucianism from the external and formal to the internal and spiritual continued. This was the period when Chinese Buddhism took up into itself much of the practical teachings of Confucianism which have ever since constituted the practical ethics found in Chinese and Japanese Buddhism. But not until the days of Riku-Shōsan, Shushi and Ōyōmei did Confucianism develop a real metaphysical and religious basis for its teachings. These philosophers and their followers were always talking about the "Ri" and the "Ki" and the relation between the two. That is, where the older Confucianism was always talking about the human relations these Neo-Confucianists were more concerned with the problem of the relation of the human to the divine, of the finite to the infinite, of the phenomenal world to the noumenal world. The "Ri" becomes in Confucianism what the "Tao," or Way, was in Taoism, and what the Eternal and Monistic Substance or the Rational Principle was in Mahāyāna Buddhism. And the "Ki" in Confucianism takes very much the same place which the transitory and phenomenal world occupies in Buddhism. The chief difference is that the "Ri" in Confucianism is usually more than a mere Rational Principle but frequently has a moral quality. That is, it is the personification of Moral Wisdom rather than the personification of mere Reason. In some writers the conception of this Moral Wisdom approaches very near the conception of a personal God, though in others it remains rather pantheistic. And as the Absolute is thought of in terms of Moral Wisdom rather than mere Reason, the relation of man to the Absolute is also thought of more as a moral relation, *i.e.* man's chief duty is expressed in terms of righteous conduct rather than in terms of right knowledge, as is usually the case in Buddhism.

While these two Neo-Confucian schools are alike in that both are the expression of a union of Confucian and Buddhist thought, they differ somewhat from each other in other respects. The Shushi school regards itself as a true transmitter of orthodox Confucianism and consequently lays a great deal of stress upon a knowledge of the classics and erudition in general. The Ōyōmei school, on the other hand, while claiming to be a follower of Confucius in spirit, is more free in what it regards as orthodox. It lays not so much stress upon erudition as upon intuitive knowledge. Very much like the Zen Sect in Buddhism, which holds that the true teaching of the master is transmitted from heart to heart and not through books, so the Ōyōmei school holds that books are only guideposts to the truth and that the heart must find the truth in itself. Or as Kumazawa Banzan, one of the chief representatives of the Oyōmei school in Japan, has so well put it when he compared books and the teachings of wise men of the past to the foot prints of a rabbit which one wishes to catch. Obviously the foot prints are a help in catching the rabbit, but they are not the rabbit itself. But if one has once caught the rabbit the foot prints are no longer necessary. Where Shushi said, know before you act (and by knowing he meant a knowledge of what wise men of the past have said), Ōyōmei said that one can know fully only as one acts. Both schools lay emphasis on practical moral wisdom, but the one looks upon transmitted knowledge as a guide to conduct and the other rather emphasizes the mutual influence of knowledge and action which alone gives true wisdom.

It is not our purpose to give here a detailed account of the introduction of this Neo-Confucianism, nor of its real place in the life of Japan. As already stated before, it was brought in gradually by priests of the Zen Sect who have always been among its chief exponents. The first representatives seem to have been two Chinese Buddhist scholars, Sōgen and Ichizan, the former coming to Japan in the latter part of the thirteenth century. These were followed by other Chinese teachers and by Japanese scholars who studied in China, but the political strife and bloodshed which caused Buddhism to degenerate in Japan also kept Confucianism from gaining much of a hold. It was not therefore until the famous trio, Nobunaga, Hideyoshi and Ieyasu, had restored peace that Neo-Confucianism became fully established in the person of the scholarly Fujiwara Seigwa (1561–1610) who is usually regarded as the first real exponent of the Shushi school in Japan. He was followed by Hayashi Razan (1583–1672), also a descendant of the great Fujiwara family. Both these illustrious scholars had been Buddhist scholars and the latter became a Buddhist priest after retiring from his position in the Tokugawa government. His opposition to Christianity was pronounced and the account of his interview with one of the Jesuit missionaries is of special interest to the student of Christianity in Japan. Other great lights regarded as disciples of the Shushi school in Japan are such men as the scholarly Muro Kyuso, the famous educator Kaibara Ekiken, Yamazaki Anzai and a whole host of strong and earnest men.

Just as the Shushi school had been recognized in China as the orthodox school by the government during the Ming era (1402–1644), so it was made, as we have said above, the authorized system of education by the Tokugawa shōguns. Ieyasu and his successors encouraged this teaching because of its great emphasis on loyalty and obedience which a subject owed to the ruling powers. So general became this teaching and so deeply was it planted into the Japanese mind that we see its effect to this day in the intense loyalty and patriotism so characteristic of the people of Japan. In fact, it was the spirit of this teaching so zealously fostered by the Tokugawa shōguns which finally, in the teachings of the Mito branch of the Shushi school, resulted in the overthrow of the shōguns and the restoration of the emperor as the real ruler of Japan.

But while the Shushi school was recognized and encouraged as the official teaching and while opponents to this system were often suppressed, there were in Japan, as there had been in China before, men whose thought-life could not be confined to a fixed rut by government edicts or persecutions. These became the followers of Ōyōmei and constituted the Ōyōmei school. The first and in many respects the greatest of these was Nakae Tōjiu, the Sage of Ōmi. In his philosophy of life Japanese thought reaches in many respects its loftiest form, and it is not strange that he is still regarded with great reverence. Some say he was really the only true sage Japan has produced. His conception of the nature of the "Ri" and man's relation to it and to his fellowman was indeed a close approach to the best Christian thought, and should be a real schoolmaster to bring men to Christ. Another man of this school was Nakae's greatest disciple, Kumazawa Banzan, who was perhaps the most independent thinker of all these Neo-Confucianists and whose views on Buddhism and Christianity are of special interest. The Ōyōmei school, like the Shushi school, counted among its exponents many of the leading men of the Tokugawa era. In fact the stream of Confucianism in this school kept purer and fresher than in the official Shushi school, for the latter was too closely hemmed in by official regulations to allow the freedom so essential for the spiritual life. The official school became really corrupt and helped rivet upon Japan that formalism [34] and dead uniformity so characteristic of much of the life during the Tokugawa period.

In addition to these two Neo-Confucian schools, found both in China and Japan, there developed in Japan, during the latter part of the seventeenth century, a third school of Confucianism known as the Classical school. The founders of this school were Yamaga Soko and Itō Jinsai, of whom the latter is of greatest importance, though the former is of peculiar interest in that he is regarded as the father of Bushidō, "The Way of the True Knight." This school may be said to be a protest against the emphasis which both the Shushi and Ōyōmei schools were placing upon the thought-life as over against the life of action and emotion. That is, Confucianism was becoming much like Buddhism, which conceives of life too much in terms of the intellect and not enough in terms of the feelings and the will. The school has a right to be called the Classical school in that it made a conscious effort to get back to Confucius and even back to the life-ideal of the wise rulers before him and of which he was only a transmitter; but, after all, the philosophy of life held by the chief exponents of this school is a great advance over the older Confucianism. Particularly is this true of the philosophy of Ogiu Sōrai. Though he claims to go back to the teachings of the sages that preceded Confucius, it is clear that his lofty conception of the divine and man's relation to it and to his fellow-man is more than the exposition of these ancient texts, but rather shows that, keen scholar that he was, he was a true heir of all the ages. Ogiu Sōrai and Nakae Tōjiu represent the best blending of what is loftiest in the teachings of the old philosophies and religions of Japan. Other great names in this Classical school are Itō Togai and Dazai Shundai, the latter being of special importance as a vigorous opponent of Buddhism.

Of less importance in the life of Japan during the Tokugawa period than the above three schools of Confucianism is a fourth one, known as the Eclectic school. The tendency towards eclecticism is always strong when too many schools of philosophy and religion occupy the field, and there were a number of such movements in Japan at this time. But

this Eclectic school of Confucianism must be distinguished
from the others in that it professed to draw its material only
from the existing Confucian schools. When it is remembered,
however, that the schools of Neo-Confucianism are themselves a syncretism of Confucianism, Taoism and Buddhism,
this so-called Eclectic Confucian school is really a wider
eclecticism.

Now from this brief summary of Confucianism in Japan
during the Tokugawa age it is clear that Buddhism had indeed a strong rival, for while, as we have said, this Confucian
thought was first introduced by Buddhist priests as a part
of Buddhist teachings, the movement gradually became
independent of its foster mother and in some cases even
opposed. In fact, some of the most bitter enemies which
Japanese Buddhism ever had were among these great Confucian scholars who came to Confucianism through Buddhism.
Gradually the intellectual leadership and the guidance in
matters of moral education passed from the hands of the
Buddhists into the hands of men who drew their inspiration
from Confucian thought. The function of the Buddhist
priests was more and more limited to matters pertaining
to the future world and to taking care of men's dead bodies
rather than directing their daily lives. The official world
in Japan and the military classes and men of affairs had
indeed little to do with Buddhism and so it became more
and more the religion of the ignorant masses, who knew
nothing of its better teachings or of its past glory. Even
the better minds in Buddhism could not cope with the new
situation. When challenged by the progressive Confucianists to state their religious views in terms applicable to Japanese life they could not do it acceptably. The simple truth
of the matter is that the Buddhist philosophy of life, being
itself the expression of a world-weary civilization, cannot
be made a constructive force in an age of reconstructions.[35]

5. *Neo-Shintō Opposition to Buddhism.* — But Neo-Confucianism was not the only force with which Buddhism had
to divide the field after the rise of the Tokugawa shōgunate.
There developed also what might be called a Neo-Shintō.

We saw how at the beginning of the ninth century Shintō and Buddhism were merged into one system known as Ryōbu Shintō. What this really meant was that Shintō was virtually swallowed up by Buddhism. Not that Shintō disappeared entirely, for the religion of the masses in Buddhism was often more like the old Shintō than Buddhism, but that it was Buddhist thought which dominated the minds of the thinking sections of society. But when, through the civil wars that preceded the Tokugawa age, Buddhism had been weakened, the spirit of the native Shintō came to life again. It is rather difficult to account for this, but one factor in the matter seems to have been a growing national consciousness caused, on the one hand, by the influx of the Neo-Confucianism, and on the other hand, by the enforced unification of the empire under Ieyasu. That is, the growing knowledge of things Chinese naturally led men to think of things Japanese by way of comparison. We know, *e.g.*, that Hayashi Razan and other Confucian scholars went so far as to work out a theory of a relation between Japan's first emperor, Jimmu Tennō, and the Chinese Emperor Taikaku of the Shu era, and that these views led Tokugawa Mitsukuni (1628–1700) to gather together many great scholars into an institution called the "Shōkō Kwan" for the purpose of investigating Japanese history. It was these scholars of the Mito branch of the Shushi school who wrote the Dai Nihon Shí, "Great Japanese History," which was to play such a big part in the Restoration of 1868. But this movement in the Mito school was only a part of a wider movement, namely, a movement to know and restore things Japanese.

A better knowledge of things Japanese showed men that Buddhism, which had dominated Japan so long, was really a foreign importation and that it could be justly blamed for having played a big part in the civil wars which had for centuries devastated these beautiful islands. In fact, it could be shown with a degree of fairness that Buddhism had broken the spirit of the native Shintō, the heart of which was loyalty to the ruler and a deep patriotism. Of course,

Confucianism was also a foreign element and for that reason there was some opposition to it on the part of certain Shintōists, but still Confucianism, with its emphasis on filial piety and loyalty, was much nearer to Shintō in spirit than was Buddhism, whose highest ideal was the celibate monk, and which treated human life and the world as evil. As time went on, therefore, this Neo-Shintō gained momentum until finally in the persons of Motoöri Norinaga and Hirata Atsutane it became a fierce opponent of Buddhism and all for which Buddhism stood. "Back to the pure Shintō of the early days!" was the cry of these men. "Back to the religion which is the only real basis for the teaching that the Imperial household descended from the Sun Goddess Amaterasu." Buddhism had made of emperors mere puppets to plotting priests and so destroyed the very foundations of the Japanese state.

Even among Buddhists themselves there was a searching into the facts of the past which helped weaken its hold on Japan and shook men's faith in its authority. Attacked from all sides and on historic grounds, some of the more earnest priests took a more critical attitude towards their own religion, and we have what we might call the birth of higher criticism in Japanese Buddhism. Two learned men, Tominaga Nakamoto and Hattori Tenyū, were elected to make a special study of the Buddhist canon; and particularly the work of the former, though attracting little attention at the time, laid the foundations for future criticisms. We shall speak of his work in the Chapter on the Buddhist Canon, but we wish to state here simply that he came to the general conclusion that Mahāyāna Buddhism was not the pure Buddhism of the founder. It is only natural that such views should have a rather serious effect on the minds of those who placed all the emphasis on external authority.

Now this religio-patriotic movement led by the Shintōists and the Confucian scholars of the Mito school not only undermined the authority of Buddhism, branding it as a foreign and undesirable importation, but it also reacted on the Tokugawa shōgunate itself, which had been instrumental in establishing the Shushi school. If Buddhism was a usurper in the spiritual world, then surely was the shōgunate itself a worse criminal, for had it not robbed the emperors at Kyōto of all real authority? Little did Tokugawa Mitsukuni dream that when he founded the "Shōkō Kwan" at Mito and encouraged the scholars to study Japanese history he was helping in the overthrow of his successors. We would not say that this was the only factor in the situation, for the Tokugawa shōgunate, long before it was viewed as a usurper, had degenerated and lost its control over the powerful clans in the south, but still the leaders from these southern clans, which took the lead in the movement that ended in the Restoration of 1868, drew much of their inspiration from the Mito scholars. The Restoration was, of course, hastened by the appearance of Commodore Perry's ships in 1853, but it was not really caused by this as some Westerners fondly imagine. It was really a very minor factor in a very complex movement the core of which was in the religious and philosophic life of the nation during the two centuries preceding.

G.   *Buddhism in the Meiji Era*

With the passing away of the Tokugawa shōgunate and the restoration of the emperor as the real ruler of the empire Buddhism passed into a new world. However much opposition there had been to it during the Tokugawa period and however much it had lost its intellectual and moral leadership to men reared in a Confucian atmosphere, it still occupied a place as a state religion. Even the fierce advocates of the native Shintō could not succeed in dislodging Buddhism from its nominal position as the religion of the land or in breaking the union of Shintō and Buddhism. But a few years after the Restoration, namely, in the year 1870, Buddhism was finally disestablished as the state religion and separated from Shintō. An attempt was even made to make the divorced Shintō the state religion, but this was pressing matters too far and did not succeed. Instead Shintō was separated into two parts, namely, Shintō as a religion and Shintō as a system of rites and ceremonies to be used on state occasions as the official form for such things. This second division (Shinshoku) takes charge of all national shrines and tombs of great statesmen and patriots which are not officially regarded as having any religious significance. Shintō as a religion (Shintō shūkyō), on the other hand, with the granting of the Constitution in 1889, was placed on the same footing with Buddhism as one of the religions of Japan, In fact, the Constitution of Japan recognizes the principle of religious liberty, and so puts all religions on the same footing before the law. The fact, however, that the government takes its ceremonies for state occasions from Shintō and has Shintō priests officiate at such times, and the fact that the great Shintō shrines are made national shrines gives the impression to the people that the government regards Shintō as the state religion. The distinction in Shintō referred to above has no meaning to the average Japanese and all the explanations of government officials as to what they mean by it has not changed matters much. The simple fact is that the people at large regard the great Shintō shrines as having religious significance and as more than simply nurseries for patriotism.[36]

As a result of this disestablishment of Buddhism as a state religion it has found it rather difficult to readjust itself. All through its history in Japan it had depended a good deal upon government patronage, and frequently its interests had been identical with those of the rulers of the nation. Thus to be cast off and thrown upon its own resources naturally led to a good many hardships. A good many temples have found it impossible to continue and have been abandoned, and still more are in a dilapidated condition. What impresses one who visits the numerous beauty spots in Japan so frequently occupied by Buddhist temples is that their glory belongs to a past age rather than to the present. The pilgrims who visit these sequestered spots are not so much the pious believers with their rosaries and

much repeated prayers but troops of Middle school students
out on an Autumn or Spring excursion with little knowledge
or interest in the things for which these decaying temples
stood in the past. Of course, there are certain parts of the
country where these temples still stand for the authority of
the past; especially is this true in some of the non-progres-
sive sections on the west coast of the main island, but no
serious student of Buddhist history would hold that Buddhism
plays anything like the rôle in Japanese life which it played
up to or even through the Tokugawa period.

In certain quarters, however, attempts have been made to
reform Buddhism and restore it to its erstwhile place in
Japanese life. Two or three of the leading sects seem to
have found themselves again and are succeeding fairly well
in meeting the stress of economic readjustment that has
come over Japan in our day. Some of the more progressive
leaders say that the disestablishment of Buddhism as the
state religion is really a good thing and will enable it to
fulfill its mission as a spiritual force in society. These sects
are even trying to extend the field of their activity by carrying on mission work in the newer portions of the empire
and by trying to rejuvenate the decadent Buddhism of
Korea and China. New methods of propaganda are being
adopted, taken over bodily from Christianity. Thus on
all sides we see springing up Young Men's Buddhist Associations, Buddhist Sunday Schools, Women's Societies,
Orphanages, Homes for Ex-convicts, etc. Even street
preaching and special "evangelistic campaigns" are getting
quite common, and the content of some of the sermons and
hymns is sometimes taken bodily from Christianity, only
that the name Buddha takes the place of Christ. It must be
added, however, that the recent scandals connected with
the headquarters of almost every one of the leading sects
go a long way to counteract this forward movement and
many earnest Buddhists are wondering what will be the
fate of their religion in Japan.

H. *The Buddhist Sects and Their Numerical Strength*

In the closing chapter we shall discuss more fully the place of Buddhism in the life of present-day Japan and its outlook for the future. At this point, however, it might be of value to give the names of the various sects and subdivisions of Japanese Buddhism as well as the relative strength of these.

1. *The Twelve Sects.* — Following the traditions of Chinese Buddhism, Japanese Buddhism has long since held to the number twelve as the proper number of sects. This has necessitated a readjustment from time to time as old sects died out and new ones came into existence. The old way of enumeration was as follows when given in their chronological order :

1. Sanron   introduced in   625 A.D.
2. Jōjitsu   introduced in   625 A.D.
3. Hossō   introduced in   625 or 653 A.D.
4. Kusha   introduced in   658 A.D.
5. Kegon   introduced in   736 A.D.
6. Ritsu   introduced in   754 A.D.
7. Tendai   introduced in   805 A.D.
8. Shingon   introduced in   805 A.D.
9. Jōdo   founded   in 1175 A.D.
10. Zen   introduced in 1191 A.D.
11. Shin   founded   in 1224 A.D.
12. Nichiren founded   in 1253 A.D.

Four of these sects have died out, namely, the Sanron, Jōjitsu, Kusha and Ritsu, and their place is made up by regarding the three main divisions of the Zen Sect as independent sects and counting the small Yūdzū Nembutsu and Ji sects, so that the list is as follows :

1. Hossō
2. Kegon
3. Tendai
4. Shingon
5. Yūdzū Nembutsu
6. Jōdo
7. Rinzai (Zen)
8. Sōtō (Zen)
9. Shin
10. Nichiren
11. Ji
12. Ōbaku (Zen)

2. *Subdivisions of the Sects*

1. Hossō: Hossō-shū. (1)
2. Kegon: Kegon-shū. (1)
3. Tendai: Tendai-shū, Jimon-ha, Shinsei-ha. (3)
4. Shingon: (Old School) Kōya-ha, Ōmuro-ha, Daigo-ha, Daikakuji-ha, Tōji-ha, Senyūji-ha, Yamashina-ha, Ōno-ha. (The last four are sometimes grouped as one.)
    (New School) Chisan-ha, Hōzan-ha, Ritsu-ha. (11)
5. Yūdzū Nembutsu: Yūdzū Nembutsu-shū. (1)
6. Jōdo: Jōdo-shū, Nishiyama-ha. (2)
7. Rinzai (Zen): Tenryūji-ha, Sōkokuji-ha, Kenninji-ha, Nanzenji-ha, Myōshinji-ha, Kenchōji-ha, Tōfukuji-ha, Daitokuji-ha, Enkakuji-ha, Eigenji-ha, Hōkōji-ha, Butsuji-ha, Kakutaiji-ha, Kōgakuji-ha. (The last two are sometimes classed as parts of other branches.) (14)
8. Sōtō (Zen): Sōtō-shū. (1)
9. Shin: Hongwanji-ha, Ōtani-ha, Takada-ha, Kōshōji-ha, Bukkōji-ha, Kibe-ha, Izumoji-ha, Yamamoto-ha, Seishōji-ha, Sammonto-ha. (10)
10. Nichiren: Nichiren-shū, Kempon Hokke-shū, Hommon-shū, Hommon Hokke-shū, Hokke-shū, Hommyō Hokke-shū, Nichiren Fuji-ha, Nichiren Fujufuse-ha, Nichiren Fujufuse Kōmon-ha. (9)
11. Ji: Jishū. (1)
12. Ōbaku (Zen): Ōbaku-shū. (1)

3. *Relative Strength of the Sects*

	TEMPLES	PRIESTS	PROPA-GANDISTS	MONKS AND NEOPHYTES NOT PROPA-GANDISTS
1. Hossō	41	17	69	121
2. Kegon	32	12	15	—
3. Tendai	4711	2789	6695	1754
4. Shingon	12,717	7741	9696	2567
5. Yūdzū Nembutsu .	363	408	275	135
6. Jōdo	8371	6149	7721	1067
7. Rinzai (Zen) . .	6142	4410	5068	3410
8. Sōtō (Zen) . . .	14,211	9499	13,675	12,770
9. Shin	19,447	15,787	22,340	23,709
10. Nichiren	5074	4181	6239	876
11. Ji	513	208	413	230
12. Ōbaku (Zen) . .	569	347	540	—
Totals	72,191	51,548	72,746	46,639

(The "Priests" in column two are some of them included also in column three and others in column four, so that they are really counted twice in the above figures.)

It is impossible to say just how many adherents the various sects have. This is due to two things. First is the fact that during the Tokugawa period everybody was required to register in one or another of the temples, and thus many still call themselves Buddhists even though they have practically no connection with any temple or sect now that this registration is no longer required. The other reason why it is impossible to give the number of adherents is the simple fact that nothing special is required to be a Buddhist. Not even the simple confession, "I take refuge in the Buddha, the Law and the Priesthood," once used as a test of discipleship, is required of the general run of people who are claimed as Buddhists. The numerical strength of Buddhists in Japan to-day, therefore, can be measured only by such figures as we have given above, and even this is rather misleading, for the simple fact that practically all those numerous temples are an inheritance of the past and it is exceedingly doubtful whether many of them will be kept up or rebuilt as the economic pressure continues to increase.

CHAPTER IV

The Buddhist Canon as Known in Japan

THE Christian Bible is a collection of books, sixty-six in all; the Buddhist Bible as known in Japan is a good-sized library. It is the boast of Buddhist priests that their sacred Canon contains no less than 6771 books. This may be an over-statement of the facts, but still is it true that the Canon of Northern Buddhism does contain upwards of 5000 books, which according to Nanjo's Catalogue of the Chinese Tripitaka represent 1662 different works. Edkins in his "Chinese Buddhism" makes the statement that the Buddhist scriptures in some of the standard Chinese versions are about 700 times as large as the New Testament, and as Japanese Buddhists include books not found in the Chinese collections their scriptures are even more voluminous.[1] The Pali Canon of Southern Buddhism, made known to Western students through the splendid efforts of the Pali Text Society, is only about twice as large as the English Bible. A simple calculation would show then that the Northern Canon is about one hundred times larger than this Pali Canon. When it is remembered that even this comparatively small Bible of southern Buddhists is still very little known by Western students, though the great bulk of the scholarly work done on Buddhism has been done on the Buddhism of the South, it will not seem strange to say that the huge Northern Canon is practically an unknown library to all but a handful of scholars. It will take the untiring efforts of several generations of students before even the more valuable of these numerous books can be made accessible to scholars not familiar with the puzzling Chinese characters. The

Sacred Books of the East series edited by Max Mueller contains a few translations and represents a noble beginning, but it is a pity that the work has not been carried further.

Strictly speaking, of course, there is really no such thing as a Canon of Northern Buddhism, for the line between books included and those excluded is not drawn very clearly. In fact, some of the books included are mere names and are no longer extant, whereas there are books used in Japan by the various sects which are not ordinarily included in the Canon, but which for all practical purposes have supplanted the canonical writings.[2] Throughout the history of Northern Buddhism the Canon has constantly been changing; old books once included have disappeared and new ones have taken their place. This comes very clearly to light from a study of the introduction to Nanjō's Catalogue referred to above. A few facts about the thirteen existing catalogues of the Chinese Canon or Canons may be summarized as follows:

The oldest catalogue in existence dates from about 520 A.D. It mentions 2213 works, of which 276 can be identified with those in existence at the present day.

The second oldest catalogue (594 A.D.) mentions 2257 distinct works in 5310 books. This does not mean, however, that these were all in existence at that time, for some were known only as names.

The third catalogue (597 A.D.) gives 1076 different works in 3325 books as admitted to the Canon at that time. Perhaps the reason why two lists published so closely together should differ so widely in the number of books given is because the third catalogue includes only the books then positively known to be extant, while the second catalogue includes all books once recognized as canonical though many had been lost.

The fourth catalogue (602 A.D.) mentions 2109 works in 5058 books.

The fifth catalogue (664 A.D.) gives 2487 works in 8476 books, but of the works actually in existence at that time only 799 are mentioned.   These comprised 3364 books and made 45,626 leaves.

The sixth catalogue (664 A.D. ?) gives 1620 works in 5552 books.

The seventh catalogue (695 A.D.) mentions 3616 works in 8521 books.   Besides these, it says, there were 859 works in 3882 books admitted to the Canon at that time.   It also gives a list of 228 works in 419 books as spurious writings.

The eighth catalogue (730 A.D.) is perhaps the best one in existence.   It gives the names of 2278 different works in 7046 books.   It states, however, that of these, 1148 works in 1980 books were missing at the time and were known only from references.   This catalogue gives also a list of 41 other catalogues, the great majority of which were no longer in existence.   This eighth catalogue itself comprised 20 books.

The ninth catalogue (730 A.D.) is an abridged reproduction of the last part of the eighth catalogue.

The tenth catalogue (730 A.D.) enumerates 163 translations in 645 books made in China between 664–730 A.D.

The eleventh catalogue (1285–1287 A.D.) gives 1440 works in 5586 books.

The twelfth catalogue (completed in 1360 A.D.) was based entirely upon the eleventh.

The thirteenth catalogue (1368–1398 A.D.) was originally a catalogue of the Canon of southern China published in Nanking, but is now used also for the edition published at Peking 1403–1424 A.D., with 41 works added later.   This thirteenth catalogue forms the basis of Nanjō's "Catalogue of the Buddhist Tripitaka" which he compiled by order of the Secretary of State for India and which was published in English by the Oxford University Press in 1883.   Nanjō gives the names of 1662 works in Chinese, in Sanskrit (when it is originally a Sanskrit work and the name is known), and in English.   He also adds a few explanatory notes to each work listed and gives such data as the name of the author, translator, dates, size of the scripture, etc.   This catalogue is a large-sized volume.   When the mere names of the books in the Canon of Northern Buddhism make a large volume, the reader may imagine how bulky the Canon itself is.

From the above summary, then, it should be clear, as we have said, that strictly speaking there is no such thing as a real Canon of Northern Buddhism. It would almost seem as if at times any book produced by Buddhists was given a place within its wide bounds, and the only reason that in the modern period the Canon has become more or less fixed is because Chinese Buddhism has decayed and ceased to produce any literature of value. In Japan, where Buddhism continued in vitality longer, books of value were produced later, and, as stated above, there is a tendency to give these a place among the sacred scriptures of Buddhism even though they may not be included in what is technically regarded as the Canon.

The standard edition of the Canon as held in Japan to-day is probably the one published by a group of Japanese scholars in 1885 and is known as The Official Canon of Japan (Dai Nippon Kōtei Daizōkyō). It is a rather critical work carried out by men who have had some training in modern methods of criticism, though it should not be supposed that it will satisfy the scholar of the future. It is based upon four older editions published in Korea and China from the eleventh to the sixteenth centuries. These are the following: (1) The Kōraibon, published in Korea at the beginning of the eleventh century and containing 1521 different works in 6467 (or 6589) books. A copy of this was brought to Japan between 1469–86 and is in the possession of the Zōjōji of Shiba Park, Tōkyō. Only two volumes are missing from the original collection. (2) The Minzō (Chinese, Min Tsan) edition of the sixteenth century, consisting of 1662 works. This edition is very widely circulated both in China and Japan, and a copy of what is essentially the same is to be found in the India office in London. (3) The Sōzō edition, which appeared in China in 1239 and which contains 1421 works in 5714 (or 5916) books. This was brought to Japan in 1275 and is to be found at the Zōjōji in Tōkyō. (4) The Genzō edition, which appeared in China at the

M

end of the thirteenth century and which consists of 5397 books.

The first copy of this standard edition of the Japanese Canon to be sent abroad was sent to the Bodleian Library at Oxford, where Western students have access to it; but as it is written in the difficult Chinese characters it is not very likely that its contents will become public property very soon. Even in the university libraries of Japan these sacred books have a forbidding air about them and none but a few students of oriental philosophy ever look into them. A few copies are finding their way into the older Buddhist lands of Asia and there among the more zealous disciples of the Buddha they may be read with interest, but for the average modern student in the Orient the majority of these books have only an antiquarian interest. A few of the books, as we shall see later, still exercise an influence over certain sections of Japanese society, and these may be said to constitute the real Bible of Japanese Buddhism.

From what we have said thus far it is already clear that there is an enormous difference between the scriptures of Northern Buddhism and those of Southern Buddhism preserved best in the Pali Canon. At least there is the obvious difference in size. But the difference is more fundamental than simply that of size; it pertains to the content equally well. The Northern Canon contains practically all that is found in the Pali Canon, but it also contains a great many treasures and a great deal of rubbish peculiar to itself. The Pali Canon was, of course, a growth and represents several centuries of development. That is, it is not simply the teachings of the Buddha and his immediate disciples handed down from generation to generation, but it is the expression of the religious experience of several centuries, guided more or less by the original impress communicated by Gautama. The Northern Canon, however, is more than the evolution of a few centuries of Indian thought; it is really a library of books written during a period extending over many centuries and by people of varying civilizations on subjects as varied as are the interests and whims of humanity. The oldest of these books date probably from about the middle of the third century B.C., while the last ones were added as late as the fourteenth century. Their contents vary all the way from the most profound speculations as to the nature of the Absolute to the most childish twaddle about the trivial things of life. One critic speaks of the Northern Canon as a house in which nothing old and worn out has ever been thrown away, though many new things have been added from time to time. The reverent Buddhist, however, sees in this bewildering variety a wise provision for the varied needs of humanity. He says the Buddhist Bible is like a well-stocked apothecary shop, and the wise druggist knows to which of the countless bottles and cases he is to turn for the specific disease he is called upon to help.

As a result of this conglomeration of books written over a period of many centuries and by thinkers of different civilizations, it is not surprising to find the most flagrantly contradictory teachings and practices represented. We speak of the differences among Christians, and an Abelard was able to write his *Sic et non* of the Catholic Church, but these differences are rather small when compared with what we find in these scriptures of Northern Buddhism. The differences and contradictions extend to the very fundamentals of fundamentals. In fact, there is as much agreement. between the varied systems of religion and philosophy which have occupied the hearts and minds of men in the West during the past 2500 years as there is in the teachings of Northern Buddhism. There is nothing that has ever entered the heart or mind of man which does not find its counterpart somewhere in these Buddhist scriptures.

And yet in spite of these glaring contradictions in the Buddhist Bible in both essentials and non-essentials, all Buddhists claim to follow the teachings of the founder Gautama, though it should be added that at least one sect in Japan, the Shin Sect, does not lay very much stress upon this point.

As we have already intimated in Chapter I, the Southern Buddhists do not find very much difficulty in tracing their central teachings back to the founder; for it is probably correct that the Pali Canon contains the core of Gautama's teachings, though, as we have said above, it also represents several centuries of development.[3]   But when we come to the Northern Canon the problem is quite different.   To say with some modern Buddhist apologists that Mahāyāna Buddhism is simply the developed form of what was really contained in germ in Gautama's teachings, is to say that a system may develop to a point where it is practically the exact opposite of what it was at the beginning.   That there is a historical connection between Southern and Northern Buddhism is beyond doubt, as we have shown in Chapter I, and in that sense the latter is, of course, a development of the former.   But the development was in some points so revolutionary that often the new remained Buddhist only in name.   Original Buddhism, as we saw in Chapter I, was itself a development of Brahmanism, whose fundamental ideas about the Absolute and the human soul it rejected, though other teachings of Brahmanism, such as the doctrine of Karma and Transmigration, it accepted.   Some 500 years later, however, Buddhism had developed (or degenerated, if one speaks from the standpoint of Gautama's views) to the point where it affirmed again these very conceptions which it originally either denied or ignored as idle speculations.   In short, the old theories about God, the soul and the future life reasserted themselves, and they have always played a rather vital part in at least some of the sects of Northern Buddhism, as we shall see in the succeeding chapters.   To this change in fundamentals were added from time to time many minor things; so that gradually the sacred Canon gathered up into itself, like a rolling snowball, everything which Buddhism found on its way through central and eastern Asia.

Of course, few Buddhists will admit that there is such a radical difference between the teachings of the founder and the later doctrines of Mahāyāna Buddhism.   They either hold, as stated above, that Mahāyāna Buddhism differs from the teachings of the founder only as the full-grown plant differs from the seed, or else they resort to the convenient theory, long held by Northern Buddhists; namely, that the founder taught all these varied and apparently contradictory doctrines, but that some of them must be regarded as provisional and accommodated teachings, while others are the undiluted and perfect truths.

The Buddhist Canon as a whole is therefore divided by Northern Buddhists into two great divisions. These are the Little Vehicle (Sansk., Hīnayāna, Japanese, Shōjō) and the Great Vehicle (Sansk., Mahāyāna, Japanese, Daijō). Many Japanese writers make three divisions, namely, adding the Provisional Mahāyāna (Japanese, Gondaijō). A few writers even speak of five Vehicles and, in a less technical sense, it is sometimes said that there are as many Vehicles of salvation as there are differences between the various living beings to be saved. Ordinarily, however, the division of the Buddhist Canon into Hīnayāna and Mahāyāna is the accepted division. These terms were invented by Mahāyāna Buddhists and bear on their face a record of the controversy which raged during the early centuries of the Christian era over the very question as to what were the real teachings of the founder. The second half of the two words, viz. *yāna*, means Vehicle, a vehicle of salvation which carries men safely across this life into the next and better life. Hīnayāna means Little Vehicle and is really a term of contempt. The name indicates the nature of the teachings which this vehicle of salvation contains, namely, the Little Teachings, or the undeveloped and provisional doctrines. Mahāyāna, on the other hand, means Great Vehicle and is a term of boastful superiority. It contains the Great Teachings, the full and perfect doctrines which the master is supposed to have taught after his disciples had been prepared for them through their knowledge of the Hīnayāna. We shall state a little later how this theory was worked out in greater detail by the founder of the T'ien T'ai Sect in China in what is known as the Five Periods of Gautama's ministry.

Now each of these two great divisions of the Canon — Hīnayāna and Mahāyāna — is subdivided into three divisions called Pitakas, Baskets (Japanese, Zō). Some say that the divisions were called Pitakas because when scholars classified the sacred scriptures the books were put into baskets. A better explanation is to see in this term rather the idea of how the scriptures were handed down from one generation to another. In the Orient it is a common custom to have workmen stationed in a line who hand from man to man a series of baskets filled with something to be removed from one place to another. (It is something like a bucket line in a fire drill.) So we are to understand by this term Pitaka a long line of teachers who have handed down to generation after generation the teachings of the founder of Buddhism.

The three Pitakas, or Tri-pitaka, are the following:

1. Sūtra-pitaka (Japanese, Kyōzō).
2. Vinaya-pitaka (Japanese, Ritsuzō).
3. Abhidharma-pitaka (Japanese, Ronzō).

The Sūtra-pitaka contains teachings in the form of collected sayings, dialogues between the Buddha and his disciples and sermons with stories and parables which relate and illustrate the things which happened at that time.

The Vinaya-pitaka contains the precepts and rules given by the master for the instruction of those who have given themselves to the following of the doctrine. It is a sort of Set of Rules for the brotherhood of the elect.

The Abhidharma-pitaka is a collection of treatises and commentaries and contains often the most profound philosophical discussions on points growing out of the teachings contained in the Sūtra-pitaka. The contents of this third division are not regarded as the Buddha's own words, but as explanations of his teachings presented from the standpoint of psychology and philosophy.

It is needless to say that this classification is rather elastic; for the Vinaya-pitaka sometimes contains sermons and discourses, and the Sūtra-pitaka often has in it discourses on points of discipline, while both of these divisions frequently have the characteristics of the third division. In fact, this threefold division, while fairly accurate for the

Pali Canon, really breaks down entirely when applied to the Northern Canon, for the simple reason that many of the leading sūtras, though put into the mouth of the Buddha, are no more his teachings than is the whole Abhidharma-pitaka. The classification should therefore not be taken too seriously and should be regarded as one of those convenient expedients of the human mind by which a bewildering multiplicity is reduced to a unity by simply affixing a label.

This gives us, then, a double Tri-pitaka for the Buddhist Canon taken as a whole; namely, a Hīnayāna Tri-pitaka and a Mahāyāna Tri-pitaka. The relative sizes of the two may be seen by a reference to Nanjō's Catalogue of the canonical writings to which we have referred above. Nanjō's divisions are a little different from what we have just given, but they are enough alike to throw a little light on the subject. He makes four Pitakas instead of three, adding the so-called Samyutka-pitaka, *i.e.* Mixed Works. The 1662 works enumerated by him are classified as follows:

A. Sūtra-pitaka
    I. Mahāyāna sūtras . . . . . Numbers   1–541
    II. Hīnayāna sūtras . . . . . Numbers 542–781
    III. Mahāyāna and Hīnayāna sū-
          tras which were added to
          the Canon 960–1368 A.D. . . Numbers 782–1081

B. Vinaya-pitaka
    I. Mahāyāna vinayas   . . . Numbers 1082–1106
    II. Hīnayāna vinayas   . . . Numbers 1107–1166

C. Abhidharma-pitaka
    I. Mahāyāna abhidharmas . . Numbers 1167–1260
    II. Hīnayāna abhidharmas . . Numbers 1261–1297
    III. Mahāyāna and Hīnayāna
          abhidharmas which were
          added to the Canon 960–
          1368 A.D. . . . . . . Numbers 1298–1320

D. Samyukta-pitaka — Mixed Works
    I. Works of Hindu teachings . . Numbers 1321–1467

II. Early Chinese works   . . .   Numbers 1468–1621
III. Chinese works added to the
    Canon 1368–1644 A.D. . .   Numbers 1622–1657
IV. Works missing in the North-
    ern Chinese collection and
    taken from the Southern
    Chinese . . . .   Numbers 1658–1662

Nanjō's classification of the Canon is based largely upon the older classifications made by Chinese scholars and therefore should not be regarded as a real critical analysis. It is but one way among others. For example, a handbook on Buddhism published in Tōkyō a few years ago makes the following sweeping classification, using the books in the Canon rather than the different works as the units of division:

A. Mahāyāna sūtras . . . . 2883 books
B. Hīnayāna sūtras . . . . 680 books
C. Mahāyāna abhidharmas . . . . 555 books
D. Hīnayāna abhidharmas . . . . 695 books
E. Hīnayāna vinayas . . . . 441 books
    Total . . . . 5254 books

Now according to the orthodox section of the Mahāyāna school the Canon with these divisions of Mahāyāna and Hīnayāna and the subdivisions of Sūtra, Vinaya, and Abhidharma was fixed in the main the year after Gautama's death at a great council of his disciples gathered at Rajagriha. It is of course quite probable that, as Buddhist tradition claims, a council was held by the Buddha's disciples soon after his death; but it is utterly out of the question that the Canon should have been fixed then and there in anything like its present form. Not even in the more simple form as preserved in the Pali scriptures could it have been finished at such an early date; for as it appears now the Pali Canon is really only the Canon of one of the sects of early Buddhism and has on the face of it traces of later dates. And as for the Northern Canon, or rather series of Canons, one has but to look at the thirteen Chinese catalogues mentioned above to see how absurd such a claim is.

It is doubtful whether or not any part of the Canon was committed to writing immediately after Gautama's death. The Pali Canon, *e.g.* was not fixed on the written page until the first century B.C.   Great portions of the Northern Canon, even great sections of the sūtra division, could not possibly have been fixed in their present form before the beginning of the Christian era.   But while this is true, we do not mean to say that no books in the Canon were fixed at an early date.   Even if they were not written down immediately after Gautama's death it seems quite likely that sections of the Vinaya-pitaka were fixed more or less definitely at the Rajagriha Council or soon after.   At any rate, the core of these Monks' Rules, it would seem, must have taken shape almost from the beginning.

If, then, portions of the Canon were fixed before they were committed to writing, may it not be that the Pali Canon was fixed long before it was committed to the written page in the first century before Christ?   And is it not therefore the oldest and most authoritative Canon of primitive Buddhism in existence, and so should be made the norm by which Buddhism as a whole is to be measured?   We may admit that the Pali Canon was fixed, at least by one sect, before it was committed to writing.   We may also admit that it contains the main teachings of Gautama, though it has in it more than simply the teachings of the founder. And still further, we must admit that, taken as a whole, the Pali Canon comes much nearer representing the teachings of original Buddhism than do the Northern Canons taken as wholes.   But this does not mean that it should be taken as the only source for Gautama's teachings, nor should it be assumed that those portions of the Northern Canon which are essentially the same as portions of the Pali Canon, *e.g.* the four Nikāyas (Agamas) were taken from the latter. In fact, it seems quite likely that some of the Sanskrit scriptures of the Northern Canon and some of the Pali scriptures go back to an older redaction in Magadhi, the language of Magadha which S'akyamuni probably used.   So it is quite possible that the Northern Canon has in it books just as

authoritative as those found in the Pali, and, perhaps, even
something of the founder's teachings not found in the latter.
Of the old redaction in Magadhi we have only a few traces
in the Pali Canon and in the edict of Bairat issued by King
Asoka in the third century B.C.   The following is a diagram
of the probable relationship of the various redactions of the
Canon of Buddhism:

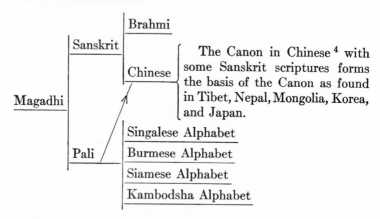

It may be said that if we have no traces of Buddhist
scriptures older than the third century B.C. and if even the
Pali Canon was not committed to writing until the first century B.C., then we are indeed far removed from the possibility of having any of the real words of the founder of
Buddhism.   It is true that Buddhism cannot lay any claim
to have worked its way back to the historic Buddha and
his sayings as Christian scholars have done in the case of
their Master; but we should not forget'that even if the transmission of the Buddha's teachings was by word of mouth
rather than through the written page, there is still the possibility of having a rather accurate transmission.   This is
made possible by the form in which the teachings of Gautama's day were usually cast, namely, a style which to the
Western mind seems like a weary repetition, but which made
it comparatively easy to be remembered.   Another factor
which made for accuracy of transmission is the phenomenal
power of memory of the Oriental mind.   The whole system

of education in the East has been for centuries a system of committing to memory what others have said. It is astonishing how much the human mind can retain when trained from youth on in this way. It is said that even today there are men in India who can, *e.g.*, recite the whole Rig-Veda — 1028 songs, many of them rather long — without a single slip. So it is not at all unlikely that we have in the Pali Canon and in some of the scriptures of the Northern Canon something of the real teachings of the founder and sometimes his actual phraseology. But after this has been said, it is none the less absurd to hold with some Buddhists of Japan that the entire Sūtra-pitaka and Vinaya-pitaka, especially of the Mahāyāna school, go back that far. Even King Asoka, in the third century B.C., apparently, knew nothing of the threefold division of the sacred scriptures; and, as we have said in Chapter I, the whole system of Mahāyāna Buddhism had not been born in his day. The most that we can say is that there were only tendencies pointing in that direction. In short, then, we may grant to the Buddhists of China and Japan that in their voluminous Canon they have as truly the teachings of the founder as do the Buddhists of the South, and they may even have some things of the master's teachings not found in the Pali Canon, but we cannot admit that the scriptures which they usually regard as the very words of S'akyamuni's deepest teachings, namely, the distinctively Mahāyāna scriptures, are such. Many of the most popular books in Japan cannot go farther back than the beginning of the Christian era.

The sweeping division of the Buddhist Canon into a Hīnayāna Tri-pitaka and a Mahāyāna Tri-pitaka did not overcome all the glaring contradictions found in the Northern Canon. In the last half of the sixth century A.D., the learned Chinese priest Chi K'ai, founder of the great T'ien T'ai Sect, worked out an elaborate scheme of harmonization. He divided Gautama's teachings into five great periods, and into these he tried to fit the various scriptures by arranging and rearranging them back and forth until he had cleared away, as he thought, all the difficulties and contradictions.   Briefly stated the scheme was as follows:

1. The first period of the Buddha's long ministry extended over a space of only two or three weeks following immediately upon the hour when the Great Enlightenment had dawned upon him.   In this first period he preached the undiluted and perfect truth as he saw it in his Buddhahood. His audience were not the ordinary people of India, but the innumerable Bodhisattvas, gods and heavenly beings. This period is called in Japanese the Kegon period and the teachings are recorded in the famous Kegonkyō (Buddhavatamsaka-Mahāvaipulya-sūtra) which has been used, perhaps, as widely by Buddhist scholars in Japan as any other scripture.

2. When the Buddha realized that his exalted teachings were beyond the capacity of the average human being, he began to dilute his teachings, as it were, and accommodated them to the understanding of the common man.   It was during this period that he taught the Four Noble Truths about suffering and salvation from suffering and the Noble Eightfold Path.   To know these truths and to follow this path led to the Arhat state which is the goal of Hīnayāna teachings.   This second period extended over twelve years, and the teachings are to be found in the ordinary Hīnayāna scriptures.

3. But when the master perceived that his disciples took this accommodated teaching of the Hīnayāna scriptures as the full truth, he began to show them that he had yet many things to say unto them and that what he had taught them thus far was only preparatory to the higher truth.   He now began to teach them the way of true enlightenment, the enlightenment not of the Arhat who seeks only his own salvation, but that of the Bodhisattva who is interested also in the salvation of others.   This period is called the Hōdō period and lasted eight years.   The teachings of this period are recorded in the ordinary Mahāyāna scriptures.

4. Now when the disciples heard these lofty teachings of the third period they felt that they were too high for the average man and that for him the Hīnayāna doctrines were

better suited. Only the one destined to be a Bodhisattva, they felt, could comprehend the profound truths of the Mahāyāna teaching. The Buddha thereupon showed them that nothing hindered even the average man from becoming a follower of Mahāyāna truth and attaining true enlightenment. The disciples were thus led to see that there was no chasm between the Hīnayāna and the Mahāyāna, but that the former was really a vehicle for the first part of the journey and from it the passenger could transfer to the latter and continue his journey till he arrived at his true destination. This fourth period is called the Hannya period and extended over twenty-two years of the master's long ministry. The leading scripture containing the teachings of this period is the voluminous Mahāpragnāpāramitā-sūtra which teaches the deep Mahāyāna doctrines in simplicity.

5. Finally when the Buddha reached the advanced age of seventy-two, he began to preach the deepest and highest truths of all, namely; that all sentient beings are able to attain Buddhahood and enjoy the blessings of Nirvāna. For this purpose he had left his heavenly home and endured hardships during many incarnations that he might lead all living beings into the bliss of Nirvāna. These teachings are contained in the famous Lotus Scripture, Saddharma-Pundarīka-sūtra (Myōhō Renge-kyō, or Hokkekyō). In this closing period the Buddha preached also the teachings of the Paradise Scripture (Mahāparinirvāna-sūtra (Nehankyō), in which he showed that all beings, animate and inanimate, have the nature of Buddha and so can attain Buddhahood. This period is called the Nehan or Hokke period and extended over eight years.

According to the Amida sects of Japan, to this last period also belong the teachings of the famous Paradise or Amida scriptures; namely, The Larger Sukhāvatī-vyūha (Daimuryō-jukyō), The Smaller Sukhāvatī-vyūha (Amidakyō), and Amitā-yur-dhyāna-sūtra (Kwammuryōjukyō). These scriptures teach the great doctrine of salvation through faith in the Buddha Amida, who has prepared for those who trust in him his Western Paradise.

Thus far Chi K'ai's classification of the founder's teachings. It was undoubtedly an ingenious piece of work and would do credit to some of our modern harmonists. For a period of about one thousand years it allayed the doubts of the skeptics and gave authority to the most contradictory teachings found in the sacred scriptures. Just as men used various means of transportation, so in religion there are various ways of salvation. The founder of Buddhism knew all these ways and taught them all, and the pious Buddhist must recognize in this a wise provision for the varied needs of humanity; yea, a provision for the needs of all beings, for the Buddha heart seeks to save all. But in the eighteenth century, when in Japan the Neo-Confucian and Neo-Shintō movement began to make itself felt, the Buddhists, too, began to question the explanation of the Five Periods. As we stated in the last chapter, a man by the name of Tominaga began to advance views which were calculated to upset this convenient solution offered by Chi K'ai. Tominaga's contention, in short, was that the scriptures which Chi K'ai assigned to the first, fourth, and fifth periods of Gautama's ministry were in reality the products of later centuries, and that his real teachings were contained in the Hīnayāna Tri-pitaka. Though these views attracted comparatively little attention at the time, they did mark the beginning of that Higher Criticism among Japanese Buddhists which is finding more and more champions as the years go on, and which some day ought to help solve the great problems which the Canon of Northern Buddhism presents.

The following is a brief summary of the stage which the controversy between conservative and liberal Buddhists has reached on this question: [5]

(1) The conservative position as represented by one of the leading Buddhist scholars of the day, Dr. Inouye Enryō.

a. Mahāyāna is not inconsistent with Hīnayāna. It is found in germ in the latter and has developed from it. The one is as truly the direct teaching of the founder as the other.

b. Mahāyāna was given in secret by the master to his

disciples to be kept secret until the time came when the world was ready to receive it.

c. The Buddha himself taught the Mahāyāna, but after he had entered Nirvāna it proved too lofty for the majority of mankind. For this reason it was little known in the early period of Buddhism. Only by the time of Asvaghosha [6] and Nāgārjuna was the world ready to receive it, and these two great teachers were the ones who made known this lofty teaching to the world.

d. Though the Buddha taught both Mahāyāna and Hīnayāna, the former was of such philosophic depth that the simple-minded inhabitants of South and Central India could not grasp it and only the people of North India comprehended this wisdom. Thus it was quite natural that five or six hundred years after the death of the Buddha the people of South and Central India did not even know that there ever was a Mahāyāna; and therefore when, at the time of Asvaghosha, — a time when non-Buddhist ideas were prevalent, — Mahāyāna was brought to these people, they declared that it was not the master's teachings, but that only the Hīnayāna came from him.

(2) And now let us give a brief statement of the liberal wing as represented by Nukariya Kaifu, a learned priest of the Zen Sect.

a. The Buddha's direct teachings are found, with perhaps some modifications, in the four Āgamas (Nikāyas) and in the Vinaya-pitaka as preserved in the present Chinese Tripitaka.

b. About the time of King Asoka (middle of the third century B.C.) a beginning was made to commit the commandments and teachings of the master to writing. Down till that time they had been handed on by word of mouth.

c. The present Āgamas were compiled after the council convened by King Asoka.

d. In the course of the development of the Hīnayāna there came into existence some eighteen or twenty schools or sects of Buddhism.[7]

e. From some of these Hīnayāna branches developed the Mahāyāna school.

f. Some Mahāyāna scriptures were written as early as the first century A.D.

g. The last of the true Mahāyāna scriptures, *e.g.* such scriptures as the Mantra-sūtras, were composed as late as the seventh century.

h. The Chinese Tri-pitaka contains also scriptures composed by Chinese Buddhists.

This, then, is in short the attitude of the conservative and liberal wings among modern Buddhists toward the problem of the relation between Hīnayāna and Mahāyāna Buddhism. The conservative wing holds that both Hīnayāna and Mahāyāna are in substance the very teachings of the master himself, *i.e.* essentially the position held by Chi K'ai ; whereas the liberal wing recognizes the fact that Mahāyāna Buddhism is a much later development and is only the teaching of the Buddha in the sense that it developed historically from primitive Buddhism. The majority of Western scholars who are in a position to have an intelligent opinion on this vexed problem side with the liberal wing; but they would go a step farther and say that Mahāyāna is not simply a developed form of Buddhism, but that it also has in it much which is not strictly Buddhistic. It has historical connection with primitive Buddhism, but it also has vital connections with other systems and streams of life, so that in many of its phases it is Buddhist only in name.

But the problems which confront the scholar who attempts to trace the historical development of Buddhism and unravel the many strands — Buddhist and non-Buddhist — which go to make up the Canon of Northern Buddhism are so stupendous that it may take centuries before even an outline of a satisfactory solution will be worked out. No one set of scholars, whether Oriental or Occidental, is sufficient for the task. It is like digging a long tunnel in which the work must be carried on from both ends. The Western scholar must dig through Greek, Roman and Near-Eastern civilizations, while the Oriental scholar will have to try to meet this tunnel from his end through Indian, Japanese and Chinese civilizations. The center of the tunnel is in the life and civilization of the people which once occupied Central Asia — that part of the world about which we know least. In fact, it seems very doubtful as to whether we shall ever know enough to pierce this great *terra incognita* in which lie hidden the secrets of those centuries of Buddhist history during which the Mahāyāna school came into being.

But this search is a fascinating work and one which has many interesting and valuable by-products; for even if we fail in our main problem of discovering a historical connection between Buddhism and Western thought, or of showing that there was no such connection, we shall at least be able to show on a very large scale that the human race is one in its needs and in its attempts to meet these needs. If East is East and West is West and never the twain have met historically (*i.e.* in ancient times), it does not follow that "never the twain shall meet." The more we know of the thought-life of the East the more do we see the kinship of all races; and this, we hold, will be one of the by-products of the scholar's work who is trying to unravel the many strands that go to make up Buddhism. A second by-product will be a deeper appreciation of the Christian religion. "What can they know of England who only England know?" So it is with religion; it is impossible to have a keen appreciation and full understanding of Christianity unless one sees it in the light of the world's other great religions. It is high time that Western scholars take a wider outlook upon the world, and through a knowledge of Oriental thought help lay the foundations for that sympathy for Asia's millions which alone can make the inevitable meeting of East and West a blessing rather than a curse. But this is a digression and we must return to the subject in hand.

While theoretically all Japanese Buddhists regard the Canon as sacred and as embodying the teachings of the founder, in practice the different sects manifest rather divergent tendencies in their attitude toward the scriptures. As may be seen from what has been said above, the Bible of

N

Northern Buddhists is entirely too voluminous to be used as a whole in a practical way. Even the Christian Bible is too large for most Christians and many portions of it remain closed books; and how could a Buddhist be expected to make use of his big Bible with its more than 5000 books? There are in general three different attitudes taken by the Japanese sects. At one extreme are sects like the old Sanron and the Tendai which make a pretense of using all the scriptures, regarding each scripture as having its own peculiar function. At the other extreme is the Rinzai branch of the Zen Sect which holds that no scripture can be really a vehicle of truth, for truth cannot be transmitted by the written page but must be communicated from heart to heart, or must be discovered in one's own heart through silent meditation. The sacred scriptures are only the footprints on the sands of time made by the wise men of the past who walked in the way of the truth. Between these two positions are to be found the majority of the sects which for practical purposes make a selection of one or more books from the Canon and make these their Authoritative or Basal Scriptures and the ones to be specially used by the adherents of the sect. Thus we have, *e.g.*, the Amida sects selecting as their Authoritative Scriptures the three Amida books; namely, the Daimuryōjukyō, the Amidakyō and the Kwammuryōjukyō. The Shingon and Nichiren sects regard as specially sacred the famous Lotus Scripture, though each of these add several other books as Basal Scriptures. The old Kegon Sect was founded on the Kegonkyō, the Sanron Sect on three scriptures. An so it is with other sects, each regarding certain scriptures as specially valuable and authoritative for the teachings of the sect, without, however, denying thereby the teachings of other scriptures in the Canon which may seem quite contradictory. As we have said before, the average Buddhist philosopher is exceedingly tolerant of other views and regards even direct opposites as but two sides of the same shield.

It might be interesting to know how the Tendai Sect, which theoretically claims that every scripture has each its special

place, succeeds in making a practical use of them.   There are
two sides to the answer; one a bright side and the other a
dark side.   As a matter of history the Tendai Sect of Japan
has furnished practically all the great men who founded
the sects which arose after the ninth century.   This is due
directly to the fact that Tendai teachers have always encouraged a wide study of all the scriptures.   Of course, the
result of this was disruption, but still it also meant a broader
development of Buddhism as a whole.   The dark side of the
picture is the way the Tendai Sect ministers to the spiritual
needs of the common people.   Only the scholarly priest had
access to the wealth of scriptures; the common man could
not do anything with them even if he had access to them.
To begin with, very few of the scriptures, until very recently,
have been translated into the language of the people, though
Buddhism has been in Japan some thirteen centuries.   The
texts are in difficult Chinese which only an educated Japanese can read.   Rather than translate all these writings the
clever priests have resorted to much more simple methods of
giving their followers the benefits of their contents.   Among
other things they have introduced from China a Chinese invention of the sixth century, namely, the huge revolving
bookcase in which the sacred scriptures are placed, and the
turning of the case by the pious ignorant believer becomes a
popular substitute for the reading of its contents.   The believer is told that "it is impossible for any one to read all
the Buddhist scriptures as their number is so great; namely,
6771 books.   Therefore if any one turns this case three times
around he shall have as much merit as he who reads the books
through.   Moreover to such a one is promised long life,
prosperity, and protection from all misfortune."   We might
add for the reader's edification that our first introduction to
the Buddhist Bible of Japan was of this nature, but unfortunately the only profit we gained by this method of
reading was simply an appreciation of the weight of these
many books, for it takes quite an effort to make such a
huge case revolve even with the assistance of the attendant.
His profit was more substantial than our own in the form

of a few coins which we gave him for his assistance in enabling us to master these sacred scriptures so easily.

Another method in use in the Tendai Sect is what a visitor to the famous Tennōji in Osaka, *e.g.*, may see. The priests, eight or ten in number sitting in a row, read the scriptures by simply letting the pages glide through the fingers so that each reader can finish a set of ten books every two or three minutes.

But even the sects which choose only a few scriptures from the voluminous Canon do not always succeed in making these the common possession of their adherents. The number of Japanese homes which have Buddhist scriptures is very small, and still fewer are the homes where the scriptures are read. The scriptures are considered too profound in their content to be understood by the masses, and these are taught to worship blindly the books rather than to know what these books have to say. This is especially true of such a sect as the Nichiren. It has as its chief scripture one of the loftiest in the entire Canon, and if its contents were really known by the people, it would have a profound influence on their lives, but the average disciple of Nichiren is taught a superstitious reverence of the book and nothing more. The prayer, Namu Myōhō Rengē-kyō, "Hail Thou Scripture of the Lotus of the Wonderful Law," is on every disciple's lips, but what that Wonderful Law might be, few indeed have the slightest idea.

This superstitious reverence for the sacred scriptures as such, irrespective of knowing their contents, has found expression in many ways. For example, it has always been regarded as a work of great merit to be engaged in copying the scriptures, and at times even emperors and princes have labored faithfully in the capacity of scribes of the sacred law. There are some manuscripts in existence written in human blood, the zealous scribe thus literally pouring out his life-blood for the transmission of the holy text. In China it was regarded as a meritorious work to pick up any piece of paper on which anything was written, for the writing might be words from the scriptures. In the face of such reverence among pious Buddhists for the very paper and ink with which their scriptures are written, it becomes clear at once that the Christian worker who comes to these people with a "Thus saith the Bible," thinking that therefore he will be heard, will be sadly disappointed. Unless he can show from the contents of his Bible that it is the word of the Lord, his mere dogmatic claim that it is such will not go very far. With the advance of education this line of approach is being made more easy, for it is, after all, only the ignorant who are held by their reverence for their scriptures without knowing what these contain. The more progressive Buddhists are trying now to give the people access to the best parts of the Canon. They are publishing in attractive form, and in Japanese, either whole books or selections from a number of the best books. Such selections are grouped topically and even the uneducated can thus get some first-hand knowledge of the teachings of Buddhism. Then in addition to this the leading sects are publishing in Japanese what might be called Sectarian Bibles, *i.e.* each sect is publishing its own Basal or Authoritative Scriptures in very attractive bindings. Some of these have had a rather phenomenal success. Thus, *e.g.*, the volume issued by the Shingon Sect passed through forty-five reprints in four years, and the Zen Bible through eighteen in about the same length of time. Just how successful this undertaking will be, remains to be seen. Thus far the average Japanese, however much he may have absorbed from the semi-Buddhistic atmosphere in which he lives, knows very little indeed of what Buddhism stands for in general or what the various sects stand for in particular. So much is this the case that the foreign student of the history or philosophy of Buddhism will often seek in vain to find out much from the average man he meets, and even among the priests there are very few who seem to have a grasp of the subject. Still fewer are those who have any definite conviction as to Buddhism's mission to modern Japan. This condition, we believe, is largely due to the fact that Buddhism has no Bible in any real sense, for however much truth those thousands of pages of the Canon may contain, it is so covered up with the rubbish of centuries that it is impossible to extricate it and make it a living force to-day. Nothing will give a Christian a deeper appreciation of the value of his Bible and the marvelous Providence which has kept it so pure and so "practically small" as a study of the clumsy Buddhist Bible. He will thank God as never before for this Book of Books.

CHAPTER V

IN giving an outline of the main doctrines of Japanese Buddhism one is naturally tempted to follow the general divisions into which the fundamentals of Christianity are usually divided by modern writers on Systematic Theology. This has the great advantage of enabling the reader to constitute a comparison between the main teachings of the two religions, and for this reason we shall not depart entirely from such a course of procedure in this chapter. But to be true to the subject in hand, we must depart from this course at least at the beginning and deal first with subjects which are very fundamental but which in books on Systematic Theology are usually left to works on philosophy and psychology.

A. *Summary Statement of Teachings*

Perhaps the most concise expression of the essence of Buddhist teachings is the pregnant phrase, "Tenmei Kaigo." "Turning from error and opening understanding." Man is in error and ignorance and he must turn from this and open his understanding. The whole mode of the Buddhist salvation is expressed primarily in terms of right thinking rather than in terms of right moral purpose, and the great obstacle in man's way is error rather than sin. Enlightenment is the great word of Buddhism, and Enlightenment means to know the truth. We do not mean to say that Buddhism does not also have a good deal to say about sin and righteous conduct but only that these are secondary.

To the pregnant expression given above are sometimes added two other expressions, and all three taken together give a comprehensive summary of Buddhist doctrines. The complete statement is, "Tenmei kaigo, riku tokuraku, shiaku shuzen." "Turning from error and opening understanding, escaping from suffering and obtaining bliss, ceasing from evil and doing good." All living beings have beclouded the reason of things and so through error they commit evil deeds and in consequence are doomed to suffer. Through the teachings of Buddhism man is to learn the truth. This will show him what is the right, and by obedience to the right he escapes from suffering and enters bliss. Or to put it in Western thought, man is to think the truth, do the good and feel the beautiful. This, in short, is the general summary of Buddhist teachings, and when given in this general form there would seem to be little difference between Buddhism and Christian thought. But when we come to inquire into what is meant by the true, the good and the beautiful, we shall find great differences between Buddhist and Christian thought and also between the different schools and sects of Buddhism.

B. *Theory of Knowledge*

The first step in the exposition of Buddhist doctrines must necessarily be in the line of a few remarks on the problem of knowledge. This problem is, of course, important in any system of thought, but in Buddhist philosophy it is peculiarly so, and it is quite impossible to make any headway in our understanding of it unless we ever bear in mind what Buddhists mean by knowledge and truth.

As the expression, "Turning from error and opening understanding" implies, all human knowledge may be divided into two great divisions; namely, Error and Truth. Such a division is, however, too clear-cut, for there is much of our knowledge which can be called neither pure truth nor absolute error; and so Buddhists usually divide knowledge into three divisions; namely, Illusion, Relative Truth and Absolute Truth. Or in case we divide knowledge into Error and Truth, Truth itself is divided into two divisions; namely, Relative or Accommodated Truth and Perfect or Absolute

Truth. All human knowledge, then, is either Illusion, Relatively True, or Absolute Truth. An ancient and popular illustration of this threefold division is that of a piece of rope seen in the twilight. Seeing its general shape, one may take it for a snake (Illusion). One may see that it is a rope and not think any further as to its constituent elements (Relative Truth). Or one may know that it is a rope made of grass, *i.e.* understand its real make-up (Absolute Truth). The knowledge of the average man is largely illusion and error. He holds a naïve realistic view and thinks that everything is in reality just what it appears to be. Relative or Accommodated Truth is a step towards perfect knowledge or Absolute Truth. This kind of knowledge penetrates somewhat into the reality of things, but it does not see things in their real essence. To this class of knowledge belongs practically all our so-called knowledge of the phenomenal world and the things we deal with in our practical life. In our practical life, *e.g.*, we make distinctions between things. We say this is good and that is bad, this is beautiful and that ugly, this is large and that small, this is light and that heavy, etc. All these distinctions have a practical value, and such knowledge is to be regarded as knowledge when contrasted with error; but, after all, this is only relative knowledge. These distinctions which we make in the world of phenomena may seem important and real, but in the last analysis they are not what they seem. They are mere appearances of a reality in which these distinctions have no real meaning. The wise man must go beyond this sort of knowledge of reality, he must attain perfect knowledge of the Absolute Truth and see things as they really are. He must get back of the appearances to the things themselves. He must know not merely the phenomena but the noumena, or rather the Noumenon, "Das Ding an Sich" of Kant.

The Western student of philosophy is, of course, quite familiar with Kant's epoch-making work on this problem of human knowledge. He knows what a great contribution Kant made when he showed that in all our thinking the thinking subject contributes something to the object perceived so that what we know seems a sort of "construct" composed of the object known and the knowing subject. That is, knowledge is not a mere impress of the object on the thinking subject, or a mere writing on an empty tablet, but the thinking subject is active rather than passive in the process. So much of Kant's theory of knowledge must be accepted as valid. But when Kant proceeded to show how our knowledge is a knowledge not of things as they really are in themselves but only as they appear (with the implication that appearance does not give us reality), we cannot follow Kant. And especially when Kant tries to draw a line between what he calls the Empirical Ego and the Transcendental or Ontological Ego, and says that we know the former but not the latter, we must reject his epistemology at this point altogether. The self knows nothing better than the self of self-consciousness, and if this is not the real self, or the noumenal ego, then there is no noumenal ego, nor has Kant even the right to express the judgment that the empirical ego is not the noumenal ego.

Now Buddhism makes this same distinction between the phenomenal and the noumenal world and says that all our ordinary knowledge is only of the phenomenal world and so is only relatively true. The knowledge of the noumenal world is possible only to the one who has reached perfect enlightenment, *i.e.* to one who has attained Buddhahood. He who has attained this stage is able to see that the distinctions which the ordinary man makes between things have no real existence in being but are due to the unenlightened mind. Not that existence is absolutely void, but that the phenomenal world appears to us as it does because we are what we are, rather than because it is so in itself. The enlightened one knows that the complex and multiplicity of the phenomenal world is really a simplicity and Oneness of Being. On the high plane of Absolute Truth one enters the "Dharma of non-duality" where all distinctions and antitheses are absorbed in a higher synthesis, where one can see the "identity of differences" and the "indifference of opposites." (And we might also add, one enters the realm of Fichte's Absolute in which, as Hegel put it, one is in "the night in which all cows are black.") Even the distinction between error and truth disappears, "because," says a modern exponent, "those who have entered a meditation in which there is no sense-impression, no cogitation, are free from ignorance as well as from enlightenment. This holds true with all the other dualistic categories." When one has entered this stage, one has entered the Nirvāna of true Buddhahood, the heaven in which even the distinction between existence and non-existence has no meaning.

According to the orthodox Buddhist theory of knowledge, then, all ordinary human knowledge deals but with the phenomenal world and not with reality itself. This knowledge of the phenomenal world is "Hōben," Accommodated Truth, *i.e.* it is the truth accommodated to meet the needs of unenlightened minds. There is an Absolute Truth and a perfect knowledge, but only for the fully enlightened, *i.e.* for those who have attained Buddhahood.

If it be asked on what grounds Buddhism makes the assertion that there is an Absolute Truth for the enlightened mind, the answer is that this must be taken on the authority of those who have attained Buddhahood. Manifestly to make the statement that our knowledge is only relative and of the phenomenal world, implies a knowledge of the real or noumenal world; and this judgment that our knowledge is relative but that there is an Absolute Truth, can therefore not be made by ordinary man as a matter of knowledge but must be accepted on faith. That is, the ordinary Buddhist accepts on faith this theory of truth that what the unenlightened mind regards as true, is true only relatively and that the Buddha knows reality as it is in itself. The Buddhist theory of truth is, then, in the last analysis a "credo ut intelligam."

Of course, even Christian epistemology would not claim that human knowledge is perfect knowledge of the truth, and would say that only God can know the truth perfectly.

That is, Christian epistemology also may speak of human knowledge as relative, but not relative in the Buddhist sense. It is relative in the sense that it is fragmentary and not complete, but not that it is wholly erroneous when compared with perfect truth. In the words of Paul, "We know in part, and we prophesy in part; but when that which is perfect is come, that which is in part shall be done away." That is, our partial knowledge is the real stepping stone to the full truth, and it is true knowledge as far as it goes. A Buddhist illustration will bring out the difference between the two views of truth; namely, the illustration of the shield. The shield seen from one side seems convex in shape, and from the opposite side, concave. To say that the shield is convex in shape, is a true statement. But the Buddhist would say that it is only relatively true, because one can say from the opposite point of view that it is concave in shape. "Therefore," proceeds Buddhist epistemology, "the shield is both convex and concave, and because these are opposites, it is neither the one nor the other, and so its real nature can not be known." Christian epistemology would say that the shield as we see it is convex. This may be only a partial view of the object. If it is also concave when seen from the other side, then the two appearances must be harmonized so as to do justice to all the facts known about the shield. They cannot be harmonized, as Buddhist epistemology tries to harmonize them; namely, by saying that we really know nothing about the object we call a shield. But if our knowledge of an object contains contradictions, we must proceed upon the basis of the knowledge we have till we clear these away. At any rate we must trust our knowledge of things as true knowledge even though we admit that it is not perfect, and that only the absolute mind can know the full truth.

The Buddhist theory of knowledge is, however, not adequately understood until one gets the Buddhist explanation of the origin of ignorance, or the theory of Nescience. All human knowledge is really a Nescience. If the phenomenal world does not represent the noumenal world, how is it that the phenomenal world appears at all? Either it appears without a cause, or if it has a cause, the cause is present in the phenomena in some way, and to that extent at least the noumenal world can be known through the phenomenal world, one should think. That the phenomenal world does appear to us no one can deny without ending in absolute skepticism. The question is, why does it appear and to what does it appear?

The orthodox Buddhist reply to this question is the so-called theory of Nescience. The phenomenal world as known to man has no existence as such; and if by existence we mean the things that appear to us, Buddhism holds that existence is void. It is, however, not void in the sense that nothing at all exists, but only in the sense that nothing really exists in the way in which it appears to us to exist. That is, Buddhism asserts the reality of a noumenal world, and the true Mahāyāna school even affirms the presence of the noumenal in the phenomenal, but denies that the phenomenal world is in reality such as it appears to us. It appears so to us only because of our ignorance. "Everything that is subject to the law of birth and death exists only (i.e. in the way it appears to exist) because of ignorance and Karma."

But how does ignorance arise, and by what process do we come to look upon things as we do? The first answer to this question is that our present state of ignorance arose, according to the law of cause and effect, from past states of error and illusions, and our present state, by the same law, will give rise to future states of ignorance. Our past states of ignorance were produced by the law of Karma from states of ignorance still further back, and so this chain of ignorance stretches backwards into an indefinite past, just as it will stretch forwards into an indefinite future unless it is broken by the "gospel of enlightenment."

It is possible to distinguish twelve links in this Chain of Ignorance, the so-called Twelve Links of Cause and Circumstance (Jūni inen).[1]   These links give us one form of the Buddhist conception of the nature of man. If the reader does not clearly understand just what they mean — and we venture to think that he will not — he should remember that it is due to the fact that Western psychology does not recognize such divisions, and also because it is impossible to get English terms to convey the exact meaning of the oriental originals. The following are the twelve links (Nidana) :

1. Ignorance — the error of lusts and desire in a previous life.

2. Latent Impressions — the deeds of good and evil of a previous life.

3. Thought Substance — the beginning of the psychic aspect of the uterine life.

4. Name and Form — the physical beginnings of the uterine life.

5. The Six Roots — the development of eyes, ears, nose, tongue, body and will during the uterine life.

6. Contact — the Six Roots of number five come into contact after birth with the Six Dusts, i.e. the physical environment.

7. Sensation — the feeling of pain and pleasure arising from the organs of sense.

8. Desire — the lust of the flesh.

9. Clinging to Existence — the passion and pride of life which drives man on to actions which produce a new Karma of good or evil.

10. Becoming — the completion of Karma in the present life.

11. Birth — the new life which shall be born in the future as a result of the deeds done in the present life.

12. Decrepitude and Death — the pain, trouble, sorrow, old age and death in the future.

Numbers 1 and 2 refer to the lusts and actions of the previous life. Numbers 3–10 refer to the present life beginning with the beginnings of the uterine life and ending with death. Numbers 11–12 refer to the birth, pain, sorrow and death in the next incarnation. Death at the end of our present life means only the continuation of the Karma-chain (unless it is broken by the gospel of Buddha) in which, in the future as in the past, the above twelve links are discernible. The twelve links become, each in turn, the effect of a preceding cause and the cause of a succeeding effect.

Some writers leave the explanation of the origin of ignorance with this description of the various links in the Karma-chain, though Ignorance constitutes the first link in the chain and so leaves the explanation just where it began. But if it be asked, How explain the origin of the first link? the reply is that it arose from preceding links ad infinitum. And if the question is pushed still further, the reply is that the very question as to the origin of ignorance is ignorance itself, and how can one demand that a rational answer be given as to the origin of the irrational; or still better, why explain the origin of that which really does not exist? for on the high plane of true enlightenment one can see that ignorance has no real existence.

Some Buddhists, however, recognize the fact that such answers are either quibbling with words or that it is reasoning in a circle, and so they meet the question as to the origin of ignorance with the bold assertion that the irrational is an original element of existence. That is, some hold that it is coeternal with the rational (a sort of dualism), or that it is inherent in the Absolute and arises spontaneously. Ignorance, which is really synonymous with consciousness — for without consciousness there would be no ignorance — is caused by "the waves of mentation which are ever stirring up the ocean of eternal tranquillity." What causes these "waves of mentation," no one can say beyond that it is a part of the eternal nature of things as they appear to ignorant man.

Ignorance, then, is the real source of the phenomenal world as it appears to us, since it is the first link in the Karma-chain by which the Absolute individualizes itself and becomes conscious in man. Man's finite mind, in turn, gives rise to the phenomenal world as known to the common man. "Things are fundamentally and in themselves non-existent; only through the law of cause and circumstance have they come to be." "All things are the product of circumstance. Apart from the law of cause and circumstance all things are invisible." From the standpoint of Absolute Truth ignorance has no real existence and therefore the phenomenal world as it appears to man has no such existence; for, as we have said, from this high plane even the difference between truth and error, being and nonbeing have no meaning. The Enlightened One has reached the "Dharma of non-duality" in which there is an "identity of differences" and an "indifference of opposites."

C. Buddhist World Views

Upon the Buddhist theory of knowledge is naturally built the Buddhist world view; or rather, world views, for there are three more or less distinct ones. These are the Hīnayāna, the Provisional Mahāyāna, and the True Mahāyāna. From the standpoint of the Mahāyāna school the other two are only relatively true and so correspond to the second division of human knowledge mentioned above, i.e. Relative Truth. The world view of the ignorant masses corresponds to the first division; namely, Illusion; whereas the True Mahāyāna world view corresponds to Absolute Truth.

Both the Hīnayāna and the Provisional Mahāyāna, we said, are regarded by Mahāyāna Buddhists as relatively true. They are said to be two extremes, and the truth lies in the middle, the Middle Path of Mahāyāna. We shall state briefly what these two extremes are and then what the true Middle Path is.

1. *Hīnayāna World View.* — The Hīnayāna view is more or less a realistic world view. It does not, of course, accept the naïve realism of the unenlightened masses who hold that the world is just what it appears to be and that there is no mystery about it. It approaches the problem with a critical spirit and by an analytical method it seeks to penetrate into the inner nature of existence. To begin with, it divides reality into two great spheres; namely, the phenomenal and the noumenal, or Nirvāna, spheres. The

phenomenal sphere it divides into two subdivisions; namely, the physical and the psychic. It treats the phenomenal sphere as having a real objective existence but as being in a constant flux and therefore lacking the element of permanency. Of the Nirvāna sphere it has little to say except that it is void of everything found in the phenomenal sphere. The Nirvāna sphere cannot therefore be known through the phenomenal sphere, for there is no real connection between them. The object of Hīnayāna philosophy is to free man from the wanderings of the phenomenal world into the Nirvāna sphere by showing him what is the real nature of his life and the whole realm of phenomena.

Thus Hīnayāna philosophy proceeds further to analyze the things which make up the world of phenomena. The analysis begins with man himself, for he is the best example of the two aspects of existence; namely, mind and matter. Man is shown to be made up of the so-called five Skandhas [2] — Form, Feeling, Notion, Predisposition and Discrimination. Of these five Skandhas, the first is physical and the remaining four are psychical. The physical aspect of man is then divided into the Five Indriyās (Jap. Gokon), *i.e.* the five organs of sense, and into the five Ālambanas (Jap. Goriki), the five senses as distinguished from the organs as such. The psychic elements are divided into two groups, the first three constituting one group and the fourth standing by itself. The fourth, *i.e.* Discrimination, is said to be the Mental King, and the other three; namely, Feeling, Notion and Predisposition, are spoken of as servants of the Mental King. Sometimes the analysis is carried still further and the upshot is that by this division of the psychic and physical of man's life, Hīnayāna Buddhism tries to account for the phenomena of our mental life, and reaches the startling conclusion that the self of self-consciousness is but an illusion and is simply the product of this aggregate of Skandhas.

The world without, Hīnayāna seeks to understand by the same analytical process. Thus it holds that matter in general is made up of minute particles, which correspond

o

very much to the atoms of modern science. These minute particles are composed of the four Great Kinds (Jap. Shidaishu, or Shidai); namely, Earth (Solids), Water (Liquids), Fire (Heat) and Wind (Movability). These four great elements, or natures, remain ever the same, and by combining in different degrees, constitute the various kinds of atoms; and these, in turn, compose the things which make up the phenomenal world.

While Hīnayāna asserts the reality of both the psychic and the physical aspects of existence, it shows a monistic tendency in that it regards the four Great Kinds, which make up the physical world, as qualities rather than elements, and holds that if the process of division were carried far enough (some say, seven raised to the seventh power in the case of an atom) matter would change into spirit. The real dualism in Hīnayāna philosophy is the dualism of the phenomenal and Nirvāna spheres. It asserts the reality of both, though it has little or nothing to say of the latter.

2. *Provisional Mahāyāna World View.* — The Provisional Mahāyāna world view also begins by speaking of the two great spheres of existence, *i.e.* the phenomenal and the noumenal. But where Hīnayāna philosophy divides the phenomenal sphere into two subdivisions and speaks of both as real, Provisional Mahāyāna denies the reality of the outside world and holds it to be the product of impure thought. The outside world exists only in the mind and has no objective existence. "In Buddhism the mind is made the source from which all laws (phenomena) come." "Mind takes the form of hell, devils, brutes, heavenly beings; in fact all that has shape and form is the product of mind." Starting with the analysis of the nature of man advanced by the Hīnayāna school, Provisional Mahāyāna speculation goes a step further and not only declares the self of self-consciousness to have no real existence, but also tries to show how this illusion arises in the mind and how the mind produces the illusions of the outside world and everything that appears in consciousness.

A great deal of Buddhist literature seems to give expression to this world view, and Western writers usually take this as the real Buddhist position. Everything is regarded as mere illusion and as devoid of reality. As we said above, even the self is said to be non-existent and an illusion. One might well ask how this can be; for if the self, too, is an illusion, it must be an illusion to something, and at least that Something must exist. A Something does exist according to the Provisional Mahāyan school; namely, the noumenal world, but of this really nothing can be affirmed. The one thing that can be done is to destroy the errors and illusions of the phenomenal world. That is, progress in truth is achieved only by destroying error. Thus, *e.g.* the old Sanron Sect, which is the best representative of this school in Japan, held that all advance in truth is made through a denial of all affirmations. "Add a negation and you clear away all illusion, you destroy and deny thus every error and misconception. If, *e.g.* you hold to the principle of birth, clear it away with the idea of death; and if you hold to death as a principle, destroy it with the principle of birth. If you hold to a non-death non-birth principle, destroy it with the non-non-birth non-non-death principle and so on and on. Since we have relative and finite minds we must clear away everything; for, after all, not one thing in our minds is real." Thus negation follows upon negation ad infinitum.

3. *Mahāyāna World View.* — But this world view which denies the reality of the outside world is regarded by the True Mahāyāna school as an extreme view. The view is correct in so far as it seeks to destroy all illusions but not in making the phenomenal world an absolute void. Mahāyāna holds that the phenomenal world is real because it is identical with the noumenal world. That is, the noumenal world is in the phenomenal world and the phenomenal rests upon the noumenal. But this does not mean that reality is as it appears to the unenlightened mind. The Mahāyāna school also says that the phenomenal world as it appears to the average man is a shadow world and has

no existence as such. Even the self known in self-consciousness has no real existence in the way it appears to exist, but it is not an absolute void. It has no individual and distinct existence as it appears to have when we are conscious of the difference between the ego and the non-ego, but it, like all phenomena, is a manifestation of the Noumenon (Shinnyō) concerning whose real nature no definite assertion can be made. That is, Mahāyāna holds that there is a noumenal world and that the noumenal is present in the phenomenal world, but the phenomenal world does not reveal to the unenlightened mind the real nature of the noumenal world. This assertion, as we said above, manifestly cannot be made by man as he is, but must be accepted on faith in the authority of the Buddha, or Buddhas, who alone know what is the nature of real existence. For any but the Enlightened the nature of real existence is incomprehensible.

"The essence of all things is incomprehensible. To attempt to realize their essence is as vain as to make real one's dreams which come to nothing the moment one awakes."

"In trying to understand the various worlds, one finds that they are like flames, shadow-pictures, sounds, dreams, visions or specters."

"Zengen said to the Buddha, 'Thou hast taught that all things are without reality, being like dreams, sounds, shadows, flames or visions, and that their real nature or individuality is neutral. How is it, then, that there are such differences as the laws of good and evil, sensuous and supersensuous, determined and free?' To this the Buddha replied, 'O Zengen, the common man knows not that his thoughts are like dreams, like shadows, like visions and specters. That is why he clings to what are mere shadows and does deeds of good and evil, happiness and misfortune in his body, words and will. In reality there are no such differences even though it may seem that there are.'"

But when it is said that the differences which the common man makes have no real existence, it is not meant that existence is altogether void. Back of the apparent plurality

of the phenomenal world is the all-inclusive Oneness of the
Real World. Back of change and the temporal is the change-
less and eternal. This is spoken of as the Substance of the
Universe and is conceived of as a unity which includes all
dualities; namely, the "Dharma of non-duality"; it is the
Spiritual True Likeness (Shin Shinnyō).

"Shin Shinnyō is that which underlies the two worlds of
matter and mind. It is boundless as to space and endless
as to time. It is constant as to past, present and future.
Extending into the Ten Worlds, it is unlimited, and the whole
universe is but the manifestation of it."

"Shin Shinnyō is the body of law which underlies the
entire universe. This is the so-called Spiritual Essence which
is neither born nor perishes. The apparent differences in
the world are but the product of impure thought. Outside
the mind there are no real differences. Therefore the real
essence of the universe is not to be expressed in words, nor
can it be reduced to any fixed formula. It is incomprehensible and ultimately it is a Oneness in which there is neither
change nor difference. It is indestructible and because it
is a Oneness it is called Shinnyō."

"Whatever exists is evolved from the One Body of Shinnyō's Law-nature (Shinnyō Hōjō no Ittai) by the law of
cause and effect, and therefore everything is substantially
one and the same."

"Shin Shinnyō is that which is the essence of all things
and principles; it is the ideal changeless and imperishable.
The distinctions and differences in things are but the product of our illusory ideas, and these differences do not exist
apart from the mind. Therefore the laws of all things are
originally and in their real essence identical, changeless, without real differences and imperishable when all explanations,
nomenclatures and thought are subtracted from them. And
because they are all one Mind they are called Shinnyō."

This third view of what constitutes the essence of reality
— and as we have said, this is the orthodox view of the
Mahāyāna school to which most Japanese sects belong —
holds, then, in short, that while for practical purposes in

our state of ignorance we may say that there are real differences (Sabetsu) in things, in reality Existence is a oneness or a sameness (Byōdō) concerning which no further assertion can be made.   Even the statement that the universe is Being would be too specific and must be balanced by the conception of Non-Being, if one would keep in the Middle Path.   "We cannot say," writes a modern Buddhist, "that things either are or that they are not.   If we ask whether things are fixed in their Being or fixed in their Non-Being, we can give no positive answer to either question.   We can only say that things are, or that they are not, or that they are midway between Being and Non-Being."   If this seems strange to the reader, let him remember that our own Hegel has tried to show that the essence of Being is Being plus Non-Being, whatever that may mean.

But the Mahāyāna Buddhist, too, recognizes that, after all, we live in a world where differences seem very real and where we must treat them as real in spite of their supposedly metaphysical identity.   And so if we would make progress in our understanding, we must leave this problem of the ulitmate nature of reality and this high plane of the "Dharma of non-duality" and come down to the world as it is, or at any rate as it appears to be.   We shall, however, not leave the above theories of knowledge and theories of the essence of reality too far behind, for they crop out in almost every problem that is discussed.   In fact, we must remember that all exposition and explanation belong to the realm of Relative or Accommodated Truth and not to the realm of Absolute Truth.   And so when we expound certain definite views regarding the cosmos, God, man, salvation etc., we must always be ready to add at the end that these are views expressed in terms of Accommodated Truth.   This is exceedingly maddening to the average Western mind, for just when one thinks that one has finally reached solid ground as to what Buddhism really teaches on this or that point, one must be prepared to have the foundation knocked from under this stately mansion of knowledge by the consciousness that these ideas are expressed, but in the concepts of Accommodated Truth and therefore are not really true. And we should add here that it is this theory of truth which makes Buddhist teachings so inconsistent when taken as a whole, and so tolerant of views which may be the direct opposite. For if in the last analysis all differences are really a sameness, then it would be folly to insist very much on any view. All contradictions are but opposite sides of the same thing whose real nature transcends the power of finite mind to comprehend. Therefore, as we said, Buddhism is very tolerant; at least this is true of Buddhist philosophers.

D. *The Pluralistic World of Experience*

If the universe is Sameness from the standpoint of Absolute Truth, from the standpoint of Accommodated Truth it is a universe of Differences. The world of experience is a pluralistic world even though the last word of speculative thought may be a monism of one sort or another. Now this pluralistic world Buddhism divides in many ways, and in these divisions all schools agree in general. That is, the distinctions between Hīnayāna, Provisional Mahāyāna and True Mahāyāna do not have much meaning here. The differences are rather sectarian and pertain more to the religious application of the teachings than otherwise.

1. *The Two Spheres.* — First of all Buddhism divides all existence into the two great spheres mentioned above; namely, the phenomenal sphere and the noumenal sphere. This has already been discussed, and we mention it here simply because even this distinction belongs to the realm of Accommodated Truth and not to the realm of Absolute Truth.

2. *The Three Worlds.* — The second great division which Buddhism makes is what is called in Japanese, Sanse, Three Worlds, *i.e.* the Past, the Present and the Future. In western thought we are, of course, familiar with this division of time, but in Buddhist thought it is not so much a division of time as a division of the Causal Nexus which runs through all things. The Past world caused the Present

world and the Present world becomes in turn the cause of the Future world. There is really nothing in the Present which was not in the Past, and there will be nothing in the Future which is not in the Present, so that the Past cause may be seen in the Present effect and the Future inferred from the Present cause. The universe is really a closed system and it repeats its perpetual rounds in strict conformity to the law of cause and effect.

3. *The Timeless, Boundless Cosmos.*—According to Buddhist cosmology the cosmos had no real beginning and has no end in time. It has always existed and it always will exist. It passes, however, through various stages as time goes on. Four stages are recognized; namely, (1) Completion, (2) Inhabitation, (3) Destruction and (4) Voidness. In the state of Completion the world is being formed from the great Void and prepared for living beings. In the state of Inhabitation it is filled with all manner of living beings. In the third state, the state of Destruction, the cosmos is disintegrating and preparing to enter the fourth state, the state of Voidness. This last state is, however, not an absolute void nor does this state continue forever, for after an immeasurable length of time the cosmos will again form from out this void and enter once more upon the first of the above mentioned states, and so a new cycle begins. One such cycle follows upon another in endless succession. Each stage in a cycle is millions of years in length, so that a single cycle is immeasurably long. And when it is said that such cycles follow each other in endless succession it becomes clear that this is simply an attempt to express in finite terms the infinity of Time. The cause of the destruction of the cosmos in the third state is said to be a destructive fire which breaks out and consumes everything with a fervent heat. The cause which reforms the cosmos in the first state is a cool wind which arises spontaneously and blows across the hot waste. Lest the reader take this too literally let him be reminded that this Wind is really the "Wind of Ignorance" which stirs up the "waves of mentation" on the "Ocean of Eternal Tranquillity." That is, the origin

of the cosmos is really due to ignorance which spontaneously springs up in the Absolute and causes it to individualize and objectify itself.   When this ignorance has been destroyed or exhausted the cosmos disappears again in the great void of Perfect Tranquillity.

The universe is not only timeless but also boundless as to space.   The cosmos spoken of above is the cosmos known to man.   But this is only one among numberless worlds. Thus Buddhist speculation says that "a thousand such worlds make a 'group of Lesser Thousand Worlds,' a thousand such groups make one group of 'Middle Thousand Worlds,' and a thousand groups of 'Middle Thousand Worlds' constitute a group of 'Larger Thousand Worlds.' And finally one such group makes one of the so-called 'Three Thousand Greatest Thousand Worlds.'"   All these worlds pass through the four stages of Completion, Inhabitation, Destruction and Voidness mentioned above.   Thus the universe is infinite both in Time and Space.   Let the reader, however, be reminded again not to take this too literally, for space and time are regarded as but the laws of thought, and everything which appears in space and time as but the product of unenlightened minds.

4.   *The Three Realms.* — We said that the second stage of each world is the state of Inhabitation, *i.e.* the state when a world is inhabited by living beings.   These living beings Buddhism divides roughly into three great classes or realms; namely, the so-called Sankai, Three Realms [3] (Sk. Trailokya).   These are the Realm of Desire (Yokukai, Sk. Kāmadhātu), the Realm of Color or Pure Form (Shikikai, Sk. Rūpadhātu) and the Realm of No-Color or Formlessness (Mushikikai, Sk. Arūpadhatu).   The first is called the Realm of Desire because all beings in this realm, or state, are subject to the bondages of sexual desires, eating, drinking, sleeping, and all that goes with physical existence.   The Realm of Color, or Pure Form, is a kind of ethereal world. The beings in this realm are free from the ordinary lusts of the flesh, but their state is still a sort of bodily existence; namely, a bodily existence of a refined and etherealized sub-

stance. The Realm of No-Color, or Formlessness, is the realm of pure spirits. The beings in that realm have neither matter nor form. In fact, the highest beings in this realm are not only free from bodily existence, but their state is even more refined than spirit and reaches almost the vanishing point, for they are said to have entered the heaven of No-Thought and No-Non-Thought. What this means is that such beings have reached the borderland of the phenomenal world where it recedes, as it were, into the noumenal world and so eludes our grasp; for as we have repeatedly said, our knowledge is but a knowledge of the phenomenal world and not of the noumenal world. Our knowledge can therefore reach up to the very threshold of the noumenal world but it cannot go beyond.

5. *The Six Ways.*— Another division of phenomenal existence which covers the same range of beings as the Three Realms but in greater detail is what is known as the Six Ways (Rokudō, Sk. Gāti). The Six Ways are really six great classes of beings. Within these great divisions there are many subdivisions and grades. In fact, one is very much reminded of the Monadology of Leibniz which arranged all beings in an ascending or descending scale, so that no two were exactly alike — all being of the same essence but in different degrees. It is exceedingly important to understand this Buddhist "scale of beings," for it is but another way of stating the two great doctrines of Indian thought which have been the common property of Hinduism and Buddhism; namely, the doctrine of Karma and its corollary, the doctrine of Transmigration. Without a knowledge of this "scale of beings" it is also impossible to understand the absence in Buddhism of a clear line between God and man on the one hand, and between man and other creatures on the other hand. The ease, therefore, with which men are exalted into gods, and gods made to appear as men or lower beings, will be understood only after one gets clearly fixed in one's mind at least the main outline of the doctrine of the Six Ways. The following are the Six Ways given in an ascending scale:

(1) Hell (Jigoku, Sk. Nāraka or Noraya), (2) Hungry Spirits (Gaki, Sk. Pretas), (3) Beasts (Chikushō), (4) Fighting and Bloodshed (Shura Sk. Asuras), (5) Man (Ningen) and (6) Heavenly Beings (Tenjō, Sk. Dēvas).

These Six Ways, or Realms of Beings, are localized with reference to Mt. Sumēru (Jap. Shumisen) regarded as the center of every world. Hell is located many leagues below this central mountain. It has eight great subdivisions located one below the other and each of these has four gates with four antechambers at each gate, thus making really a total of one hundred thirty-six hells. These are all hot hells, but there are also eight great divisions of a cold hell.[4] The picture which Buddhism gives of the lot of the beings in these various hells surpasses the imagination of Western readers even though they may be steeped in Dante's Inferno.

The Realm of Hungry Spirits has two great divisions; one being located under Mt. Sumēru but above Hell, and the other above the surface of the earth in the air near the base of the mountain. The characteristics of beings in this realm are greed and passion which exist in various degrees.

The Realm of Beasts has also two main divisions; one being in the " great sea " and the other on land around the base of Mt. Sumēru. Folly and passion are the characteristics of beings in this realm and their variety is as great as the number of living beings in the waters and on land, with man excluded.

The Realm of Fighting and Bloodshed has again two main divisions, one being in the sea and the other on land. Pride, strife and cruelty are the characteristics of beings in this realm. Some Japanese Buddhists omit this fourth realm, for it is not quite clear just what is really meant by it. The beings in it seem to be a sort of hybrid between beasts and man.

When we come to the fifth way or realm; namely, the Realm of Man, we come to an existence which has two sides to it. On the one hand human life is a life of sorrow and suffering, and on the other hand it is a life of joy and happiness. As compared with the four lower realms it is highly to be desired, but still it is not an existence in which one should care to remain forever. Sorrow and suffering outweigh the happy side, and all pleasures in this life are fleeting.

The last and highest of the Six Ways is the Way or Realm of Heavenly Beings. This is the great realm into which Buddhist speculation places all the gods and superhuman beings of Brahmanism and other religions, i.e. beings that are superior to man but which have not entered the Buddhist Nirvāna. The Realm of Heavenly Beings has numerous divisions, heaven rising above heaven in endless numbers. They are divided into three great groups, the first group being the heavens of the Realm of Desire, the second, the heavens of the Realm of Form, and the third, the heavens of the Realm of Formlessness. These are located one above the other and separated by immense distances. The lower heavens of the Realm of Desire are located on the upper slopes and top of Mt. Sumēru, while the upper heavens of this lower group are located hundreds of thousands of leagues above this central mountain, whose own height is said to be 84,000 yodjanas above the surface of the ocean and whose depth extends an equal distance downwards. As the upper groups of heavens are separated by immeasurable distances from this lower group, it follows that they extend upward into infinite space. As the heights of these numerous heavens vary, so does the length of life in them vary. In the lowest of the heavens of the Realm of Desire, e.g. life lasts 500 years, but twenty-four hours in this heaven are equal in length to fifty years on earth. In the highest of this lower group life lasts 16,000 years, but twenty-four hours are equal to 1600 years on earth. In the heavens of the Realm of Form and the Realm of Formlessness life can only be measured by Kalpas, and a Kalpa may be measured in years by adding from seventeen to ninety ciphers to the figure one. The following outline may give the reader a glimpse of this immense structure of oriental imagination. We give both the Japanese and Sanskrit terms, and, where possible, the meaning in English.

Tenjō (Dēvas), Heavenly Beings.
1. Roku Yokuten (6 Dēvalōkas), Six Heavens of Desire.
   (1) Shiōten (Tchatur mahārādja kāyikas), Heaven of Four Dēva Kings; namely, the four kings who rule over the regions on the four sides of Mt. Sumēru.
   (2) Tōriten (Traiyastrimsas), Heaven of thirty-three cities or beings, probably, the heaven of the ancient Vedic gods.
   (3) Yamaten (Yama).
   (4) Dosotsuten (Tuchita), The heaven in which all Bodhisattvas are reborn before they appear as Buddhas upon earth. Maitreya, the Buddha of the Future, is now there preaching Buddhism to the inhabitants.
   (5) Kerakuten (Nirmanarati), Heaven of Delight in Transformation.
   (6) Takajisaiten (Paranirmita Vasavartin), Heaven where dēvas remain unchanged while others change. This is the highest of the Six Heavens of Desire and the abode of Māra, the Buddhist tempter.
2. Shizen (4 Dhyānas), Four Meditation Regions.
   (1) Shōzenten (First Dhyāna), First Meditation Region.
      a. Bonshūten (Brahma parichadya), Assembly of the Brahmas.
      b. Bonhōten (Brahma purōhita), Heaven of Brahma's Attendants.
      c. Daibonten (Mahābrahma), Heaven of the Great Brahma.
   (2) Nizenten (Second Dhyāna), Second Meditation Region.
      a. Shōkōten (Parittābha), Little Light Heaven.
      b. Muryōkōten (Apramabha), Boundless Light Heaven.
      c. Gokukōjōten (Abhasvara), Superior Pure Light Heaven.
   (3) Sanzenten (Third Dhyāna), Third Meditation Region.
      a. Shōjōten (Parittasubha), Limited Purity Heaven.
      b. Muryōjōten (Apramānāsubha), Boundless Purity Heaven.

      c. Henjōten (Subhakritsna), All Purity Heaven.
(4) Shizenten (Fourth Dhyāna), Fourth Meditation Region.
      a. Fukushō (Punyaprasava), Happy Birth Heaven.
      b. Muunten (Anabhraka), Cloudless Heaven.
      c. Kokwaten (Vrihatphala), Vast Merit Heaven.
      d. Munetsuten (Asandjnisattva), No Heat Heaven.
      e. Musōten (Avriha), No Thought Heaven.
      f. Mubonten (Atapa), No Passion Heaven.
      g. Zenkenten (Sudrisa), Virtue Seeing Heaven.
      h. Zengenten (Sudarsana), Virtue Appearing Heaven.
      i. Shikikukyōten (Akanichtha), Final Limit of Desire Heaven.
3. Shimushiki (Arūpadhatu), Four Formlessness Regions.
    (1) Kūshōten, Empty Place Heaven. One is born into this when body is regarded as void.
    (2) Shikishōten, Imaginary Place Heaven. One is born into this heaven when both body and mind are regarded as void.
    (3) Mushōten, No Place Heaven. One is born into this heaven when body, mind and all phenomenal existence are regarded as void.
    (4) Hisōhihisōshōten, No Thought No Non-thought Place Heaven.

The reader is not expected to master all the details in the above outlines of the Six Ways, but simply to get a general idea of the conception which Buddhism has of living beings. All these beings, from the lowest hell to the highest heaven, are bound together by the one inexorable law of Karma. Beings pass from one state to another, either up or down, according to the law of merit and demerit. If merit outweighs demerit, a being will be born into a higher state, and if demerit is the greater, the birth will be in a lower state. No state is a permanent condition. Even the beings which have obtained birth into the highest heaven are still in the clutches of the law of Karma and Transmigration. Their life may be a happy one and it may last for thousands of years, but at the end of that time, unless they heap up further merit, they are doomed to sink again in the "scale of beings." Yea, the very bliss of the highest heaven makes their lot all the worse when they must leave it. Such a being is said to suffer sixteen times more than beings in the lowest of hells, "for only a King can mourn the loss of a kingdom." "If man does not cut the coils of evil deeds, he is doomed eternally to drift about in this ocean of life and death. And even though he has obtained birth into a world where life lasts eighty thousand years (*i.e.* in the higher heavens mentioned above), when this happiness ends he is doomed to fall into the way of the Three Evils." The beings in the Six Ways, then, are one and all still bound to the Wheel of Life and compelled to wander about in the "dread cycle of existence."

6. *The Four Holies.* — Now Buddhism offers a salvation from this "dread cycle of existence" by opening unto all beings a way of escape. This way is the way of the Four Holies (Shisei). These are the four great stages of enlightenment, beginning with those who hear the law of Buddha and ending with those who have fully attained Perfect Enlightenment, or Buddhahood. These four stages are the following: (1) Hearers (Jap. Shōmon, Sk. Srāvaka), (2) Enlightened One (Jap. Enkaku, Sk. Pratyēka Buddha), (3) Bodhisattva (Jap. Bosatsu, Sk. Bodhisattva), (4) Buddha (Jap. Butsu, Sk. Buddha). There are several degrees in each of these four stages of holiness, as may be seen at a glance from the following outline:

Four Holies (Shisei)	1. Shōmon (Srāvaka)		a. Sudako (Srotāpanna), a beginner in the way of Enlightenment.
			b. Sudagon (Skridagamin), one who returns but once to the Three Worlds.
			c. Anagon (Anagamin), no return to the Three Worlds.
			d. Arakan, or Rakan (Arhat), a true saint, free from evil and one who has attained the first stage of Buddhahood.
	2. Enkaku (Pratyēka Buddha)		One who has broken the twelve links in the Karma Chain. The state is also called Dokugaku, Self enlightenment. This enlightenment is still shallow and this kind of Buddha, like the Arhat, seeks salvation only for himself.
	3. Bosatsu (Bodhi-sattva)	The Bodhi-sattva makes four great vows	a. To save all beings.
			b. To destroy all passions.
			c. To know and teach others all laws.
			d. To lead others to understand all Buddha's ways.
		and practices the six virtues (Pāramitās)	a. Almsgiving and teaching the ignorant.
			b. Keeping the Commandments.
			c. Patience and Long-suffering.
			d. Diligence (in fulfilling the vows).
			e. Meditation.
			f. Wisdom (for self and others).
	4. Butsu (Buddha)		a. Ōjin Butsu (Nirmanakāya), Buddha in human form like the historic Buddha S'akyamuni.
			b. Hoshin Butsu (Sambhogakāya), Buddha as an ideal person or the personification of virtue and wisdom such as the Buddha Amitābha.
			c. Hōshin Butsu (Dharmakāya), Buddha as the Absolute or the Noumenon that underlies all phenomenal existence.

To appreciate the respective values of these different stages of holiness the following section from the Sūtra of the Forty-two Sections should be read :

"The Buddha said, 'It is better to feed one good man than to feed one hundred bad men. It is better to feed one who observes the Five Precepts of Buddha than to feed one thousand good men. It is better to feed one Srotāpanna than to feed ten thousand of those who observe the Five Precepts of Buddha. It is better to feed one Skridagamin than to feed one million Srotāpanna. It is better to feed one Anagamin than to feed ten millions of Skridagamin. It is better to feed one Arhat than to feed one hundred millions of Anagamins. It is better to feed one Pratyēka Buddha than to feed one billion of Arhats. It is better to feed one of the Buddhas, either of the present, or of the past, or of the future, than to feed ten billions of Pratyēka Buddhas. It is better to feed one who is above knowledge, one sidedness, discipline and enlightenment than to feed one hundred billions of Buddhas of the past, present, or future.'"

7. *The Ten Worlds.* — The Four Holies and the Six Ways are sometimes placed together in one great scale of beings known as the Ten Worlds (Jūkai). This gives us the most comprehensive classification, as it includes all beings both within the Three Realms and above the Three Realms. The following diagram illustrates the matter at a glance:

The Ten Worlds		
	1. Hell.	
	2. Hungry Spirits.	
	3. Beasts.	The Six Ways, or the Three Realms. The World of Ignorance.
	4. Fighting and Bloodshed.	
	5. Man.	
	6. Heavenly Beings.	
	7. Srāvaka.	The Four Holies, or Above the Three Realms. The World of Enlightenment.
	8. Pratyēka Buddha.	
	9. Bodhisattva.	
	10. Buddha.	

As we said above, it is not necessary that the reader master all the details of these various ways in which Buddhists divide the phenomenal world, but it is exceedingly worth while to keep these things before one in a general way and to remember that all these grades of beings, from the lowest hell to the highest heaven, yea to the Buddhas who are above the highest heaven, are all bound together by the law of Karma into a sort of monistic whole. This should be remembered whether one discusses the Buddhist God-idea, the

P

nature of man, the way of salvation, the future life, or any other cardinal doctrine. It affects the way of approach to all of these and explains why the clear lines we draw in Western thought between God and man, truth and error, right and wrong, etc. do not usually obtain in Buddhism. And especially should the reader remember that this whole scheme of graded beings is but a presentation of things as they appear from the standpoint of Accommodated Truth, and not as they really are when seen from the high plane of Absolute Truth; for from this standpoint these differences have no real meaning. They are but ripples caused by the Wind of Ignorance on the Ocean of Sameness. Even the beings of the lowest hell are substantially one with the beings of the highest realms, for "in every passion there is a Buddha," and "in every living being dwells the essence of Buddha."

We have now reached the point where we can take up more specifically what from a Western standpoint would be regarded as the cardinal doctrines of religion. The first of these is naturally the doctrine of God.

E. *The God-idea of Japanese Buddhism*

What is really the conception of the Divine held by Japanese Buddhists? The answer is a very complex one.

In our first chapter we discussed briefly what seems to have been S'akyamuni's teaching on this point. We saw that he regarded the speculations about the Brahman as an idle waste of time, and on the other hand, the numerous gods of the common people he robbed of their glory either by ignoring them altogether, or by assigning them a much lower place than that of one who like himself had attained enlightenment; for the gods too, according to S'akyamuni, were still subject to the laws of birth and death and the dread cycle of existence which is incurably evil. In our second chapter we saw how the idea of a Supreme Being reasserted itself in Buddhism as it spread through northwest India and then into China, and that S'akyamuni him-

self was exalted into a being like God, or at least was regarded as a special manifestation of the Supreme Being.
We saw how Buddhism in its onward march gathered up into
itself practically everything with which it came in contact,
so that by the time it reached Japan it had assumed a complexity rather difficult to analyze. As was the case with
other cardinal doctrines, so its God-idea was no longer
one God-idea but many, ranging all the way from a low
animistic nature cult through ancestor worship and various
stages of polytheism to a philosophical monism which in
some branches was atheistic, in others semi-theistic, and in
still others pantheistic. And what Buddhism was in China
before it reached Japan, it has been and is to-day in Japan,
only that here it has added to itself the legends and myths
of the primitive Shintō which saw in every phenomenon a
special god and regarded particularly the Imperial family as
the descendants of the gods and as worthy to become gods
after death. Thus it is clear that if one would set forth the
conception which Japanese Buddhists have of the Divine,
no clear-cut presentation need be expected, and it is no
wonder that there is such a divergence of opinion among
writers on Buddhism as to just what is the Buddhist conception of God.

But while it is difficult to make a clear-cut presentation
of the subject we shall try to analyze in a measure at least
this maze of contradictory ideas. To begin with, we must
again refer the reader to the scheme of gradation of beings
which we have given above. There are ten great realms
of living beings in the Buddhist universe, and man finds
himself near the middle of this scale. That is, he is superior
to some and inferior to others. Those above man, though
differing from one another in excellence, may be regarded
as gods. And as all beings are bound together by a universal causal nexus, so that the higher may return to the
lower and the lower to the higher stages of existence, the
boundary between the human and the divine or any other
stage naturally disappears. Thus men can become gods
and gods become men. And still further must it be remem-

bered that all these graded realms of beings are superior or inferior only as seen from the standpoint of unenlightened man, but that from the standpoint of true enlightenment these differences have no meaning; for all are mere manifestations of what is essentially one and the same reality. This one reality is the Absolute of Buddhist philosophy. Western writers usually speak of the Buddhist conception of the Absolute as being a pantheistic conception and say that Buddhism as a religion is pantheism. Perhaps Pantheism is the best word we can use in English to designate the Buddhist God-idea, but only so because it is a very vague term open to an almost indefinite number of shades of meaning. As a matter of fact, Buddhist philosophers do not use the term. The Ultimate of Buddhist thought is not All-God, but a Oneness which transcends the categories of all being as known to man. The Absolute is really the Great Unknowable, and the agnostic attitude is the proper one for all true Buddhist philosophers.

But while the agnostic attitude is regarded as the most profound and should issue logically in silence on this great problem, few Buddhists are consistent on this point and, like Herbert Spencer, have a good deal to say about the Great Unknowable. What they have to say differs rather widely, for with some the conception of the Divine is practically atheism, *i.e.* the God-idea ends in zero, with others the conception is not far removed from theism, and with still others, who represent the majority, the conception fluctuates between atheism and theism, so that it may be designated by the vague term pantheism. The conception held by the general run of believers is incurably polytheistic, for polytheism is not, as some suppose, inconsistent with pantheism, but its necessary complement. That is, polytheism and pantheism are but two sides of one and the same shield; the former being the pluralistic view of everyday experience, and the latter the monistic view of the speculative thinker.

If then we speak of the God-idea as held by Japanese Buddhists, it depends largely upon what Buddhists we are

talking about. The uneducated classes in all sects are poly-
theists, and the philosophers are usually monists of one sort
or another, varying, as we have just said, all the way from
atheism to a semi-theism. We shall take up the philosophic
views first and then the popular ideas.

While for the sake of convenience we shall discuss the
God-idea of the thinking classes under the three heads
of Atheism, Theism and Pantheism, we do not wish to give
the impression that these are clear divisions, or that they
are held so in actual practice. There are two reasons why
these divisions cannot be clear-cut. The first reason is
that all three have in the religious life of the average adherent an undergrowth of polytheistic nature worship with
a strong admixture of ancestor worship which ever grows
up and chokes any clear distinctions which the philosophers
might seek to make. The second reason is that Atheism,
Pantheism and Theism, in the very nature of the case,
cannot be marked off clearly one from the other. For
example, if in Theism one lays great stress on what in Western
thought is called the Immanence of God, one is not far
removed from Pantheism, and the lower end of Pantheism
which denies consciousness to the One-All is not far from
Atheism. It is best then to think of the Buddhist God-idea
as a tree whose stem is pantheistic, with atheistic branches
on its shady side and semi-theistic branches on the sunny
side. Or to use the Hegelian mode of thought, Atheism
might be regarded as the thesis of original Buddhism and the
Buddhism of those Japanese and Chinese sects which have
kept nearest to the teachings of the founder. Theism is
the antithesis posited by the worshippers of Amida, and
Pantheism is the synthesis of the two, and stands for Buddhism as a whole; for not only the sects which stand
avowedly for the pantheistic conception, but even the
atheistic and semi-theistic sects would not object to being
classed as pantheists. It is the glory of Buddhism, and
always has been, that it is comprehensive in its thought,
and what can be more comprehensive than the vague Pantheism which allows both Atheism and Theism as equally

true; or as the Buddhist would say, two opposite sides of the same shield?

1. *Atheistic Buddhism.* — It may seem a contradiction in terms to speak of an atheistic God-idea, but the student of Buddhism should not be too sensitive about using contradictory terms if he would advance in his understanding of its mysteries. Even an atheistic Buddhist will call his philosophy of life a religion, though according to our Western mode of thought a religion without a god would hardly be regarded as religion. It can at least be a religion of humanity as we Westerners have been taught by Comte and his followers; and in reality atheistic Buddhism is far more than this, for while the God-idea does seem to end almost in zero, the Buddhist of this type gives at least a passive worship to the mystery of the unknowable Absolute.

Atheistic Buddhism finds its best representative among Japanese Buddhists in the three branches of the Zen Sect; namely, the Rinzai, Sōtō and Obaku sects. It is the boast of the Zen Sect that it is nearest to the teachings of the founder of Buddhism. It often calls itself the Buddha Heart Sect. The student of primitive Buddhism must admit that the Zen, both in theory and in practice, is far nearer the religion of the founder than are the other Chinese and Japanese sects. As we said in our first chapter, Gautama may not have been an out-and-out atheist but he certainly had very little to say about God. If he did not deny the existence of the gods of the common people, he robbed them of the glory they once had. And so these true modern followers of Gautama may not deny the existence of beings higher than ordinary man — beings which the ignorant may fear and worship as gods — but such beings would not be regarded as gods or as God, worthy to be worshipped. And just as Gautama held that through self-discipline man can attain enlightenment and Buddhahood which is higher than all the gods, so the Zen philosopher of to-day holds that man can, in his own strength through self-discipline, attain unto the highest condition of existence. If the reader will again consult the chart of the Ten Worlds given above,

he will see that above man is the realm of heavenly beings
with grades upon grades. The Zen philosopher may not
deny the existence of these beings, but they are not gods
to him. Above the realm of these heavenly beings are the
Four Holies, each of which represents higher and higher
stages of enlightenment and all of them are far above the
realms of heavenly beings, which latter still belong to the
realm of individual existence with all its limitations. And
furthermore, all of these grades of beings with their differences are in the last analysis but the product of impure
thought and so have no real existence outside the mind
of the thinker. He who has entered the highest meditation
of Zen thought, "the white silence of truth," will see that
these differences do not exist and that all individuality is
swallowed up in the ocean of the Eternal.

But what about the Four Holies and especially the highest
of these, the Buddha state? If the Zen philosopher ignores
or denies the existence of God or the gods, is not Buddhahood
itself, which man may attain, the God of Zen teaching? If
the Zen philosopher believes in a god at all, we might say
it is Buddha. But then the question arises as to what
is meant by Buddha. Is Buddha regarded as a personal
being, and does he exist now as a personal being?

The historic Buddha Gautama existed as an individual
human being (or what appears so from the standpoint of
Accommodated Truth). But when that historic being attained enlightenment and entered into Nirvāna he became
free from the bondages of individual existence. He passed
out from the Three Worlds and so ceased to exist in the
sense that one can predicate anything of his state of being.
Or it may be said that he entered a state which transcends
all the categories of beings known to man. Therefore if
anything is asserted about him, it must be in the form of
negating any particularization, and the wisest attitude is
one of silence. Buddha is certainly not a personal being,
not a personal God; nor can one assert anything about
him. The Zen Sect thus consistently lays great stress on
meditation which should lead to silence, not only of words,

but also of thought of all particulars. The true Zen student seeks to enter a Holy Vacancy in which no thought of individual being appears. Even to say that Zen teaches atheism in regard to the God-idea is not quite accurate, for that would be asserting something definite inasmuch as every negation is really an affirmation.

It might be asked, then, whether the Zen philosopher teaches that all existence is God, and that the God-idea is an idea which includes everything. To this the answer is that the words "all existence" represent to the person who uses them something definite, *i.e.* a summary of all individual beings. But all so-called individual beings have merely a phenomenal existence; and so it cannot be said that the Ultimate of Zen philosophy is the One-All, for the All itself does not exist in the sense in which the mind predicates existence of anything. Thus the height of Zen philosophy does not only deny the existence of God and gods, but it refuses to assert the opposite, or to make a synthesis of the two and assert Pantheism. The consistent Zen philosopher passes through Atheism and Pantheism into absolute Agnosticism which ends consistently in silence. If this silence is broken at all, it is to assert merely the existence of the Great Unknowable towards which the philosopher may take an attitude of reverence and even worship it with a passive spirit, but this can hardly be compared with the conscious fellowship which the Christian has in his experience of God.

Sometimes it is claimed that the Zen believer experiences that mystical communion with the Divine which Christian mystics claim to have, and this may be so; but when this is a real communion of the soul with God it transcends what Zen theology holds to be true. The true Communion in Zen teaching is the communion of self with self, for there is no Divine with which to commune except within the heart of him who communes. That is, the real God of Zen is man's own heart — the heart freed from the distractions of particular thought. This God may be called the Higher Self, and this may be identified with the Universal Self which constitutes the core of all existence; but such language is really too definite and savors too much of philosophic theism to be quite true to orthodox Zen thought, though some moderns writing for Western eyes are inclined sometimes to use such phraseology. The weight of Zen thought is against the conception of God as a Personal Spirit transcending the universe though immanent in it; and in fact it recognizes "no God except such as man can and has become by the attainment of Buddhahood"; and the Buddha state, as we have said, is not that of personality but transcends the categories of all beings.

2. *Theistic Buddhism.* — Theistic Buddhism finds its best representative among Japanese Buddhists in the four Amida sects; namely, the great Jōdo and Shin sects and the two small Yūdzū Nembutsu and Ji sects. Let us, however, state at the outset that strictly speaking we cannot call these sects theistic, for they make some allowances for other gods or Buddhas beside Amida, and in the last analysis, as we shall see, they really deny the personality of God as the Absolute, and, like all Mahāyāna sects, hold that the Absolute is neither personal nor impersonal but transcends human knowledge.

But while the Amidaists make room for other Buddhas and gods, on the whole the Buddha Amida occupies such a unique place, and his name is on the lips of his followers so much that we speak of the Amida sects as theistic, or at least semi-theistic sects. They hold that to worship Amida is sufficient, for he embraces all others; he is, as it were, the *pleroma* of the God-head. Some moderns, influenced by Christian thought, speak of Amida as the Creator and the Father, and ascribe to him practically all the attributes which a Christian would ascribe unto God. And even in some of the older canonical scriptures we find, *e.g.*, such sentences as this, "Buddha (Amida) said, 'My mercy towards all ye heaven and earth-born creatures is deeper than the love of parents towards their children.'" And in the famous Lotus scripture we read, "Now are the Three Worlds mine and all living beings in the same are indeed my children.

But great and many are their afflictions and it is I alone that can save them." The Nirvāna sūtra speaks in much the same strain when it says, " If a man have seven children and one of these be ill, his love though equal towards all, will go out in a special way to this one. Thus it is with the love of the Nyōrai ; though it is equal towards all beings, it hovers in a special manner over those who are in sin." These may not be exactly characteristic thoughts of Amida Buddhism, but there is enough of this element in it to make one feel that it is indeed an approach to the Christian conception of God. This will come more clearly to light in what we have to say under the heading of Salvation, and has also been touched upon in Chapter III, in the section on the Shin Sect.

In our second chapter we spoke of the beginnings of the Amitābha (Amida) faith. We saw how early in the Christian era this Buddha was known to Asvaghosha and Nāgārjuna, though they saw him only " as through a glass darkly." By the beginning of the fifth century Kumārajīva seemed to have had a clearer conception of him as the supreme Personal God. But the name which is great among the Amida sects is that of Zendō [5] who lived at Sin-an-fu, China, in the first half of the seventh century. In 635 A.D. there arrived in the same city the Nestorian mission under Olopun, which must have been rather successful, as may be inferred from the celebrated memorial stone, the Nestorian Monument, erected in 781 A.D. Is it stretching the imagination to suppose that Zendō may have been influenced by the Christian conception of God, taught by these Nestorian missionaries? Not that the Amida doctrine is a Christian product pure and simple, for as we showed in Chapter II, it may have had its origin in purely Indian or Persian thought, but it does seem possible, if not probable, that Nestorian Christianity in China strengthened this theistic tendency in Buddhism of singling out one of the many Buddhas and making him the one and only Buddha. All the more does this theory seem plausible when it is remembered that Zendō's teachings were regarded by other Buddhists as heretical doctrines. Zendō's teachings were taken to Japan, where they were spread by Genshin and others till finally they were crystallized in the formation of the Amida sects mentioned above. These have perpetuated and developed the Amida doctrine and made it the common possession of millions of Japanese Buddhists; namely, four sects with a total of more than 28,000 temples, or about three-sevenths of the whole.

As we have stated above, the God-idea in Amida Buddhism is not strictly a theistic idea. On the one hand, the Amidaist makes room for other gods or Buddhas beside Amida; and on the other hand, the Amida philosopher really denies that Amida as the Absolute is personal. First let us give a few characteristic quotations from Amida theologians to show how Amida must share his glory with others even though he occupies the central place. "The Gods, Buddhas and Bodhisattvas are numberless," says a recent theologian of the Shin Sect, "but since all these are branch bodies of Amida they are ultimately contained in the six characters Na-mu A-mi-da Butsu (I worship Thee Thou Buddha of Boundless Life and Light). For this reason it is sufficient to worship the one Buddha Amida and not necessary to worship these many deities separately. Rennyō says, 'As the body called Namu Amida Butsu includes all Gods, Buddhas and Bodhisattvas, and everything good and every good work, what is the use of worrying your mind about various works and things good?'" But to make sure of being comprehensive the writer goes on to say that the good Amidaist "worships the deities worshiped by others. Every God and Buddha worshiped by man deserves reverence and worship. Speaking from the standpoint of human expediency, reverence and worship must not be neglected, and much less should the believer in the Nyōrai (i. e., Amida) neglect this duty of mankind." Speaking on this same point another writer says, "Not even in dreams should one make light of any of the Buddhas or Bodhisattvas, nor should one despise or reject any god and his ways. Though through the ages and the various stages of life we have practiced many good things by the boundless help of all the Buddhas and Bodhisattvas, we still cannot escape mortality through our own efforts; but having been urged on in past existences by all the Buddhas and Bodhisattvas we have now come under the benefit of the gracious vow of Amida. To speak evil of any of the Buddhas or Bodhisattvas, not knowing their benevolence, is indeed to show the deepest ingratitude."

But the Amida doctrine breaks down as a theistic conception also for the reason that no Buddhist philosopher is willing to think of the Ultimate in terms of personality. Amida is spoken of as a personal being, but the term Personal is what Buddhist philosophers of all schools would consider as an accommodation of language when used of the Ultimate. Even in the West it is a common objection to the doctrine of a Personal God to say that personality implies limitation, and that therefore God as the Absolute cannot be personal. The Buddhist philosopher raises the same objection and says that if Amida is spoken of as personal, it is only by way of accommodation to suit the doctrine to the intelligence of the average man who cannot think in the concepts of philosophy. The Christian theist admits, of course, that God as the Absolute necessarily transcends man's comprehension, but he holds that the term Personality represents the highest conception which can be held of God, so that we must think of God either as personal or as sub-personal. Super-personal concepts are beyond us. The Buddhist philosopher, regarding the idea of Personality as inadequate to express the nature of God, rejects it and without realizing it lapses into the sub-personal. Instead of getting an idea more adequate than the conception of a perfect Personality he either gets one less so, or the concept ends in the zero of Agnosticism, or in the confusion of Pantheism.

But to understand more clearly in just what sense these semi-theistic sects regard Amida as a personal Buddha, we must take up at this point what is known as the doctrine of the Three Bodies of Buddha (Sanshin, Sk. Trikāya). This doctrine is not peculiar to the Amida Buddhists, but it throws special light upon the God-idea as held by these

sects. If the reader will again consult the chart of the Ten
Worlds, he will find that the tenth, or the highest, is the
Buddha World. Now Buddha may be thought of in three
different ways, and these three ways are the so-called Three
Bodies of Buddha. These are: (a) The Law Body of
Buddha (Sk. Dharmakāya, Jap. Hosshin Butsu), (b) The
Compensation Body of Buddha (Sk. Sambhogakāya, Jap.
Hōshin Butsu), and (c) The Accommodated Body of Buddha
(Sk. Nirmanakāya, Jap. Ōjin Butsu).

The first of these three, or the Law Body of Buddha,
means Buddha conceived of as the embodiment of Law. It
is Buddha regarded as the essence or underlying substance
of the universe, or Buddha as the Noumenon back of the
phenomenal world. Or if the doctrine be stated in the
language of modern thought, it is almost synonymous with
the Laws of Nature conceived of as metaphysical entities
and constituting a monistic whole of which nature is a visible
and pluralistic expression.

"Buddha makes Law his body."

"The realm of Law is the Nyōrai and this is the true
body of Buddha."

"The Law Body is the Law without birth and without
death. It exists neither in the past nor in the future, for
it transcends time."

The Law Body of Buddha, then, means Buddha conceived of as the Absolute and the underlying substance
or essence of all reality, and as such Buddha is not a personal
being.

The second way in which Buddha may be thought of is
what is called the Compensation Body of Buddha. The
meaning of this conception is rather difficult to state clearly,
but in it lies the key to the understanding of theistic Buddhism and the explanation of what is meant by the so-called
personal Buddha, or God, Amida. We have already said
above that according to Buddhist philosophy the Absolute
as such is not personal, but personality is something which
is evolved in the process of phenomenal existence and,
like all phenomena, personality cannot be a permanent

state of being. In other words, there was a time when the Buddha Amida did not exist as Amida, and likewise it is impossible to affirm that Amida is a personal being now. He is spoken of as personal simply because this is a practical conception for the religious needs of the average man.

According to the Buddhist cosmogony this universe has always existed very much as it exists to-day; at least the essence of the universe has always existed. The material of the universe at times is organized and at times is in a state of chaos, so that chaos and order follow each other at great intervals. Thus there have been millions of universes and millions of states of chaos or voids, and in the future there will be millions of universes alternating with millions of periods of chaos and void. Where in Christian thought we say, "In the beginning God created the heavens and the earth," the Buddhist would say, "In the beginning was the substance of the universe, or the Law Body of Buddha." In the course of time, namely ten Kalpas ago, there was a Buddha in this world whose name was the Buddha of Perfect Freedom. This Buddha had a disciple, Hōzō Bosatsu, who, casting away his kingly rank, became zealous in religion. He took pity on all living creatures and made a vow that he would not enter the bliss of Buddhahood until he had prepared a way of salvation for all beings. When he had fulfilled his vow he attained perfection and became the Buddha Amida. That is, the Buddha Amida was first the man Hōzō Bosatsu. The latter, as a resultant of his good works and the fulfillment of his vow to save all living beings, obtained the Compensation Body and became Amida. Hōzō Bosatsu as a man was, of course, a personal being, and as Amida he became the embodiment of mercy and wisdom. Amida may therefore be regarded as the ideal personification of mercy and wisdom, but not as a personal being whose characteristics are mercy and wisdom. And he is not the Eternal Personal God, but only man become God. In the words of Professor T. Inouye, "Buddhism knows of no God except such a one as man can and has become by the attainment of Buddhahood." And as Amida

is not God from the beginning, but only one who has attained
Buddhahood, it is not surprising that Amida philosophers
deny that Amida has any personal existence now. He is
spoken of in personal terms simply by way of accommodation
of language and not because he is personal.

Amida, then, is an example of the second sense in which
the term Buddha is used; namely, the Compensation Body
of Buddha, or the Body of Reward for good works achieved
by a human being who as such was personal, but who as
Amida is not a real personal being but only the personification
of the qualities of mercy and wisdom; for when Hōzō
Bosatsu really entered into Buddhahood he, as an individual being, was merged in Buddha as the Absolute, which is
neither personal nor impersonal.

"Mercy is the Nyōrai and the Nyōrai is Mercy."

The third way in which Buddha may be thought of is
what is called the Accommodated Body of Buddha. This
means Buddha regarded as a historical personage, such,
e.g. as S'akyamuni, the founder of Buddhism. Such Buddhas
have existed by the thousands and millions in the past
cycles of time. They are said to be as numerous as the
grains of sand on the sacred Ganges. "Buddha's body (i.e.
the Law Body of Buddha) fills the ends of the universe.
It is revealed to all living beings everywhere and always in
a manner suited to meet the needs of life to which it appears" (i.e. the Accommodated Body of Buddha). "The
so-called gods," says Rennyō, "are but the transformations
of the Buddhas and Bodhisattvas. But since it is difficult
for men in this world to approach the Buddhas and Bodhisattvas, deity is revealed by accommodation as gods (i.e.
the popular gods of Shintō and polytheistic Buddhism).
Thus connection with mankind is made and man is brought
finally into Buddhism."

The historical being whom we know as Gautama, the
founder of Buddhism, was therefore not the manifestation
of the Eternal Personal God, but simply one of the many
forms of individual existence, and he no more truly represented the nature of the Ultimate than did the inanimate

ground of India on which he walked. For neither the personal nor the impersonal represents the essence of reality; both are but different expressions of one and the same Whole.

From the above it must be clear, then, that when we speak of theistic Buddhism and call Amida a personal God we are using language in a very loose sense. While the average Amidaist prays to Amida and speaks of him in personal terms, the Amida philosopher looks upon him as merely the personification of a principle, or the idea of mercy and wisdom. In Christian language we say, "God is love." If by this we meant that God is simply the personification of love and not that love is the expression of a real personal being, we would have a parallel case with the Buddhist idea of Amida as the embodiment of Mercy.

Of the Three Bodies of Buddha mentioned above the Law Body is the most ultimate, and in so far as the Amidaists recognize this they agree with all the Mahāyāna sects that, while for practical purposes they may make room for the idea of a personal god or of personal gods, the ultimate as such cannot be said to be personal. It is the Great Unknowable concerning which no affirmation can be made.

3. *Pantheistic Buddhism.* — Pantheistic Buddhism finds its best representative in such sects as the Tendai and Shingon. It asserts the reality of the Divine and so is perhaps a little more positive in its God-idea than are the sects which we have designated as atheistic. In the second place pantheistic sects see the divine in everything, and so differ somewhat from the so-called theistic sects which tend to see the divine primarily in the Buddha Amida. The pantheistic God-idea is the true philosophic basis for the polytheism of the common believer who is to be found in every sect. Even if in the pantheistic sects there are some gods who seem to occupy a peculiar preëminence, and the Buddha Vairochana, *e.g.*, is spoken of as the Supreme Buddha, the lesser gods and Buddhas will be considered as so many manifestations of these supreme beings, and these supreme beings will not be regarded as having an independent personal

existence but only as existing in the various lesser beings. And not only are the gods of polytheistic Buddhism the manifestation of the divine, but all things are equally its manifestation. "In every living being dwells the essence of Buddha."

It was this pantheistic basis of Buddhism which enabled Kōbō Daishi and the men of his day to bring into the already overstocked Buddhist pantheon the myriads of gods of the old Shintō, and form what is known as the Two-Sided Shintō. Every popular god of the native Shintō could easily be regarded as but the Japanese form of Buddhist deities or as new manifestations of the Divine, which is infinite in its modes of existence and manifestations.

Under theistic Buddhism we spoke of the Three Bodies of Buddha, and said that the first of these, the Law Body of Buddha, is regarded by all Mahāyāna sects as the deepest reality and the underlying essence of all things. Both the so-called atheistic and theistic branches hold this view. Pantheistic Buddhism, too, recognizes this threefold distinction and makes the Law Body the deepest reality. It is simply more insistent in its religious application of the idea upon making all individual beings, especially the gods of the common people, the real manifestation of this ultimate divine reality. Or to put it the other way around, the ultimate reality has no existence except as it exists in individual beings. All things are not merely the manifestation of the Divine but they are the Divine. While there may be forms and manifestations of the Divine unknown to man, the phenomenal world with its gods many and Buddhas many is the Divine. The Accommodated Bodies of Buddha are the Law Body and the Law Body is in the Accommodated Body. The phenomena are the Noumenon, and the Noumenon is in the phenomena.

If, then, there appear personal beings in the phenomenal world, the essence of reality is personal to that extent, but the Infinite is personal only as it is personal in the finite, or God is personal only in so far as he is personal in human beings and in the gods of popular polytheism. But inas-

Q

much as the personality of each human being and these popular gods is regarded as but a temporary state brought about by certain conditions which are constantly changing, God is not permanently personal in any one being. The Divine is permanently personal in finite beings only in so far as it has always manifested itself in them and probably always will. The Great Ocean of Reality is ever breaking up into waves. No wave, however, is permanent, but soon sinks back again into the waveless depths. In the same way the Divine ever wells up into personal beings, but none endure as such, and soon sink back into the depth of Being which is neither personal nor impersonal.

The God-idea, then, of pantheistic Buddhism is that God is personal in finite personal beings and impersonal in finite impersonal beings; the latter are as truly the essence of the Divine as the former. To the question as to whether God is personal, the reply would be both Yes and No. That is why we said at the beginning of the section on the God-idea that Pantheism is the synthesis of the thesis Atheism and the antithesis Theism, including both and being neither. Speaking in the figure of a shield, Pantheism is the main body of the shield. Atheism is the smooth and barren concave surface, while the convex surface represents the theistic phase. The convex surface faces the foe of practical life and it may have on it one central decoration (Semi-theism), or it may be decorated with many symbols (Polytheism). Whether they be many or only one they are, after all, only surface decorations. The surface decorations may be the picture of those who have attained Buddhahood and so are an encouragement to the one who bears it, but they can be hardly more than that; for again let us remember that Buddhism really knows of no personal God except such as man can himself become, *i.e.* the Divine is only such as is within man.

4. *Polytheistic Buddhism.* — While philosophic Buddhism is monistic with a strong bent towards agnosticism, popular Buddhism is pluralistic and realistic. The average Buddhist believer is incurably polytheistic, and the philosophical dis-

tinctions between atheism, theism and pantheism, which we have made above, do not mean much to him, for these monistic concepts are beyond the uneducated masses. They are at best mere shadowy backgrounds of the picture, the foreground is occupied by gods innumerable. Just as in the political life of Japan there has always been but one dynasty and one emperor recognized but kept far removed from the common people by the various ranks of officials who acted as intermediaries, so in the religious life of Japan the monistic Absolute was too far removed from the needs of practical life and the realistic gods of popular polytheism have functioned instead.

We give here a list of the more popular deities. Some of them are of Indian or Chinese origin gradually taken on by popular Buddhism; others came from Shintō and are regarded as Shintō deities but are worshiped by most Buddhists, and still others are a mixture of Indian, Chinese and Japanese elements. The order is alphabetical rather than according to importance.

Amaterasu, the Sun Goddess, the leading Shintō deity, but as ancestress of the Imperial family is worshiped by Buddhists and Shintōists alike. Other names under which this goddess is known are Daijingu, Shimmei and Ten-Shōkō-Daijin.

Amida, worshiped by the masses as a god or a Buddha among many Buddhas rather than as the one and only Buddha of theistic philosophy.

Atago, a Shintō deity worshiped as the god who protects against fire.

Benten, or Benzaiten, one of the seven deities of good luck. The other six are Bishamon, Daikoku, Ebisu, Fukurokuju, Hōtei, and Jurojin. Benten may be known by the serpent or dragon as her symbol.

Binzuru, a God of Healing, is very popular with the ignorant classes and his image is frequently adorned with hood, bib and mittens. The famous image at the Asakusa Kwannon temple touched by all who have pain is a real spreader of disease, but so strong is the faith in its healing power that the more enlightened official world has not dared to forbid the practice.

Bishamon, one of the seven deities of Luck, also a god of War, and so is represented with armor, spear and toy pagoda.

Daikoku, one of the seven deities of Luck, especially the God of Wealth, usually seated on bales of rice, the main item of wealth in old Japan.

Dainichi Nyōryai, worshiped as the God of Wisdom and Purity rather than as the Eternal Buddha of philosophic Buddhism.

Daiseishi, usually associated with Amida and Kwannon.

Ebisu, one of the seven deities of Luck and usually represented with a fishing-rod and a tai fish. He is the special patron of honest labor.

Emma-O, the ruler of the Buddhist hells.

Fudo, probably a God of Wisdom, which characteristic is represented by flames. This symbol has led many to worship him as God of Fire.

Fugen, a special patron of those who practice a certain ecstatic meditation. His image is frequently associated with that of S'akyamuni.

Gongen, a general term for Shintō deities regarded as temporary manifestations of Buddhas; frequently, however, this term is applied to Ieyasu.

Hachiman, the God of War.

Inari, the Goddess of the Rice, symbolized by her servant the fox whom many regard as the goddess herself.

Izanagi and *Izanami,* the Creator and Creatress of Japan.

Jizo, the very popular deity of those who are in trouble, especially the patron of travelers, pregnant women and little children. The images of this popular deity are perhaps more numerous than any other. It may be recognized by the staff in one hand and the jewel in the other, and especially by the pebbles heaped upon it by the numerous devotees.

Kishi Bojin, like Jizo, a protector of little children.

Kompira, a deity held in special regard by seamen and travelers.

Koshin, a deification of the day of the monkey in the calendar and symbolized by three monkeys, *i.e.* the blind monkey, the deaf monkey and the dumb monkey.

Kwannon, the God or Goddess of Mercy. The full name is Kwanzeon Dai Bosatsu, and the original Sanskrit word Avalōkitēsvara means The-One-Who-Looks-Down-from-Above. Perhaps no deity plays a bigger rôle in popular Buddhism, and the famous Asakusa Kwannon temple in Tōkyō is the most frequented spot in all Japan, though it must be admitted that in recent years the crowds are drawn, perhaps, more by the "movies" which flank two sides of the temple grounds than by the temple itself.

Miroku, the Buddhist Messiah, for whom the pious still wait.

Monju, an apotheosis of wisdom and usually associated with the images of S'akyamuni.

Ni-O, the two Dēva kings, Indra and Brahma, who stand guard at temple gates to keep away the demons.

Onamuji, or Okuni-nushi, the deity who gave his throne to the ancestors of the Imperial Family.

Sengen, the Goddess of Mt. Fuji, the sacred mountain and pride of Japan.

Shaka, i.e. S'akyamuni, worshiped by the masses as a god or Buddha among other gods and Buddhas. By some he is worshiped simply as the founder of Buddhism, while by others he is regarded as the incarnation of the Eternal Buddha.

Shi-Tennō, Four Heavenly Kings who protect the devotee from demons, each guarding one quarter of the compass.

Suitengu, a sea-god.

Susa-no-Ō, brother of Amaterasu, and regarded as God of the Sea, or God of the Moon.

Tenjin, an apotheosis of the great Sugawara-no-Michizane. He is worshiped as the God of Calligraphy.

Tōshōgu, an apotheosis of Ieyasu and worshiped as the Illuminator of the East.

Toyo-Uke-Bime, or *Uke-Mochi-no-Kami*, Goddess of Food or Goddess of the Earth.

Yakushi Nyōrai, the Divine Healer.

These are among the more popular deities worshiped by the masses and to them might be added a long list of other Bodhisattvas and Buddhas, angels and saints which receive more or less worship as superhuman beings. In fact, the making of gods is not altogether a lost art even in modern Japan, as may be seen from the fact that the late Emperor Meiji Tennō and Admiral Tōgo are being rapidly enshrined in the hearts of the common people as superhuman beings. This may seem strange to the Western mind, but it is a very natural process from the Buddhist or Shintō standpoint which refuses to make a clear-cut distinction between the human and the divine.

As we have said above, these realistic gods of popular polytheism play a far more important part in the life of the average Buddhist adherent than do the abstract monistic conceptions of Mahāyāna philosophy. In fact, even to the Buddhist philosopher this realistic polytheism is not altogether disagreeable and supplies more of a content to his monistic abstractions than is usually realized; for the gods of polytheism may be regarded as temporary beings like man himself which are personal now but have no ultimate existence as personal beings, they may be regarded as subject to and manifestations of the one Supreme Being (Semi-theism), or they may be regarded as mere parts of the pantheistic whole into which they, like man, are ultimately absorbed. But as we have said, the most congenial philosophic background of polytheism is pantheism. Or to put it the other way around, polytheism is the popular aspect of the philosopher's pantheism. Thus polytheism is not a coördinate division with atheism, theism and pantheism, but it is the popular complement of these, especially of the latter.

As we have already said, Buddhism was polytheistic before it reached Japan, but it became even more so after it absorbed the innumerable gods (Yaoyorozu no kamigami, Eight hundred myriads of gods) of the native Shintō. If the resultant of the union between Buddhism and Shintō is strongly Buddhistic on the philosophical side, on its popular religious side it often seems more Shintōistic. The truth is that Buddhism in Japan could win its place only by giving to the popular Shintō gods a conspicuous place in its pantheon, and while the Buddhist philosopher has reduced these gods to mere manifestations of the older Buddhist deities, to the average Japanese believer they have more or less kept their former place. This alone can explain the fact that even to this day, after thirteen centuries of Buddhist history in this land, the small shrines to Shintō deities exist by the tens of thousands, and the greater Shintō deities such as Amaterasu, Hachiman, Inari occupy a prominent place in Japanese religious life. In spite of the separation of Shintō from Buddhism made in the Meiji era, the people in general do not give their allegiance exclusively to one or the other, but regard themselves as being Shintōists and Buddhists at one and the same time.

And now let us refer for a moment to the Chart of the Ten Buddhist Worlds and see how this gradation of beings, which is essentially Indian in origin, was well adapted to absorb the Shintō cosmology. This scale of beings fixes man near the center, and provides for four grades below him and for five grades above. The grade immediately above man is the Realm of Heavenly Beings, or the Realm of the Gods. Now Shintō had no scale like this, but it, too, believed in beings lower than man and beings higher than man. The beings higher than man were the gods; in fact, the very word for God in Japanese probably meant originally simply that which is "above" or "superior." It is a rather striking fact that the realms below man in the Buddhist scale were not enriched from the Shintō cosmology. There was comparatively little of the horrible demonology of India, China and Korea in primitive Shintō. There was much of spirits and ghosts and some of these were more or less malicious, but on the whole, Shintō had little of the horrors of hell and demonology which we find in other Asiatic religions. It was rich in deities — nature deities, personifications of abstractions, apotheoses of great ancestors and heroes etc. — and these "eight hundred myriads of gods" were added to the ever-growing pantheon of popular Buddhism. And there they have remained down to our enlightened day, so that in the life of the common people they play a bigger rôle than do the abstract speculations of the Buddhist philosopher.

The God-idea, then, in Japanese Buddhism is, as we said at the beginning of this section, an exceedingly complex one. It varies all the way from a low animistic conception up through ancestor worship and a variegated polytheism until it reaches, in the minds of the philosophers and better ed-ucated classes, a monistic form which leans to atheism on one side and to semi-theism on the other, but whose real core is best expressed by the vague pantheism. And all three philosophic conceptions are in the last analysis under-mined by an agnosticism which makes every assertion about the nature of the divine futile, and seeks to remind us that all human knowledge is but seeing things from the standpoint of Accommodated Truth, and not as things really are.

But we cannot close the remarks on the God-idea in Japanese Buddhism without adding a few words by way of supplement. There is among educated Japanese quite a large number of those who would class themselves as Bud-dhists, but who know little or nothing of the specific teachings of Buddhist philosophy, and yet whose general intelligence forbids them to believe in the polytheistic ideas of the un-educated masses. It seems safe to say that many of these have at least a vague belief in a Personal God who is the Great Intelligence which controls this universe of ours, and who is the Moral Power which in some way will reward the righteous and punish the wicked, both in this life and in the life to come. And there are still more whose conception is less theistic but rather neo-pantheistic. They draw their inspiration from modern science, which in its most reverent moods recognizes dimly an eternal mysterious life or energy permeating all things. This neo-pantheism differs from the old Oriental pantheism in that it puts a greater value upon the physical universe. For while the older pantheism always held that the pluralistic world of experience is the mani-festation of the One-All, it nevertheless regarded this manifestation as inherently evil and as something to be avoided. These neo-pantheists, or spiritual monists, are reverent towards the physical world and see in it the mysterious workings of an all-pervasive energy, or life.   We might say they are disciples of Spinoza and our pantheistic poets rather than of the old Oriental school.   Their God-idea is almost theistic, with all the emphasis placed on the immanence of God, ignoring that God also transcends his universe.   This belief may not be strong enough always to restrain such men from sin and to lead them in the paths of righteousness and peace, but it is there.   It is from the ranks of such men that Christianity makes its converts, for they are the ones who have breathed most deeply the modern Western atmosphere which, though it contains much that is evil, also contains much that is Christian.

F. *Man and His Condition*

1. *The Nature of Man.* — In Christian thought there is a clear distinction between God and man on the one hand, and between man and the lower beings on the other hand.   It is true that the distinction between man and the rest of nature has been somewhat obliterated in modern thought by certain schools of philosophy, and no thinkers in the West would deny that man is linked closely with nature, at least on one side.   But after this has been granted, Western thought still maintains that man is a unique being in nature and that there is a wide gap between him and other animals; at least, man has within him capacities which, when developed, make of him a decidedly higher order of being.   In Buddhism these lines of demarcation between God and man on the one side, and between man and lower beings on the other side, are not so clear.   As we have repeatedly said, man is placed somewhere about the center in the scale of beings which inhabit the Buddhist universe.   The Ten Realms of beings into which the universe is divided merge one into the other so that the lower constantly becomes the higher, and the higher degenerates into the lower.   Man's good Karma leads him to birth into a heavenly realm, or if his

evil Karma preponderates, he is born into a state lower than the human. Thus a being which now is human may, in the next incarnation, be either a god or an animal or demon.

But what is the origin of man according to Buddhism? In Genesis we read that God created man in his own image. However modern thought in the Christian world has changed the formulation of this idea, the Christian of to-day believes as firmly as the Old Testament writers that God was prior to man and in some way created man, either outright or through a slow evolutionary process. And he also believes that man is created in God's image, *i.e.* man, like God, is a rational personal being. Buddhism does not posit a Personal God prior to the universe, nor does Buddhist thought hold that God has created man. It rather holds that where man thinks of the Divine in terms of a personal being he is creating God in his own image. The universe has always been, and man, or beings like him, have always been. And such beings probably always will be as long as the monistic whole breaks up into the pluralism of individual beings. Ever since the wind of primordial Ignorance has broken up the ocean of Sameness into the waves of individual beings, man has existed, and human beings will continue to come and go as long as the waves of mentation disturb the eternal Calm. Man is, then, not the creation of an all wise and loving God, but, like all individual existence, is an accident of primordial Ignorance which, when once it begins to function, works on and on by the law of Karma unceasingly, or till it is exhausted.

The inner constitution of man and the way in which the law of Karma works is explained by the doctrine of the Twelve Links in the Karma-chain. This has already been given above in the section on the Theory of Knowledge. This is exceedingly difficult for the Western mind to understand, largely, however, because Western psychology realizes too clearly that the self is a unity which cannot be understood by such an analytic process and by what is essentially a mechanistic conception.

It is commonly held that Buddhism denies the reality of

the self or the soul. This is true in that Buddhism refuses to hold that the ego is a permanent reality, but not in the sense that Buddhism denies the reality of the psychic in human nature. In fact, Buddhism regards the psychic as the deepest reality in human nature. The self in the Western sense Buddhism would call the Provisional Self, and would regard it as a resultant of the physical organism of the body. This, however, does not mean that the physical organism, or matter, is regarded as the deepest reality; it is itself the product of a deeper reality, which deeper reality is to be thought of more in terms of the psychic nature of man than in terms of the physical. This psychic reality is something like the Will of Schopenhauer's philosophy. It is that blind "will-to-be" which gives rise to individual beings, and especially to such beings as man, who is self-conscious and who therefore thinks that the self of self-consciousness is a permanent reality. It is not a permanent reality but only a fleeting phase of the chain of life which has as its permanent element, or core, only this psychic power, or this blind "will-to-be." It is, then, neither the self of self-consciousness, nor the physical organism, that gives rise to this self that is the permanent reality in human nature, but it is that mysterious "will-to-be" that gives rise to both the physical organism and the self of self-consciousness. This mysterious energy, strange to say, continues to "will-to-be" as long as it is ignorant of the nature of true being, and especially, ignorant of the nature of the self of self-consciousness. That is why man is born again and again into this world, and only when the blind energy which makes up the real core of his being has been enlightened will it be free from individualizing itself in human beings. Thus according to Buddhism the real source of man, as well as the source of all individual existence, is that ignorance which somehow enters reality and makes the eternal Oneness form itself into individual beings. The first link in the chain of Karma is the link of Ignorance.

This is the philosophical explanation which Buddhism makes of the origin and inner constitution of man. It is, perhaps, needless to say that the common Buddhist knows nothing about this doctrine except that he believes in the transmigration of the soul. That is, he believes that the present generation of human beings upon the earth has existed before, either as human beings, or as lower or higher forms of beings. Even this conception is not held consistently, for the average Buddhist in Japan makes some room for the Shintō explanation; namely, that the people of Japan are really the descendants of the Imperial Family, and that their ancestry goes back to the gods of heaven and earth. This is at least the orthodox Japanese doctrine which no Buddhist dared challenge in the past. The educated classes of to-day in the Buddhist fold, who are ignorant of the Buddhist explanation and to whom the Shintō explanation is too childish, naturally accept, in a vague way at least, the Western naturalistic explanation of man's origin; namely, that Nature, spelled with a capital, has somehow produced man and made him as he is. For practical purposes, they would say, we must treat the self as real, but just what the self is or what becomes of it need not concern the practical man. Religion, this type of Buddhist would say, should seek more to develop strong men who are able to do the work of the world than spend its time in speculating about the nature of the self or its final destiny.

2. *Man's Condition.* — As man finds himself near the center of the scale of living beings his condition is better than that of beings lower down in the scale, and worse than that of those above him. His is an existence of joy and sorrow, pleasure and pain. On the whole, however, the dark side of life overbalances the bright side, for all pleasures are fleeting and end in sorrow; all youth and strength end in old age, weakness and death. In our first chapter we spoke of the Four Noble Truths of Buddhism and we saw that the first of these is the truth that life is essentially sorrow and suffering. We repeat this truth here, for Japanese Buddhism, though much less pessimistic than Indian Buddhism, after all, accepts this estimate of life as substantially correct.

"Now this is the Noble Truth as to suffering. Birth is

attended with pain, decay is painful, disease is painful, death is painful.   Union with the unpleasant is painful, painful is separation from the pleasant; and any craving unsatisfied, that, too, is painful."

This thought has become the possession of the whole Buddhist world and has cast a shadow over the life of Asia which is broken only occasionally by the rays of hope of a more optimistic world view.   Japan is least pessimistic of the nations of the Orient, but even happy Japan, of whom one of its ancient poets (Hitomaru) wrote, "Japan is not a land where men need pray, for 'tis itself divine," is deeply imbued with the idea of the vanity of life and the transitoriness of all pleasure.   The following passages taken from the sacred scriptures are characteristic:

"Water flows on but does not always overflow, fire burns brightly but soon dies down, the sun rises but only to sink in the west, the moon waxes but soon wanes again.   Less permanent than all these is the glory and power of man."

"In this world every one who has been born returns unto death, and even an endless life must come to an end.   The prosperous must some day be ruined, and those who meet must part again.   Youth does not last long, and sickness overtakes those with rosy cheeks.   Manifold sufferings encompass life and continue without ceasing.   In the Three Worlds all things are transient, and there is no pleasure in the things that are."

"There are four things in this world that are transient; namely, stability which is really instability, fortune which ends in poverty, meeting which ends in separation, and health which ends in death."

"The flower of youth fades with the speed of a galloping steed."

"Like the ox whose every step brings him that much nearer to the slaughter is the life of man; for every day brings him that much nearer the grave."

"Man's life in this world is like the flash of lightning."

The Buddhist would agree with the heathen earldorman of Northumbria when he compared human life with a sparrow flying by chance into the light and warmth of the banquet hall and then passing out again into the cold and the dark. However pleasant it may be, it cannot last long, and this fact mars the pleasure while it lasts, not to mention the fact that for most men suffering and sorrow far outweigh the bright side of life.

Christianity, too, has a great deal to say about the vanity of life as lived by the average man. It, too, holds that the ordinary pleasures of life are short and that there is much sorrow and suffering for all, but Christianity speaks of the vanity of life in contrast with the abiding realities of the spiritual world. It does not regard human life as incurably evil as Buddhism does; for, after all, "the earth is the Lord's and the fullness thereof." Man is not to cut the ties which bind him to life in order to escape from evil, as in Buddhism, but by God's grace he is to triumph over the evils and difficulties, and transmute them into higher values and victory. Paul's philosophy of suffering in the eighth chapter of Romans could not have been written by a Buddhist.

3. *The Cause of Life's Evils.* — What is the cause of the sorrow and suffering in human life according to Buddhism?

We have seen above that the very origin of man is due to the primordial Ignorance, or that blind desire for individual existence which somehow is inherent in the universe. Naturally this blind desire constitutes the core of man's being, and so is the seat of his sorrows and sufferings. The second of the Four Noble Truths of Buddhism given in Chapter I is the truth about the origin of suffering, and it is formulated as follows:

"Now this is the Noble Truth as to the origin of suffering. Verily; it is the craving thirst that causes the renewal of becomings, that is accompanied by sensual delights, and seeks satisfaction, now here and now there — that is to say, the craving for the gratification of the senses, or the craving for a future life, or the craving for prosperity."

In short, then, it is the desire for the pleasures of life, the desire for self-assertion, which causes the sufferings of life. And why is it that man desires the things which, though they are pleasant, always end in disappointment and suffering? It is because man is ignorant. Ignorance is the first link in the Karma-chain. It gives rise to the formation of the individual, till in the eighth link of the Karma-chain we reach Desire, *i.e.* the lust of the flesh. This Desire leads to a clinging to existence and a passion for the things that cannot permanently satisfy. This, in turn, leads to rebirth into this world of evil, and so the Wheel of Life keeps repeating its endless revolutions.

In Buddhism, therefore, it is not so much that "the wages of sin is death" as that the wages of ignorance is suffering. Man's state is not so much a state of sin as one of ignorance. It is true that Buddhism uses the word Sin, but hardly with the import which it has in Christian thought, for without the Christian conception of God the Christian idea of sin is unintelligible. In fact, it is more accurate to say that Buddhism speaks of Evil rather than of Sin. And Evil is rather an effect than a cause; namely, the effect produced by ignorance or error. In the practical ethics of Buddhism the conception of sin seems to find a place, but hardly in the connection concerning which we are speaking now. It is better to say that Buddhism makes no distinction between sin and evil. That is, if Job is afflicted above his neighbors, it is because he is the greater sinner, and those "eighteen upon whom the tower in Siloam fell" were deeper sinners than their neighbors and deserved the punishment.

This is a natural answer for Buddhism to make, and follows directly from its cardinal doctrine of Karma. The evils of human life belong to the state of human beings, and only that being is born into the human state which deserved to be there, or rather, which through the inexorable workings of the law of Karma has caused itself to be born into that state. That is, the character of one's environment corresponds to the nature of one's being, and vice versa; so that an evil being is in an evil environment, and a good being in a good environment. This harmony between being and environment is known as the Two Fruits of Shōhō and Ihō. The evils of life are the fruits of past deeds, which past deeds may be called sins, or acts of ignorance; and the sins, or acts of ignorance, of the present life may be regarded as the cause of present and future evils.

Sin, then, in Buddhism is not to be regarded as a moral affront to God, but rather as a foolish act which necessarily brings the one who commits it a present or future evil. No true Buddhist could have written the fifty-first Psalm and especially not the words, "Against thee, thee only have I sinned." Sin is essentially folly, for what sane man would do that which is sure to bring evil upon himself? The real trouble with man is that he is ignorant, rather than that he is in moral rebellion against God's will; he needs a renewal of mind rather than a change of heart. This is why the Buddhist gospel of salvation is presented as an Enlightenment of the mind rather than a Regeneration of the heart; and the whole teaching of Buddhism is cast in the form of right thinking rather than right moral purpose. Man is to be saved from evil rather than from sin, and sin as the cause of evil is ignorance rather than wrong moral purpose. Men are not sinners so much as fools, and Buddhism seeks to make of them sages rather than saints. But this brings us to a new subject; namely, the subject of Salvation in Japanese Buddhism.

G. *Salvation*

The subject of Salvation naturally falls into two general divisions; namely, the Essence and Goal of Salvation, and the Way or Means of Salvation. Of course, it is impossible to keep these two aspects entirely separate in one's presentation of the matter, for the essence and goal of salvation are in part the way and means. Thus, *e.g.* it may be said that in Buddhism the essence and goal of salvation is Enlightenment, and that the way and means to achieve this is through Enlightenment. It is also difficult to say which of these two aspects should be taken up first, but it seems best to state first what Japanese Buddhism means by Salvation, and then show what it regards as the Way to attain this.

1. *The Essence and Goal of Salvation.* — The essence and

goal of the salvation offered by Buddhism is expressed most
generally by that mystifying word Nirvāna (Jap. Nehan).
Salvation is to enter Nirvāna.

But what is meant by entering Nirvāna?

The meaning of this word, even in primitive Buddhism,
has led to much discussion among scholars. It used to be
maintained that Nirvāna means a cessation of being, extinction, or total annihilation. Salvation therefore meant
an "escape" from life — life which is incurably evil. In
recent years, however, there has been a reaction against this
interpretation, and Nirvāna is taken to mean not only an
"escape" from evil, but also an "entrance" into a life of
bliss. But whether that life of bliss is to continue beyond
physical death is not always so clear. That question in
primitive Buddhism, as we pointed out in Chapter I, was
put among the Great Indeterminates. At any rate, it seems
true that if the founder of Buddhism believed in the continuation of the Arhat beyond death, he hesitated to say
anything very definite as to the nature of such a life. But as
we pointed out in Chapter II, when primitive Buddhism began to develop into Mahāyāna Buddhism, the doctrine of a
future life of bliss began to assert itself in one way or another.
In Chinese Buddhism the chief function of the Buddhist
priests seems to have centered about funerals and mátters
relating to the world to come. And in Japan, too, both
in popular and philosophical Buddhism, salvation means not
merely an "escape" from the dread cycle of existence, but
often the "entrance" into a present and future life of positive
content. Thus we have as one of the great summaries of
Buddhist doctrine the pregnant phrase, "Riku Tokuraku,"
"Escaping from Suffering and Obtaining Bliss." That is,
salvation is both an "escape" and an "entrance."

It is true that some philosophers say that "obtaining
bliss" simply means the "escape from suffering" and not
the obtaining of a positive good, but the majority of Japanese Buddhists would hold that "obtaining bliss" does
mean the entrance into an existence of real content. There
are various ways of interpreting the meaning of this "con-

R

tent," as we shall see. But first let us show from the very process by which the Buddhist obtains Buddhahood that salvation means an "entrance" into something good as well as an "escape" from evil.

We must again refer to the Buddhist chart of the Ten Worlds. The Human World is placed fifth from the bottom. Above the Human World is the Realm of Heavenly Beings, and above this are the Four Holies, the highest of which being Buddhahood, or the Buddha World. Now salvation consists in passing out of the Human World into the worlds above the human. Thus salvation is naturally a matter of degrees and is only perfect when one has entered into the highest of the Ten Worlds; namely into the Buddha World. This passage from the lower worlds into the higher worlds is naturally both an "escape" from evil and an "entrance" into bliss. Thus when man passes into the world above him he escapes from the sufferings and limitations characteristic of the Human Sphere and becomes a sharer of the bliss characteristic of his new environment. But as the Realm of Heavenly Beings still belongs to the Six Ways or the Three Worlds in which the law of Karma is operative, beings in this heavenly world are in danger of falling back into the human and lower worlds. Therefore entrance into the world of heavenly beings is not true salvation, however desirable it may be when compared with human life. Buddhism offers a full salvation, and so it must save man out of this realm of heavenly beings. Other religions, the Buddhist would say, may accomplish this limited salvation, but only Buddhism brings man the complete salvation; it offers salvation into the Four Holies, yea, into the Holiest of Holies, the Buddha state.

The lowest of the Four Holies is the Hearer State (Srāvaka, Jap. Shōmon), and this has four grades. To enter the lowest of these four grades is to enter the Fellowship of the Saints. He who has entered the second grade is subject to return but once more to the Six Ways or the Three Worlds where the law of Karma reigns. He who has entered the third grade is certain of ultimately obtaining absolute salvation. And to enter the fourth grade is to be free from evil, and such a one has really reached the first stage of true Buddhahood.

The second of the Four Holies is the Pratyēka Buddha State (Jap. Enkaku). He who has entered this state has broken the twelve links of the Karma-chain, and thus has escaped from the dread Wheel of Life and entered the beginnings of true enlightenment. Of course, such enlightenment as compared with that of the perfect Buddha is still very shallow. Nirvāna to such a one is void of all passions and sufferings and is filled with the bliss of knowledge.

But a fuller salvation than that of the Pratyēka Buddha is that of the Bodhisattva (Jap. Bosatsu). The one who has attained this lofty degree of salvation has not only escaped himself from the evils of life and entered bliss, but such a one finds the bliss of salvation to consist in helping others to escape from the Wheel of Life and enter a life of positive bliss. A Bodhisattva returns into the human world again and again, not because he is bound to the Wheel of Life and so is dragged down, but because he is bound by the law of love and sympathy for suffering humanity. That is, Nirvāna to a Bodhisattva is not an extinction or total annihilation, but it is a great work of annihilating the passions and sufferings in the lives of others. This he does by practicing the Six Virtues [6] of almsgiving and teaching, keeping the commandments, patience and longsuffering, diligence, meditation and wisdom in fulfillment of his Four Great Vows [7] to save all beings, to destroy all passions, to know and teach others all laws and to lead others to understand the ways of Buddha however lofty. With these characteristics it is not strange that popular polytheistic Buddhism gets its leading deities from the ranks of the Bodhisattvas.

The fourth of the Four Holies is the Buddha State. When the Bodhisattva has finished his noble work of providing a way of salvation for others, then, and only then, does he enter the bliss of true Buddhahood. Through his good work of saving others he has justified to himself the right of entering into the highest bliss, into the perfect rest and peace, into real Nirvāna.

Now from all this it is clear, as we said above, that Nirvāna, in Japanese Buddhism at least, is both an "escape" from the lower stages of existence and an "entrance" into higher stages until the highest of all, the Buddha State, is reached. Salvation is indeed a Riku Tokuraku, "An Escape from Evil and an Obtaining of Bliss."

But while it is clear that Nirvāna is an escape from, or an annihilation of, the lower and an entrance into the higher, it is not yet clear from what has been said as to what is the condition of one who has entered into the highest state. What is the condition of one who has obtained the complete salvation which Buddhism offers?

The answer to this question is that it is Buddhahood. But then what is really meant by Buddhahood? This, as the reader will observe, is bringing the subject back to what we have already discussed in the section on the God-idea. Without repeating in full what we said there, let us state briefly the substance in its bearing upon the matter in hand.

We saw that the God-idea in Buddhist philosophy falls under three general heads; namely, Atheism, Theism or Semitheism, and Pantheism. The perfect salvation which Japanese Buddhism offers to all beings may likewise be divided into three kinds; for in Buddhism as in all religions the God-idea conditions the idea of salvation, and vice versa. It is a real case of "we shall be like him; for we shall see him even as he is."

To the Buddhist whose God-idea ends practically in zero, Nirvāna also approaches the vanishing point.[8] But just as no Buddhist in Japan would say that existence is absolutely void but that the essence of existence is a Something which transcends the categories of all beings known to man, so Nirvāna, or the perfect Buddha State, is not a condition of absolute void but a state which transcends the categories of human life. It is a total annihilation of everything which makes up this present phenomenal world, but it is not therefore an absolute void. To describe such a state would be to limit it, and its very essence is that it is an existence which is no longer bound by the limitations of life as we know it. Not only should we not think of Nirvāna as simply a higher and loftier life of the self — for that would still be thinking of it in definite terms — but we are not to think of it in terms of any form of existence. Nirvāna is the state which transcends all existence known to us; yea, it is even beyond the dualism of being and non-being. It is the "Dharma of non-duality, because those who have entered a meditation in which there is no sense-impression, no cogitation, are free from ignorance as well as from enlightenment. This holds true with all other dualistic categories." Thus what the highest stage of salvation means transcends all knowledge, and the wise philosopher will make no affirmation about it. This is one answer to the question as to what is meant by Nirvāna, or the essence and goal of salvation.

To the Buddhist philosopher whose God-idea is more or less theistic, Nirvāna has a more or less positive and definite content. The Amidaist has his paradise. Paradise is the abode of Amida and all who have become like Amida; namely, all who have attained Buddhahood. Of course, in the popular presentation of this Paradise doctrine we often find very realistic pictures, but even to the educated Buddhist Amida's Western Paradise stands for something real and is conceived of in terms of our higher psychic life. Thus "Nirvāna is the abode of all those who see the reality of all principles." "Nirvāna is the name we apply to the region of all the Buddhas who have cut out all passions from their lives." It is probably true that to some intelligent Amidaists salvation and Nirvāna mean something not so very different from what salvation and heaven mean to an educated Christian. It is a life of conquest over sin and evil and a fellowship with Amida and the saints. The following quotation from a letter of an old woman illustrates this nobler type of Buddhist believers: "I am old and I am a woman, and it is not expected that a woman will know much of such subjects, but I will tell you what thoughts I have. I am weak and sinful, and have no hope in myself; my hope is all in Amida Buddha. I believe him to be the Supreme Being. Because of the wickedness of man, and because of human sorrow, Amida Buddha became incarnate and came to earth to deliver man; and my hope and the world's hope is to be found only in his suffering love. He has entered humanity to save it; and he alone can save. He constantly watches over and helps all who trust in him. I am not in a hurry to die, but I am ready when my time comes; and I trust that through the gracious love of Amida Buddha I shall then enter into the future life which I believe to be a state of conscious existence, and where I shall be free from sorrow. I believe that he hears prayer, and that he has guided me thus far, and my hope is only in his suffering love."

Another pious believer in Amida writing from her deathbed to her friends expresses herself as follows: "I have been ailing for several days past, and, believing my sickness to be a messenger of death, I am filled with joy, trusting myself entirely to His mercies. . . . The manifestation of the Tathāgata (Amida) is the earnest and pledge to us of our entrance into Paradise. Why should we doubt? . . . Should my sickness change for the worse, I shall never see you again in this life. But I shall, of a certainty, see once more, in the Pure Land, all those who are partakers with me in the faith that I have in Amida."

These are indeed noble utterances, and the faith that permeates them seems to be a real faith in a living God whose salvation alone can satisfy the heart of man. But after we have said this we must add that the doctrine of Amida's salvation and his Western Paradise, after all, breaks down lamentably in the case of the Amidaists themselves. We shall state later how it breaks down in its popular form; here we shall indicate how it breaks down philosophically. As we said above, the God-idea and the idea of salvation are inextricably connected in any advanced religion. Now in the section on the Theistic God-idea we have already shown that though Amida is popularly regarded as a per-

sonal being, his existence as a personal being is denied by
the philosophers; not only by the exceptional philosopher,
but practically by every philosopher of the Amida sects
themselves. He is regarded as but the personification of
the ideal, the ideal of mercy and wisdom. He is not really
a personal being existing now. The conception of Amida
as a personal being is said to be but an accommodation of
language. From the standpoint of real truth Amida vanishes into the thin mist of the Absolute concerning which
nothing can be affirmed, for it transcends the categories of
human knowledge. And what is true of Amida is equally
true of his so-called Western Paradise which is popularly
said to be "ten trillion worlds" away. The Amida philosopher not only denies the materialistic aspects of Paradise, so dear to the common believer, but he denies also the
higher aspects conceived in terms of our higher and spiritual
life. To him the conception of Paradise, like that of Amida,
is only an accommodation of language. Nirvāna is to him,
as it is to the atheistic Buddhist, a great void. Of course,
he would not say that it is an absolute void, but that it is a
state which transcends all categories of human thought.
Yea, even to say that it is "a state which transcends all
categories of human thought," is really saying too much.
As a result of this agnostic spirit which ever flows as an
undercurrent of Buddhist thought there is much less of the
joy of a real salvation from life's sin and sorrows, and much
less of the hope of a conquering life and an eternal fellowship with God than one would expect among Amida Buddhists. The two letters quoted above, with their note of
joy and confidence, are the exception rather than the rule.

And now what must we say as to the meaning of salvation
and Nirvāna to the pantheistic Buddhist? He, too, would
say that salvation, or Nirvāna, is a progressive "escape"
from evil and an "entrance" into a higher and higher good.
He differs from the semi-theistic Buddhist in that where
the former ordinarily thinks of Nirvāna as a fellowship of
the Buddhas, the latter conceives of Nirvāna rather as a
merging of the individual with the All-inclusive Buddha.

Salvation consists in knowing that Buddha is in all and all are in Buddha. But just what that state is in which the saved are merged with the Divine is not very clear. In fact, the pantheistic philosopher will give essentially the same answer which has already been given above as representing the atheistic and semi-theistic philosophers. As the true essence of the Divine-All transcends all human knowledge it is impossible to state in human language what is the condition of those who have attained perfect salvation. It is, of course, a freedom from the suffering inherent in all individual existence. It is a rest and peace which is void of all that characterizes our present life, but it is not therefore an absolute void. Only in negative terms can one speak of it at all, *i.e.* a negation of all that might be affirmed of life as we know it.

Thus we see that while to the question as to what is meant by Nirvāna or salvation, in Japanese Buddhism, several answers may be given; they merge in the last analysis into the same answer. They all agree that it is an "escape from evil and an obtaining of bliss," but what that highest bliss may be is impossible to say. This answer, as we have stated in other connections, grows logically from the Buddhist theory of knowledge which claims that all human knowledge is relative and of the shadow world.

"All things are unstable, for this is the law of life and death. When life and death are completely done away, extinction is happiness."

"The great and wide expanse of space is called empty space. The peace of Nirvāna is like this empty space, being an immense void. In this place lives no ruler, nor is it the abode of the ego."

"Life, death, and Nirvāna are nothing but dreams that have passed; for there is no beginning and no end, there is no coming and no going."

But while the meaning of Nirvāna and salvation in philosophical Buddhism vanishes into thin mist, it is quite the opposite in popular Buddhism. Here it is often crudely realistic. The common man knows comparatively little

of the meaning of the Four Holies and less of the ultimate
goal to which the Four Holies are supposed to lead. To
him salvation is primarily a present concrete good and a
shadowy hope of a future life of happiness. The meaning
of this "present good" differs, of course, very widely. To
some, though it must be confessed that their number is not
very large, the meaning may not be so very different from
what it is to the average Christian. These "more noble"
ones seek earnestly to conquer the lower passion and to
walk in the path of righteousness and truth to the extent of
their ability. And salvation beyond the present life they
would think of in terms of our present higher life and a fellowship with Buddha and the saints. The passages quoted
from the letters of two Buddhist women throw light on the
faith of this nobler type. There are others who would have
less to say about the help of Buddha and their hope of a
better future, but to whom salvation means something real
in the form of a higher ethical life lived in obedience to the
commandments and maxims of Buddhism. That is, there
are devout people in all the sects to whom Buddha's salvation
is something real and rather noble.

There is, however, a darker side to the picture. Just as
the God-idea as held by the general run of believers is
incurably polytheistic and often revoltingly crude, so the
conception of salvation is on an exceedingly low plane. It
is real enough. Yea, just because philosophical Buddhism
has lost itself in the clouds of abstract speculations and has
not been faithful in proclaiming the higher life in compre-
hensible terms, the common man has been left to himself,
and thus he thinks of salvation largely in terms of life on the
lowest plane. He has made gods a little higher (and sometimes a little lower) than himself, and the salvation which
such gods offer is naturally in harmony with their nature.
Thus the common man turns to one or the other of the gods
in the crowded pantheon and expects from each the help
for which the deity has special qualification to bestow. To
the various gods of Luck the worshiper turns for good luck
in various fields. Binzuru's images are worn smooth by the

touch of the thousands and tens of thousands who rub the various parts of the god's anatomy, and then the corresponding part of their own in the hope that they might be healed of their physcial infirmities. Jizo is implored by the childless for an offspring and by bereaved mothers to be merciful to their little ones whom death has snatched from their arms, and protect them from the hag on the banks of the Buddhist Styx. Or the traveler starting on a journey looks to him or to Kompira for protection and guidance. When a house is built the deities of the Four Regions must be consulted and satisfied if the future occupant is to be happy and prosperous. In war, prayers for victory are offered to Hachiman and to the spirits of departed heroes. The peaceful peasant turns to the Inari shrines for a good rice crop; the man of the sea looks upon Kompira as patron. And whatever may be needed by those in need may be obtained from the all-compassionate Kwannon whose images with many hands inspires the worshiper with the faith that he that asketh shall receive. When the various deities have done their part in giving what man needs for this life and in protecting him from bad luck and all sorts of misfortunes, then there are other gods and Buddhas who will help him in the life beyond. Emma-O, the regent of the Buddhist hell, is appeased and implored to be merciful to those under his dominion. Amida, who has prepared his Western Paradise, which each devotee fills with whatever suits his fancy, is expected by many to care for all who call upon his name.

But in all the helps which the various deities render to mankind there is a surprising absence of the higher aspects of life. Salvation as a conquest over sin and a growth in righteousness is a conception not generally shared by the great mass of those who call themselves Buddhists. In fact, it is not difficult to show that popular Buddhism is often responsible for keeping the people bound with the fetters of sin and ignorance. If anyone doubts this statement, let him visit some of the most popular centers of Buddhism and look around with open eyes. Not only are the temples frequently surrounded with the most vulgar sort of amusements and shows, but where these religious pilgrims gather in large numbers the brothels are not far away. At great religious festivals the religious element is usually so completely overshadowed by the frivolous, the superstitious and the immoral that their effect upon the participants is that of a grand spree and debauch. Whatever may be said about the lofty teachings of Buddhism as to salvation and Nirvāna, it must be admitted by the unbiased observer that Buddhism, in the lives of the great majority of its adherents, is often a real hindrance to the higher life. If the religion of the Buddha ever was a power unto salvation to Japan's millions, it cannot be said to fill such a function to-day, at least not on a very large scale.

2. *The Way of Salvation.* — If the essence and goal of salvation in Buddhism is an "escape from evil and an entrance into a life of bliss," and if the cause of evil and the hindrance to entrance into the life of bliss is Ignorance, then it follows that the Way of Salvation must be a way which leads away from Ignorance into Knowledge. Thus we have the great summary of the Buddhist mode of salvation, Tenmei Kaigo, "Turning from Error and Opening Understanding." Man is saved by knowing the truth, the Truth of Buddhism.

But what is that saving truth which man must know and which Buddhism offers him? This is a question which has a very complex answer.

There is at least one school which holds that this saving truth consists in "breaking error," *i.e.* truth has no positive content, and the spirit of truth is the spirit which denies all things, for this world is a shadow world and therefore must be destroyed by a process of negations. Light, this school would say, is not a positive reality, but simply the absence of darkness.

But just as we saw in the preceding section that the essence of salvation in Japanese Buddhism has ordinarily a rather positive content, so the way of salvation is usually not simply a "breaking of error" but also a real "opening of the understanding." The way, however, in which this breaking of error and opening of the understanding is to be achieved varied somewhat in the different sects.

It is customary to divide these various ways into two great divisions. These divisions correspond roughly to the two great divisions known in Christian thought as the Way of the Law and the Way of Grace; or the Way of Good Works and the Way of Faith. There are several ways in which the chief aspects of these two great divisions are expressed. Thus the Way of the Law is called the Holy Way Division (Jap. Shōdōmon), or Self-reliance (Jap. Jiriki, literally meaning Self-strength). In less technical language it is called the Way of Hardships (Jap. Nangyōdō). On the other hand, the doctrine of the Way of Grace is called the Pure Land Division (Jap. Jōdomon) from the fact that it teaches a salvation in Paradise which is not prepared or earned by the believer, but by Amida. In contrast with the way of Self-reliance it is called Reliance upon Another (Jap. Tariki, literally meaning Another's Strength), and in contrast with the Way of Hardships it is called the Easy Way (Igyōdō).

a. *The Way of the Law.* — The first of these two great ways of salvation; namely, the Way of the Law of Self-reliance, is, as we saw in Chapter I, the way proclaimed by primitive Buddhism. It recognized apparently no salvation except such as man can work out for himself through perfect obedience of the law and through a strict walking in the Holy Way of self-discipline. This one must do in one's own strength and without trust in the assistance of another. The majority of Japanese sects are usually classified as teachers of this rigid way, and at least one sect; namely, the great Zen Sect, really carries this doctrine into practice. As we saw in the section on the God-idea, the Zen Sect is practically atheistic, and, of course, the logical corollary of atheism is that man cannot look to God for help, but that he must save himself. Every man is the sole architect of his own future, and whatsoever he sows that shall he also reap. Not even a heavenly being can intervene and save man from the inexorable workings of the

law of Karma. He must save himself by his own wisdom
and good deeds. "A good cause brings forth good fruit
and an evil cause brings forth evil fruit." This is an inexorable law and is called Jigyō jitoku, "Self-do self-get." The
good cause which bears good fruit is the walking in the
way of self-discipline and knowledge of the truth about life.
"Self-denial, constancy and wisdom constitute the way of
deliverance." "O monks, if you have wisdom you will
not cling to worldliness. Wherefore examine yourselves
constantly that you lose not wisdom; for this according to
my teaching is the way of deliverance. If any one loses
wisdom, he is no longer in the way, nor a white-robed
man, but only a nameless one. True wisdom is a strong
ship which carries us across the sea of old age, sickness
and death. And again, wisdom is the great light which
illumines the outer darkness; it is an effective medicine
for all patients, and a sharp ax to cut down the trees of
passion."

But while one branch of Buddhism teaches a rather rigid
doctrine of salvation through one's own strength, there is
usually some room left for the doctrine that help may come
from another. Even the architect of his own future can
receive suggestions from another as to how to build that
future. Gautama himself, though he spurned the assistance
of the gods of the people and trusted not in the unknowable
God of the philosophers, felt that the way of salvation which
he had achieved would at least show the way unto others,
and so be a real help. In fact, he gave his life to the task
of showing others his way of salvation and preached it as
the way in which all the Buddhas before him had walked.
And so among Japanese Buddhists who hold the doctrine
of salvation through self-reliance, there is at least the recognition of the possibility of one man helping another to the
extent of showing him the right way. It is true that the
Zen Sect goes so far as to say that truth cannot be transmitted by the written or spoken word but must be transmitted from heart to heart, or rather, must be discovered
by each one within his own heart; and yet even the strict-

est Zen philosopher thinks it possible to help his fellow man at least to the extent of telling him that he must and can help himself. And then in practical life the Zen teacher lays a great deal of stress on the ethical principle of benevolence which naturally implies the possibility of man receiving help from another, even though that other be only a man.

Then besides the Zen Sect there are other great sects which are said to teach this doctrine of "Help Thyself," but which make equal room for the opposite truth; namely, that help may come from another. Practically every one of the great Japanese sects makes room for the Bodhisattva ideal (a main characteristic of Mahāyāna Buddhism); and what is a Bodhisattva but one who has not only achieved his own salvation but is willing to return to the Three Worlds again and again in order to help others attain that same state. Even when the doctrine of "Help Thyself" is held in the most extreme form it is usually accompanied by the doctrine that in the last analysis everything has, as the core of its real being, the Buddha nature, and so the most depraved may have a hope of ultimate deliverance from the bondages of existence even though there is no immediate prospect of entrance into a positive salvation.

b. *The Way of Grace.* — The second great Way of Salvation taught by Japanese Buddhism is the Way of Grace, or salvation through the Strength of Another. The best representatives of this way are the Amida sects, especially the Shin Sect. We saw in the section on the God-idea that the Amida sects are at least semi-theistic, and it is natural that with such a God-idea these sects should recognize more clearly the principle of Divine Grace in human life than is done by the atheistic and pantheistic sects. In fact, these Amida sects not only recognize this principle, but they seem to carry it to an extreme in their popular presentation of the matter. They do not deny that salvation through one's own strength is possible — it is possible for the few strong men, and especially was it possible for strong men back in the golden age of humanity

— but the great mass of mankind, especially in these degenerate days, need help from Another and can be saved only through the grace of Amida who has worked out a way of salvation for all living beings through his vicarious sufferings and hardships. It is not that S'akyamuni has shown in his life the way in which man should walk in order to attain enlightenment and so freedom from the evils of existence, but rather that Hōzō Bosatsu who became the Buddha Amida made a great vow that he would not enter the full bliss of Buddhahood until he had prepared a way of salvation for all living beings. This way being prepared it remains only for sinful and ignorant humanity to appropriate the heavenly good and enter Paradise through faith in the great name of Amida.

"Every one, who through the might of Buddha's Great Vow hears his name and desires to be born into Paradise, shall enter that land and never return" (that is, he shall never be born again into this world of evil).

"I have reached the time of my final doctrine. There are millions of men who are trying to master the doctrine, giving themselves to various religious practices; but there is not a single one who has attained. These are my final teachings. I say this is an evil world of Five Impurities and only one gate stands ajar; namely, the gate that leads to Paradise."

"For men of this world there is no other gate which leads from this life of sorrow than the gate which opens on the way that leads to the West." (That is, the way to Amida's Western Paradise.) "All living beings, who rejoice at hearing the sacred Name (*i.e.*, Amida) and who practice with singleness of heart the religious requirements and pray to be born into that Land, shall obtain such birth and shall sit upon thrones incorruptible."

The way of escape, then, from this world of evil is possible because Amida has prepared such a way. He has prepared a heavenly home for sinful and suffering humanity, and by his grace he leads man to this home. No matter how low man has sunk he is still worthy of being saved through this way of grace. "When I look at men," says one of the scriptures, "though I realize that they are sunk in the passions of avarice, anger and ignorance, I see in every one the wisdom of Buddha, the eyes of Buddha, and the body of Buddha. O Good Generation, every man, though sunk in passion, has within him the undefiled image of the Nyōrai, and, equipped with virtue, he is not different from myself. This image is like pure gold which cannot lose its nature even though buried out of sight and lost to knowledge for many years."

Not only do the Amida sects preach this doctrine of salvation through the Strength of Another, but we might say that all popular Buddhism, in one way or another, holds that man receives aid and salvation from the gods, Buddhas and Bodhisattvas. Each one of these many deities has his own peculiar function as a helper of man, for what is the use of deities if they cannot help man in the hour of need? The way of the Law and Self-discipline is largely confined to the better educated classes. The masses, whether Amidaists or not, as a rule expect their gods to take care of them. The gods, of course, must be propitiated through various rites and ceremonies, and to that extent man must earn their help and protection.

We said above that the salvation prepared by Amida needs only to be appropriated by man to receive the full benefit; but how is man to appropriate it? By faith and faith alone, say the true Amidaists. It is sometimes customary among believers in Amida to divide Buddhism as a whole into two great divisions, and to say that one teaches that man is saved through philosophical wisdom, and the other that man is saved solely through faith. Such a clearcut division is a little arbitrary; for in a true sense Buddhism as a whole is a faith, and the very foundation of its theories of knowledge, as we saw above, is a "credo ut intelligam." Then also the formula which the Buddhists of all sects use is a formula of faith; namely, "I take refuge in Buddha, the Law, and the Priesthood." There are many passages in the various scriptures which show that faith plays an im-

portant part in the way of salvation. The following are
but a few examples:

"A man without hands can receive nothing even though
he should come to a mountain of treasures; neither can the
man who has not the hands of faith obtain anything even
though he should meet the Three Treasures" (*i.e.* Buddha,
the Law and the Priesthood).

"Faith is the key to the understanding and knowledge of
Buddha."

"The good root is righteous faith."

"Only by faith can one venture out upon the great ocean
of Buddha's law."

"Faith is the crown of every deed and the basis of every
virtue."

"Faith is the chief treasure in the treasury."

The Nirvāna scripture, speaking of the relation between
knowledge and faith, says they are complementary. "Faith
without knowledge leads to the conceit of ignorance, and
knowledge without faith begets a stony heart. Therefore
only as these two are well blended do they become the basis
of good deeds."

But after we have said that faith is recognized by all
sects as important, it is true that faith in the sense of trust
is par excellence the characteristic of that mode of salvation
which puts its confidence in the mercy of Amida. There
are some Amidaists who rely still in part on the fruits of
their own good deeds, but at least one sect, the Shin, claims
to appropriate the heavenly good offered by Amida solely
by accepting it in simple faith and trust, for through this
act of faith the believer is said to be made one with
Amida. "The man who relies upon Amida is said to have
become merged with Namu Amida Butsu and thinks himself under his protection." And with this thought passes
away all worry of sin and good works to counterbalance
evil deeds.

Not only is the heavenly good offered by Amida to the believer appropriated by faith, but faith itself is said to be the
gift of Amida. In the words of a recent writer on this point,

s

"Faith is the gift of Another because it is not a faith which is fixed through the believer's own efforts, but entirely through the influence of the great, merciful heart of Amida. This faith is wrought through the enlightened vow of Amida, and to fill the believer's heart with faith is Amida's desire."

So far is this principle of grace carried in its popular presentation that the hearer is told that to repeat but once or a few times the prayer, Namu Amida Butsu, is sufficient to insure him birth into the Western Paradise. Some Amidaists are still too conscious of the old Karma doctrine to admit that a deathbed repentance can lead to immediate birth into Paradise. They hold that a deathbed repentance and faith in Amida will ultimately lead to birth into Paradise. Such a man's lotus, to use the Buddhist terminology, will some day, perhaps tens of thousands of years later, open up and he will thus be born into Amida's Paradise. As a rule, however, the Amida believer is taught that he will enter Paradise immediately after death and that even now he is in Paradise, for he lives in the assurance of the great hope.

Good works, the careful Amidaist says, are necessary as signs of the believer's salvation, and they should be done out of gratitude for the gift of Amida's grace. Good works are not causes of salvation but rather effects of salvation.

But there is another side to this beautiful doctrine of salvation through faith in Amida's saving grace. In practice this doctrine is often an antinomianism of the worst type. In fact, the Amidaists sometimes boast that their doctrine of grace is more lofty than the Christian doctrine because Christians seem to pay a good deal of attention to moral conduct, after all, while Amida saves every one no matter how vile. As one Christian critic who is well acquainted with the practical workings of Buddhism puts it, where the Christian doctrine teaches that man is saved from sin, *i.e. from* its guilt, pollution and power, the doctrine of these followers of Amida is that man is saved *in* sin. He is saved from the evils of existence into the Western Paradise just as he is. He may do anything he pleases, for nothing can separate him from the bliss of Paradise, not even sin. A recent Buddhist writer, speaking on the believer's life lived in gratitude for Amida's salvation, expresses himself as follows: "When we pursue our daily duties and work cheerfully and assiduously, even though we indulge in lies and sharp practices, we help spread the way of Buddha, and so even our lies and sharp practices become expressions of gratitude." To such an extreme has this doctrine of grace been carried that the indifference of the Amidaists to self-culture in the past gave rise to the jibe, "Zenshū zeni nashi, Monto mono wo shirazu," "The Zen followers have no money, the Monto (Shin) followers have no knowledge."

But not only is this doctrine of salvation through the grace of Amida much abused in its popular presentation, and often leads to a mere superstitious repetition of the prayer Namu Amida Butsu without working a change of heart or enlightening the mind; in the last analysis it also breaks down philosophically. We have already seen in the section on the God-idea that Amida is, after all, only such a "god as man can and has become." The so-called vicarious savior in Amida Buddhism is not God come in the flesh, but man through his own strength become a god. Hōzō Bosatsu was first an ordinary man and then became the Buddha Amida. Perhaps this would not be such a serious defect to many minds, for it would mean that a man has demonstrated the possibility of becoming god, and such a one could really help other men to escape from the evils of this world into the bliss of another world. But there is another weakness in this Buddhist savior-idea. The man Hōzō Bosatsu has not a shred of historicity about him, but is a mere fiction of the fertile imagination. And further, Amida, according to the Amidaists themselves, has no real personal existence but is only the personification of the idea of mercy and wisdom. Thus the savior in Amidaism is reduced to a mere savior-idea, and this idea has no real ontological reference. And if there is really no Amida and no savior, then what becomes of the Savior-idea? Those modern psychologists who hold that an idea is as good as the reality for which it stands as long as the idea functions, may be quite right. But the question is, How long will an idea function if those who hold it do not believe that it stands for a reality? Obviously it will not function long or very vigorously. If my creditor thinks that the check I hand him is worth five dollars, then it is worth five dollars to him and to me; but unless I have a deposit with the bank on which I give him the check, and unless the bank has back of the checks it issues some value equal to five dollars, then the man is a fool to accept my check. And so if back of the Savior-idea and the God-idea in Amida Buddhism there is no real God and Savior (as the Amidaists themselves admit that there is not), then it would not be strange if the savior-idea should cease to function effectively as the believer is educated in the teachings of his own religion. And that is exactly what happens in nine cases out of ten. For the ignorant Buddhist the savior-idea functions, yea functions too realistically, but for the enlightened Buddhist it, too, becomes but one of those ideas with which to allure the common herd but which must not be taken too seriously. Salvation through faith in Amida's grace is to him but an accommodation of language, and does not represent anything really true.

Thus in spite of the strong resemblance between Christianity and Amida Buddhism in this doctrine of salvation there is this radical difference; that the Christian Savior-idea has its ontological reference in the historic personality of Jesus Christ, while the Buddhist idea has confessedly no such reference. "The inexhaustible fountain of religious strength," writes Cumont in his little volume on Mithras, "which flowed from the doctrine of the Passion and Crucifixion of the Son of God never flowed for the disciples of Mithras." The same may be said with equal truth about the savior in Amida Buddhism; no real "fountain of religious strength" has ever flowed or can ever flow from him, for he confessedly never existed.

The two great divisions in Buddhist doctrine of Salvation through Man's Own Strength and Salvation through the Strength of Another, after all, merge into one, and we must say that Buddhism knows no way of salvation except such as man has worked out for himself. God cannot save man, for in the last analysis there is no real God in Buddhism except the unknowable and indifferent Absolute. And thus once more we see things vanishing into thin mist, and what to the common man may seem very real, to the educated Buddhist it belongs to the uncertainty of all human knowledge.

3. *The Extent and Speed of Salvation.* — There are some aspects of the Way of Salvation which are not brought out clearly in the above discussion but which are rather important from the Buddhist point of view. These aspects pertain to the extent and what we might call the Speed of the process of salvation.

As to the extent of salvation Buddhists are usually universalists. In fact, not only shall all mankind be saved ultimately,[9] but everything that lives and moves shall share in this universal salvation. If it is possible for an evil man by the law of Karma to be born into a state lower than the human state, then it is also possible by the operation of the same law for beings in the lower states to be born into higher and higher states until finally they enter Buddhahood. Thus we read in the Paradise sutra, "In every living being dwells the essence of Buddha," and therefore, "everything that has a heart can surely attain Buddhahood."

This doctrine of universal salvation rests on slightly different bases in the different sects, as might be expected. The pantheistic Buddhists find the ground of their belief in the thought that since every individual existence is a part of the Great-All, there can be no permanent separation or loss; or still better, the thought of separation and loss is but error, and in reality does not exist. The Amidaist, on the other hand, finds his hope of a universal salvation in the thought of Amida's boundless mercy. So great is this mercy that it cannot fail to save all that lives and moves. "The Buddha heart is great mercy. With this absolute mercy which is not bound by circumstances it saves all living beings."

As to the speed with which the salvation of any being is to

be accomplished Buddhists differ rather widely. The older Buddhists, conscious of the workings of the inexorable law of Karma, usually held that the process by which a being is to pass through the various grades of existence until it reaches the highest state of Buddhahood is a very long and gradual process. Thus Gautama is said to have lived through many incarnations before he finally attained enlightenment. But as Buddhism developed, and especially after it reached the northern peoples, Buddhists became impatient with this slow process and in one way or another developed a way by which salvation can be attained speedily. Thus we have in Japanese and Chinese Buddhism the two ways known as the Gradual Way and the Abrupt Way. These two ways are really subdivisions of each of the two great ways mentioned above; namely, the Way of Self-reliance and the Way of Reliance on the Strength of Another. That is, the goal in either of these two ways may be reached either Gradually or Abruptly.

To reach the goal gradually in the Way of Self-reliance is called Lengthwise-going-out (Jap. Shu-shutsu). That is, the way of deliverance from the Three Worlds is the long route of the path of self-discipline extending through many incarnations until, after grades upon grades of existence have been passed, the final goal is reached at last. The old Sanron and Hossō sects taught this gradual way.

To reach the goal abruptly in the Way of Self-reliance is called Lengthwise-passing-over (Jap. Shu-chō). That is, the long way which leads from the lower to the higher stages of existence is passed over rapidly. It is not necessary to go through many rebirths and so ascend gradually in the scale of beings, but the believer, having as it were the right password or the key of wisdom which unlocks all doors, can pass through gate after gate in rapid succession and reach the highest goal speedily. The nature of this password or key differs in different sects. To some it is a magic word or sign. To others it is a knowledge of the mystery of all being, a correct philosophic insight. To still others it is right conduct, or both correct knowledge and conduct.

But whatever the key may be, one who possesses it can attain the highest salvation even in this life. To this group belong such sects as the Kegon, Tendai, Shingon and Zen.

To reach the goal gradually in the Way of Reliance on the Strength of Another is called Crosswise-going-out (Jap. Wō-shutsu). That is, the one who attains salvation by this path goes through the long scale of beings which separates him from the final goal, by gradual stages. His final salvation is certain because Another (Amida) has prepared for him his Western Paradise; but he must pass through many rebirths before he can be born into Paradise. This differs from the gradual way in the Path of self-reliance in that the goal and the power to reach the goal depend not upon the believer, but upon Another. Some Amidaists walk by this way.

To reach the goal abruptly in the Way of Reliance on the Strength of Another is called Crosswise-passing-over (Jap. Wō-chō). That is, the believer passes freely over all the stages of existence which separate him from his goal because he is carried by another's power. It is not necessary to stop along the way, for Amida has cleared away all difficulties. This abrupt way differs from the abrupt way in the Path of Self-reliance in that the believer has nothing to do but to trust and believe. He need not have the key of knowledge nor the password of mystery to allow him to pass on. Sufficient for him is the hand of faith and simple trust in Amida; yea, Amida carries him like a ship across the ocean of life into his haven of rest and peace. Among the Amida sects the Shin regards itself as being the true representative of this way of salvation. All other ways are regarded as provisional ways. They are not wrong ways, for just as all roads lead to Rome, so all ways of salvation lead finally to Amida's Paradise, but it is better to go by the short and easy way provided for sinful humanity.

Practically all Japanese sects would take an equally liberal view of the ways of salvation. Each sect will maintain that its way is the best way, but would not insist that it is the only way. Buddhism is usually very charitable towards the teachings of others, for it teaches that all rivers finally flow into the ocean. However dirty, or crooked, or sluggish the stream may be, it reaches the ocean at last and in its depths all waters are purified.

H. *Things to Come*

In the Buddhist doctrine of universal salvation we have in part the answer as to what Buddhism teaches about the Things to Come. Not only is all mankind ultimately to be saved, but everything that lives is to be delivered from the bondages of individual existence into the bliss of the All-One. But when shall this consummation be reached, and what shall be the intermediary process?

To begin with, for ages to come life will go on very much as it is. The great majority of beings shall be born again and again into the Six Ways, *i.e.* they shall be born as human beings, or into the realm of heavenly beings (not the Buddhist heaven), if their good Karma outweighs their evil Karma; but if the evil outweighs the good, then their birth will be in the lower realms; namely Fighting and Bloodshed, the Realm of Beasts, Hungry Spirits, or Hell. From this dread cycle of the Six Ways it is hard to escape and, if measured by human life, this condition of things seems almost a permanent one. "A blind turtle and a floating tree are more likely to meet and see each other than ignorant and stupid humanity is to obtain the body of a man." And if the chances for man are so meager, then what must be the chances of beings lower in the scale of existence! Obviously the situation looks rather gloomy in spite of the hope of a universal salvation.

But the Buddhist speculative thinker is not daunted by time. In fact, he loves to dwell upon the endlessness of time and express this in finite terms. Thus while the present state of affairs may seem to be an endless state, it will some day be followed by another situation. First there is to come a golden age for humanity when there shall appear the Buddha of the Future, the Buddha Maitreya (Jap. Miroku). When he shall appear then life will be long and pleasant, and many shall there be who will hear the gospel of Buddha and enter from this world of evil into the bliss of Buddhahood.

And when shall that be?

To this there have been several answers. Some have held that Maitreya has already appeared, and that the rise of Mahāyāna Buddhism marked the beginning of this glorious age. The great Nichiren held that he was the herald of that golden age, and that the darkness of the age into which he was born was to be followed by the dawn. But by most thinkers this golden age is placed in the distant future.

In the section on the Buddhist cosmology we spoke of the four stages through which the universe is said to pass ; namely, the stages of Completion, Inhabitation, Destruction and Voidness. The universe is now in the state of Inhabitation. Now the length of each stage is said to be twenty Decreasing-increasing Æons. These æons are called thus because in each æon life is very long at the beginning and gradually decreases until the life of man is only ten years long. Then it begins to lengthen very gradually, until finally human life is 84,000 years in duration. The actual length of such an æon can, therefore, not be expressed in years for the rate of change is not known. We are, however, told that when Maitreya will appear human life shall be 80,000 years in length, and this shall be 5,670,000,000 years after the day of S'akyamuni who lived about 2500 years ago. Maitreya is thus to appear before the end of the present æon, *i.e.* when life is only 80,000 years in duration and not yet 84,000 years as it is to be at the end of this present æon.

When Maitreya shall appear with a body 320 feet in height (this is indicative of what will be the size of the human body in that age), then shall the trees on the earth be like golden dragons with flowers shaped like dragons, and in the midst of this splendor he shall proclaim the sacred Law three times. The first time he proclaims the Law there shall be 9,600,000,000 human beings who shall hear the Law and so enter the first stage of enlightenment, becoming Arakans, and 360,000 heavenly beings who shall hear the

law and so enter the perfect enlightenment of the Bodhisattva. The second time the Law is proclaimed there
shall be 9,400,000,000 human beings attaining the Arakan
stage and 6,400,000,000 angelic beings attaining perfect
enlightenment. The third time there shall be respectively
9,200,000,000 and 3,400,000,000 attaining the higher life.
From this it may be seen what a glorious age that will be.
Truly it will be a day when the knowledge of the sacred
Law shall cover the earth as the waters cover the sea.

This is, however, not the consummation of all things; it
is only the consummation of one Decreasing-increasing Æon.
It is the tenth such æon in the stage of Inhabitation which is
the second of the four stages through which the universe is
said to pass. This tenth æon is therefore to be followed
by ten more æons of equal length before the stage of Inhabitation shall come to an end. During each of these æons
to come there shall be Buddhas to proclaim the sacred Law,
just as before Maitreya and S'akyamuni there were many
Buddhas.

Now when the second great stage has come to an end
then the universe will pass into the third stage, the stage of
Destruction. In this stage there will be no living beings
but all things will gradually be dissolved and then the universe will reach its fourth stage. The fourth stage is the
great Void. In this stage all individual beings, whether
material or spiritual, shall have returned into the void from
which they originally came. In this void there shall be
neither being nor non-being, neither truth nor error, for all
things shall have become a Oneness which transcends all our
dualistic categories.

But we have not yet reached the end of all things; it is
only the end of the first chapter. After all things have
passed into the great Void and have remained there through
twenty Decreasing-increasing Æons then shall the second
chapter begin. That is, the universe will again enter the
first of the four stages and this will be followed by the second,
third and fourth. Thus Completion, Inhabitation, Destruction and Voidness shall follow each other in endless succes-

sion. The ocean of eternal Oneness shall again break up into the waves of individuation through the wind of ignorance which somehow or other begins to blow over the surface of the great Calm. With the appearance of the Many from the womb of the One shall come again all the anguish and suffering inherent in individual existence. Among these individual beings there shall arise again those who will attain perfect enlightenment, and who will show others how to return to the All from which they came. Beyond this Buddhist speculation does not feel called upon to go. And we, too, will stop at this point with this chapter, only reminding the reader once more that all that has been said by way of explaining Buddhist doctrines belongs to the realm of Accommodated Truth, and not Absolute Truth, and therefore must not be taken too literally or seriously.

CHAPTER VI

Buddhist Ethics

A. *General Aspects*

To discuss the ethics of Buddhism in a separate chapter may at first sight seem rather arbitrary, for the ethics of a religion would seem most naturally to belong to the very core of the religious life flowing from the fundamental doctrines. If we were dealing simply with primitive Buddhism, or with only certain phases of Mahāyāna Buddhism such a separation as we are making would be impossible, but as we are discussing primarily Japanese Buddhism the treatment is not only justifiable but essential, for in a peculiar way religion and ethics seem strangely divorced in this land.

The history of religion in all lands shows tendencies to divorce the ethical elements from the purely religious. There are various forms which this separation has taken, but three general types seem rather universal. Thus we have in the first place systems which may be regarded as ethical systems but which have no real religious basis. Confucianism and primitive Buddhism are the best examples of this type. In the second place there are systems which may be said to be truly religious systems but which have no vital ethics, *i.e.* they are ethic-less religions. Many of the animistic and polytheistic systems show this characteristic. Not, of course, that these are altogether without the ethical element, but that this is very insignificant. And in the third place, there are systems in which the religious elements and the distinctively ethical elements exist side by side without there being always a vital connection between the two, or even with a fundamental antagonism between the two; so that the ethical principles do not only fail to flow from the religious doctrines but are more or less in direct opposition to them. This type finds its best representative in Buddhism taken as a whole.

Even in the history of Christianity do we find evidence of these strange tendencies to separate the fundamental religious doctrines from the ethical principles, or at least to neglect one or the other aspect. Thus we have had periods when great emphasis was placed on certain fundamental doctrines without a corresponding emphasis on practical Christian ethics. And again there have been periods — and the present is such a one — when the emphasis was laid exclusively upon Christian ethics and the theology underlying it was regarded as suited only for a few impractical theologians. And in the third place, we see the spectacle of professing Christians being perfectly " orthodox " and scrupulously careful as to ritual and ceremony but regarding the Sermon on the Mount as a beautiful but impractical ideal.

But while the West is more or less familiar with the various tendencies to separate religion and ethics, it is in the Orient that we most commonly find the divorce of the two, and of all religions of the world no system shows the three types of separation mentioned above more markedly than does Buddhism in its various phases.

Primitive Buddhism, as we have said, shows the first type of separation; namely, the type which divorces religion from ethics by practically eliminating what to a Western mind, at least, would seem indispensable elements of religion. So much is this the case that some scholars have hesitated to call Gautama's system a religion at all, though later Buddhism no one would refuse to recognize as such. Of course, it is possible to use the term religion in such a broad sense that any attitude towards life may be called religious. Thus a Comte, after discarding religion as a phenomenon belonging to the primitive mind, advocates his own anti-religious system as the Religion of Humanity. Or again, we have in our own day materialists and atheists speaking of the Religion of

Science. In this broad sense Gautama's system was certainly a religion, and had even a better right to the title than these, for it had at least one of the cardinal elements of religion in that it had a doctrine of redemption. But if religion is essentially "a quest for the enrichment of life by establishing vital relationships with superhuman powers or persons (power or person)," then Gautama's system, with its indifference, if not opposition, to the God-idea, can hardly be called a real religion. Of course, as soon as Gautama himself was lifted into the place of a superhuman being, as happened rather early in Buddhist history, the essential elements of religion were present. But the system which he himself proclaimed may be said to be a practical ethical system which above everything else sought to make man independent of the gods and dependent solely upon himself. The Buddha did not seek to show men the vital relationships which may be established between them and the divine, but he wanted them to see the vital relationship which their present state sustains to their past deeds and which their present deeds will sustain to their future state.

But while primitive Buddhism was primarily a practical system of ethics growing out of a certain view of life; namely, the view of life summed up in the Four Noble Truths, we have even here a divorcement between this philosophy of life and some of the practical ethical teachings. The ethical teachings which have as their object the cutting of all the bonds which bind man to this life flow naturally from the view of life expressed in the Four Great Truths, but when ethical ideals center around the thought of self-discipline and self-culture, it is difficult to reconcile them with the doctrine of the non-reality of the self so important in primitive Buddhism. In short, then, many of the ethical principles even in primitive Buddhism were based upon what India had found to be practical for a moral life, but which in reality failed to grow out of the fundamental doctrines of Gautama's view of life and which were even in flat contradiction to it.

As we saw in Chapters I and II, it was not long before the fundamentals of religion which Gautama had practically ignored, found their way into Buddhism and so for the first time made it truly a religion in the generally accepted sense of the term. Unfortunately, however, the movement towards a real religion was accompanied by a movement which led away from the rather lofty ethical plain on which Gautama lived. It may almost be said that Buddhism developed from a religion-less ethic into an ethic-less religion. This may be stating the case too strongly, but it is certainly true that in spite of the change from the Arhat ideal to the more altruistic Bodhisattva ideal, the growing popularity of the old Indian deities and the deities absorbed by Buddhism as it marched triumphantly northward, somehow overshadowed the ethics of the Middle Path. That which Gautama had made central was relegated to a secondary place, and that which he had ignored or opposed as superstition was made central in the religious life of the average adherent. And thus it has remained down to the present day. So much is this the case in Japan that especially during the Meiji era religion was regarded as superstition and the real enemy of rational conduct.

It is true that, as intimated above, there was a nobler side to this development in Buddhism of the religious element which also brought with it lofty ethical ideals. Thus the self-centered ethics of the Arhat was augmented by the altruistic ethics of the Bodhisattva. The goal of ethical conduct was no longer so much the breaking of the bonds of existence, but rather the development of the self into the higher self. The Buddha was regarded as having had many incarnations, and as having finally prepared for man a way to this perfection. It became the ideal of some Buddhists to attain unto this perfection of character and to help others attain. That is, the ideal for self-discipline and self-culture and the desire to help others was an ethical ideal consistently flowing from the fundamental religious doctrines of later Buddhism. But when this later Buddhism sought at the same time to perpetuate the ethics of primitive Buddhism based upon a view of life which practically denied the reality of the self, we have again an example of ethical principles divorced from, and antagonistic to, the religious doctrines. This, however, is really an example of the third type of separation mentioned above; namely, the existence of religious and ethical elements side by side without there being a vital connection between the two.

But a better example of the third type is seen in Japanese Buddhism where we find various religious and ethical elements taken from widely separated sources existing side by side without there being a vital connection. It is this which accounts for the strange spectacle in the present educational system of the land which makes moral training the first subject in the curriculum and excludes religion not only from the course, but in many cases from the very school grounds. We do not mean to say that there are no ethical principles in Japanese Buddhism growing out of the fundamental philosophic doctrines, but that there are many which came from systems quite alien to Buddhism, and even antagonistic to its fundamental doctrines. Thus it is a common-place to say that, perhaps, the most vital elements in the practical ethics of Japanese Buddhism are taken from Confucianism, and it is an open secret that some of the progressive priests are not averse to vitalizing their moral instruction by an infusion from the ethics of Jesus. One frequently hears it said that as a philosophy Buddhism is more profound than Christianity, though the latter may be superior in its practical ethics. All of which goes to show how real is the divorcement of religion and ethics even in the minds of religious leaders. At any rate must it be admitted that they would regard the practical ethics of every-day life as belonging to the realm of Accommodated Truth, and therefore being purely relative.

Since Japanese Buddhism contains such a complex of philosophic doctrines and its ethical teachings are based only in part upon this complex and in part are taken from other sources, it becomes practically impossible to give a systematic presentation of the subject in hand. Even the barest outline of Buddhist ethics leads one to flatly contradictory positions, so that even a writer like Professor Anezaki has to say that "the moral and intellectual perfection of a personality, in spite of the doctrine of the non-ego, is the highest aim of Buddhist morality." How is it possible to say that "moral and intellectual perfection of personality" is the highest aim of a system when personality itself is said to have no real existence? It is possible only by admitting, as Professor Anezaki does admit, a flat contradiction between Buddhist ethics and one of its fundamental doctrines. The reader will, therefore, forgive us if in what follows, things do not always hang together, or if they appear contradictory.

To the extent to which Buddhist ethics is grounded in Buddhist doctrines, we might say that it has its basis and aim in the philosophy of the good. What is meant by "the Good" we have already discussed in the previous chapter under the head of the essence of salvation, and in what was said there about the essence of true enlightenment. All moral principles have as their criterion the essence of enlightenment; and since enlightenment is a matter of degrees, it follows that ethical principles are also matters of degree. There is no categorical right and wrong, but right and wrong are purely relative. The good varies with the true, and the true changes with the point of view, so that what is true and good for one being is not necessarily so for another. In the long scale of beings[1] into which Buddhism divides the world of phenomena, each being has its own laws and may appropriate the true and the good in its own way. Thus the standard of ethics is necessarily varied and relative. There is one standard only in the sense that all beings have the capacity for attaining Buddhahood, and will attain this if they obey the varying ethical principles as they advance from stage to stage.

In the beginning of the preceding chapter we gave, as the complete summary of all Buddhist teachings, the pregnant sentence, "Tenmei kaigo, Riku tokuraku, Shiaku shuzen," the last phrase of which presents the ethical side of the system; namely, "Ceasing from evil and doing good." When this thought is put by itself it reads, "Not to commit any

T

sin (evil), to do good, and to purify one's own mind; this is the teaching of all the Buddhas." To this general way of stating the core of all Buddhist ethics all Buddhists would agree, and even a Christian would have no objection to expressing his ethical ideal in such terms. But when it comes to defining more specifically what is meant by "sin" which is not to be committed, and the "good" which is to be done, then, of course, the differences begin to appear.

Roughly speaking, Buddhist ethics may be divided into two great types; namely, the older Hīnayāna type and the later Mahāyāna type. The two have very much in common in the ethical principles which pertain to man as a citizen of this world, but in so far as they pertain to man as a candidate for salvation out of this world the older type may be said to be less altruistic [2] than the later Mahāyāna ideal. It will be remembered that the Hīnayāna ideal of salvation was the Arhat, and the Arhat was above all else interested in his own salvation. He walked in the path of righteousness for his own sake; not so much for the positive good which he sought to achieve as for the sake of escaping from a positive evil. He perfected his personality in order to destroy the conditions of individuality and personality.

The hindrance to this goal of the ethical ideal of Hīnayāna Buddhism lies not so much in man's will as in man's mind. In order to overcome the obstacles in the path of righteousness the mind must be enlightened with the truth. This necessary truth is above all else the truth above the nature of existence, i.e. the nature of human life and the causes which have brought about man's present condition. Thus the beginning of all ethical conduct is correct knowledge. This knowledge is formulated first of all in the Four Noble Truths and the Noble Eightfold Path, and then in the various moral maxims suited for practical life. To be sure, the mere knowledge of the truth does not bring deliverance; man must walk by the knowledge he has received, for it is only in the union of theoretical knowledge and practical application of it to life that deliverance is found.

But what is it that gives man the motive power to walk in the way of truth as it is presented to the mind?

It is the truth itself which gives this motive power, for truth expels ignorance, and ignorance is the core of all sin. Hence to know the truth is to be free from sin and to do the good.

It is a question whether this is good psychology, and whether Buddhism does not give too much prominence to the intellectual aspect of the human personality and not enough to the aspect we call the Will. Of course, a knowledge of the truth is necessary as a step toward freedom from sin, but it does not always follow that to know the truth is to obey it. After all, there is that mysterious aspect of our personality called the Will which enables a man to choose as to whether he will obey the truth as he sees it, or not. It is true, as Buddhism says, that man is in ignorance and that ignorance is a source of sin, but sin is more than mere ignorance. It is not merely an intellectual mistake, but rather a rebellion of the will. In short, man is not simply a mind, but a personality. Personality has as its core the Will aspect as truly as the intellectual, and consequently abstract truth does not make a sufficiently strong appeal to enable man to forsake sin and do good, but the appeal must be made by a perfect personality. And here is exactly where the ethics of primitive Buddhism must inevitably break down. It can never consistently present the ethical appeal in the truth of a perfect personality, for it denies that personality is a permanent reality., It can therefore never have the drive of Christian ethics which is grounded in the perfect personality of God expressed in human terms in the historic perfect personality of Jesus Christ. It can never say to man "Be ye therefore perfect, even as your Father which is in heaven is perfect." The best it can say is, "Be ye perfect as S'akyamuni was perfect in order that ye may escape from the evils of life." The appeal which this older ethic makes is therefore more of an appeal of man's sense of fear. It is, "be good lest you suffer the consequences." This was a powerful appeal to a world-weary civilization, but it can never be as powerful as the appeal to a man's higher self which finds its ground in the thought that the universe has as its source the eternal Personal God and has as its goal the achievement of perfected personalities after the likeness of Christ Jesus. It is not strange therefore that even Buddhists admit that Christian ethics have a greater vitality and make a stronger appeal to the heart of man than Buddhism.

Now, the newer ethic of Mahāyāna Buddhism has a more positive goal than the older and it is also more altruistic in its tone. That is, it not only leads away from a positive evil but also to a positive good, and the good is both for the self and others. Its ideal is the Bodhisattva, and he is one who achieves perfection for himself, but refuses to enjoy the fruit of his labors to the full until he has helped others achieve the same benefit. In fact, the Bodhisattva is one who might say of himself, "For their sakes I sanctify myself, that they also might be sanctified through the truth." This type of ethic therefore makes a stronger appeal than the older type in that it directs itself to the higher self in man and centers more on what good he may achieve rather than on what evil he is to escape. The Mahāyāna ethic has, however, some of the weakness of the Hīnayāna in that it, too, makes the intellectual aspect of human nature central and does not give due recognition to the Will. Sin is also in this system primarily a matter of mere ignorance, and not the perversion of the entire personality. And further, while this ethic makes an appeal to the higher self, the philosophy on which it rests, after all, denies that personality is really permanent. The Bodhisattva may be personal as long as he chooses to be a Bodhisattva, but when he enters into the full Buddhahood he disappears as personal. And so it comes about that though the highest aim of Mahāyāna ethics may be "the moral and intellectual perfection of the personality," this end when achieved is really not permanent, but only a stepping into that which is neither personal nor impersonal. One might wonder why one should strive to achieve a perfect personality if the real goal is as truly the impersonal as the personal.

Approaching the subject of Buddhist ethics from the ecclesiastical standpoint, we may say that it again divides itself into two main branches; namely, the ethics for the layman and the ethics for the monk and priest. There is usually a double standard, that for the monk being higher than that for the layman and including it. Thus *e.g.* in the older Buddhist Ten Commandments the first five only are for the layman while the monk must observe the entire ten. In fact this is one of the outstanding characteristics of Buddhism — not only of its ethical teachings, but of all its teachings — that there is such a wide chasm between the layman and the priest. Not that the priest is actually so superior in holiness and learning to the layman, but that theoretically he is so. The lay Buddhist is supposed to go on in his life very much as he did before he became a Buddhist; practically nothing is required of him. But the monk and priest are expected to leave behind, not only the evil ways of this world, but also much of what is normal and good in human life. The very expression in Japanese for entering the monk's life indicates his break with the normal life. He is said to "forsake home" and to "ascend the mountain." (Most monasteries are in the mountains far removed from the world of men.) The monk alone is supposed to read and know the sacred scriptures, and with his advance in knowledge is supposed to come an advance in holiness. Only the Shin Sect has sought to spread "household religion," but even here the sect has not at all kept true to the high ideal of its founder. The writer is, of course, familiar with the fact that in Christianity, and in practically every religion, there have been these wide gaps between the layman's religion and the professional religionist's religion, but there is at least in Protestant Christianity an attempt to make the knowledge of the Lord cover the earth as the waters cover the sea, and to set up but one standard of conduct for layman and clergy; namely, the standard of perfect manhood revealed in Jesus Christ.

B. *The Vices and Virtues*

We must now leave the general characteristics of Buddhist ethics and come more specifically to the ethical teaching and moral maxims themselves. These will be seen to fall into two great groups; namely, teachings concerning the vices of life and teachings concerning the virtues of life. The contrast between ignorance and enlightenment which Buddhism makes in its fundamental doctrines is carried out in its ethical teachings by the contrast between the vices and virtues, for ignorance may be said to be the cardinal vice and wisdom the cardinal virtue. Buddhists are exceedingly fond, not only of classifying all ethical teachings under these two main heads, but of making lists upon lists of the various major and minor vices and virtues. This is often done in a rather mechanical way, and particularly do the methods of inculcating these ethical teachings frequently degenerate into a mere mechanical process which kills the real spirit of the teaching.

1. *The Vices of Life.* — The cardinal vice is the vice of egoism grounded in ignorance; or to put it the other way around, it is ignorance expressing itself in egoism. Egoism whose taproot is ignorance is the trunk from which grow all other vices, so that whatever may be the specific vice under consideration, it can always be traced back to a form of egoism, and this always grows out of ignorance; for in Buddhism all individual life is essentially nothing but the desire of Ignorance, or the expression of an unconscious desire — a blind "will-to-be."

This egoism manifests itself in three primary vices usually spoken of as the Three Poisons; namely, Lust, Anger and Folly. From these three main branches of the tree of vice come other smaller branches, twigs and leaves. The classifications which follow below overlap and are not always logical divisions. Thus we have a list of the Five Vices of Greed, Seeking for Pleasure, Hatred, Stupidity and Indifference. Following this may be given the Five Lusts of the Eye, Ear, Nose, Tongue and the Organs of Touch. The Five Hindrances are: Sensual Desire, Ill-will, Torpor of Mind or Body, Excitement and Vanity and Perplexity. The Seven Fetters are: Sensual Pleasures, Repugnance, Opinion, Perplexity, Pride, Attachment to Life and Ignorance. These Fetters are divided and subdivided until there are ten, sixteen, hundred and eight, etc. The Five Impurities are: Primary Impurity which gives rise to the following four; namely, Impurity of Doubt, Impurity of Passion, Impurity which weakens the body and Impurity which shortens life. The Five Crimes are: Patricide, Matricide, Killing a Saint, Disturbing the Peace of the Monks and Opposing the Buddha. The Seven Prides are: Pride towards Inferiors, Pride towards Equals, Pride towards Superiors, Pride of Self-confidence, Pride of Pretence, Pride of thinking oneself equal to one's peer and Pride of boasting to be able to do what one cannot do.

But the most widely known lists of vices and the warning against which may be said to form a real vital part of the practical ethical teachings of Japanese Buddhism for all classes of believers are the Ten Evils forbidden in the Ten Commandments. (These Ten Commandments differ somewhat from the Ten Commandments mentioned in Chapter I.) These Ten Evils, or Sins, are: Killing, Stealing, Committing Adultery, Lying, Exaggerating, Slandering, Being Double-tongued, Coveting, Being Angry and Being Heretical. These Ten Sins are divided into three groups. The first group consists of the first three and these sins are called Sins of the Body, or Evil Works. The second group is made up of numbers four to seven, and these are called Sins of the Mouth, or Evil Words. The third group is composed of numbers eight to ten and these are called Sins of the Mind, or Evil Desires.

It will be seen at a glance that many of the vices and sins given in these various lists are such as one would expect to find recognized by any advanced religion. And likewise would most advanced systems of ethics agree with Buddhism that the cardinal vice is a low, base egoism or selfishness. But when it is held that all sorts of egoism, even the egoism which seeks the development of the higher self, is a vice, then Christianity at least must part company with Buddhist ethics. And still further when it is held that all vice is mere ignorance and all sin is essentially nothing more than a "big mistake," Christianity again must part company, for it must ever be more accurate in its psychology and treat sin as not simply a matter of the intellectual aspect of the human personality, but also as a matter of the will and the affections; in short, as a marring of the entire personality.

2. *The Virtues of Life.* — Let us next consider very briefly the virtues of life which Buddhism seeks to inculcate. If egoism rooted in ignorance is the cardinal vice, then the suppression of this egoism through knowledge is the cardinal virtue. That is, all virtue is rooted in right thinking. Thus Buddhists regard mental discipline rather than a discipline of the will as a thing of first importance, and among the primary virtues methods of mental discipline occupy a prominent place.

But if the suppression of egoism is the primary virtue, a question arises as to whether this means the suppression of a lower egoism by the self-assertion of a higher and nobler egoism or does it mean the suppression of all egoism or self-assertion? Or to put it in another form: Is enlightenment positive knowledge or simply a "breaking of error"? Some Buddhists hold — and it would seem that to be consistent with Buddhist psychology a Buddhist must hold — that it means the latter, and that virtue is not a positive goodness but simply the absence of a positive evil. This is why most of the teachings of Buddhism are cast in a negative mold. The Ten Commandments of Buddhism are ten prohibitions, ten "Don'ts." Keeping these ten negative commandments constitutes the Ten Virtues which the average Buddhist is supposed to cultivate just as breaking them is to commit the Ten Vices mentioned above. The Ten Virtues, then, are the following: Not to Kill, Not to Steal, Not to Commit Adultery, Not to Lie, Not to Exaggerate, Not to Slander, Not to be Double-tongued, Not to Covet, Not to be Angry and Not to be Heretical. Thus, as we have said, at least according to the form in which these virtues are stated, they seem to be negative virtues, or merely the suppression of vices.

But while Buddhist ethics makes more of the suppression of vices than of the inculcation of positive virtues, there is, after all, a good deal in Buddhist ethics which is built up on the conception that virtue is the expression of the higher and nobler ego. That is, not only are the vices of a low egoism to be suppressed, but a higher self expresses itself in this suppression and goes beyond this in exerting itself in positive virtues. For example, man is not only to suppress his feeling of anger and hatred towards his fellow-man, but his heart should go out to him in sympathy and love. Even in the older Buddhism, which made the denial of the reality of the self a cardinal doctrine, one finds ethical principles based upon the conception that "the intellectual and moral perfection of the personality" is the highest aim of ethics. Thus the Noble Eightfold Path itself is a path of rather positive virtues and more than a mere suppression of vices.

In enumerating the main positive virtues one must begin with the virtues of walking in the Noble Eightfold Path, *i.e.* the virtues of Right Opinion, Right Decision, Right Speech, Right Action, Right Livelihood, Right Effort, Right Mindfulness and Right Contemplation.[3]

When the virtues are thought of in terms of psychological faculties, Buddhists speak of them as Organs, and of these they usually distinguish five; namely, Faith, Exertion, Mindfulness, Contemplation and Wisdom. Three of these are regarded as cardinal virtues and are included in every list. These three are Faith, Exertion and Wisdom; the greatest of these is Faith according to some, and Wisdom according to others. Other virtues emphasized in Buddhist ethics are the following: A Sense of Shame, Conscientiousness, Clear Conscience, Thoughtfulness, Sympathy, Gentleness, Kindness, Mercy, Pity and Benevolence; the latter being divided into the Four Benevolences directed respectively towards parents, people in general, the ruler, and the Three Treasures (*i.e.* Buddha, the Law and the Priesthood).

Of these major virtues Buddhism has been especially successful in inculcating widely the virtues of Gentleness, Pity and Sympathy. It is not strange that this is so, for especially the virtues of Pity and Sympathy for others grow directly out of the Buddhist view as to the nature of human life. Life is suffering, and sympathy (suffering with) becomes a natural attitude of mind and heart. The German words "Leid" and "Mitleid" express the relationship in a nutshell. *Das Leben ist Leid und darum ist die höchste Tugend Mitleid.* To be sure, the Buddhist conception of Pity and Sympathy lacks something of the positive element which we find in the Christian conception of Love, for it lacks the underlying conviction of the eternal value of human life. Human life seems very cheap in Buddhist lands and especially does the life of the masses seem but as the foam on a turbulent sea. But still Buddhism has done much to promote the feeling of the solidarity of the human race. Humanity is a great brotherhood of suffering, yea, even the dumb animals are our fellow-sufferers and bound to us by the strong links of the Karma-chain. Who knows but that the ox which draws the driver's heavy load is the great ances- tor of the driver, appearing in the form of an ox in obedience to the law of Karma. Shall not, then, the driver be kind to his beast?

Thus far we have spoken of what might be regarded as rather ordinary virtues. There are higher virtues which are practiced by those who are really seriously bent upon attaining Buddhahood. These are the so-called Perfections. The full list are ten[4] in number; namely, Charity, Morality, Resignation, Wisdom, Exertion or Diligence, Forbearance, Truthfulness, Persistency, Love and Equanimity. Ordi- narily Japanese Buddhism reduces these to six; namely, Charity (almsgiving and teaching), Morality (keeping the various commandments), Patience and Forbearance, Exer- tion or Diligence (in keeping the vows of a Bodhisattva), Meditation and Wisdom (for self and others).

These virtues were originally regarded as the special virtues of the few rare souls who sought to be Bodhisattvas and finally Buddhas, but in Mahāyāna Buddhism it is theoretically the purpose of every believer to become a Bodhisattva and Buddha, and so these virtues are theoreti- cally virtues which every believer should practice. But as a matter of fact, in practice, Mahāyāna Buddhism makes as truly a distinction between the ordinary believer and the candidate for Buddhahood as the older Buddhism ever did, and these Six Perfections are therefore not a very vital part of the ethics of the average Buddhist. In fact, a great many Mahāyāna Buddhists hold that these difficult steps towards perfection are not necessary as they have been taken by the various Bodhisattvas whose accumulated merits the believer may appropriate unto his own benefit by the simple act of faith. So it comes back to this, that for the common man at least, the only necessary virtue is the virtue of faith in the holiness and all-sufficient merit of the saints and Buddhas who have gone before. That is why the great formula of faith for every Buddhist is the confession, "I take refuge in the Buddha, I take refuge in the Law, I take refuge in the Priesthood." Even the sects which make the doctrine of "Save thyself" their cardinal teaching, combine with this severe injunction the comfort that somehow the goodness of the good and the wisdom of the wise who have gone before will help those who put their trust in them.

The above may be enough to give the reader a general idea of Buddhist ethics, but it is too much like a skeleton without flesh and blood. We therefore give below extracts from the sacred scriptures which set forth succinctly the ethical ideals. The reader should not think, however, that the Buddhist scriptures always maintain this rather lofty level. The extracts are choice bits, "golden words" as the Japanese compiler calls them, or "Buddhist Gold Nuggets" as we have called them in the "Transactions of the Asiatic Society of Japan," Vol. XL, from which they are taken.

C. *Buddhist Gold Nuggets*

Commit no evil, do good and purify your own **General** heart; this is the teaching of all the Buddhas. (Nehankyō)

Hate not, quarrel not, abuse no one; these are the teachings of Buddhism. (Hōzōkyō)

Fear Evil

Do not make light of little evils, thinking them harmless; for even drops of water, small as they are, will at length fill a large vessel. (Nehankyō)

Evils are born of the heart, and reacting upon it destroy it; just like rust is born of the iron which it consumes. (Hainiku)

Rather thrust a dagger into your bosom than embrace evil; and it is more desirable to be crushed under the weight of Mt. Sumēru than to commit one evil deed. (Ninnikukyō)

Do Good

Peace of mind and understanding the Way are both born of goodness. Goodness is a great armor which fears no weapon. (Ananfumbetsukyō)

A good man does good deeds and he passes from bliss unto bliss, from light into light; but an evil man does evil deeds and he goes from affliction unto affliction, from darkness into darkness. (Muryōjukyō)

Err not in Your Heart

Buddha said to Shamon, "Beware of trusting your own heart; for the heart, after all, is unreliable." (Shijunishōkyō)

Be the master of your own heart, and do not let it master you. (Nehankyō)

The heart is the source of great disasters; keep, then, this heart under control. (Hōunkyō)

Make Upright Your Heart

Stand resolute, keep your body erect and your conduct upright. Do every good, keep yourself under control and your body pure. Wash the filth from your heart, and make your words and conduct harmonize. Be sincere, frank and temperate, helping one another and praying with understanding. In this way you shall be able to heap up virtue. (Muryōjukyō)

I am not ashamed when I sit among men, and the reason I am held in esteem by them is because my heart is pure and upright. (Shōgyōkyō)

Buddha said, "O Monks, the heart that flatters

cannot conform unto the Way; therefore make your heart sincere. Moreover know this that flattery only works deception, and he who walks in the Way has nothing to do with it. Make, then, your heart upright and let integrity be your guiding principle. (Yuigyōkyō)

First examine yourself and then others; first **Examine** examine your own will and then the will of others; **Yourself** first examine your own principles and then the principles of others. (Chūshinkyō)

Man usually fails to curb his own will and yet he tries to conquer the will of others. First therefore curb your own will and then shall you be able to control the will of others. (Sanekyō)

The Bodhisattva knows nothing but his own heart. And why is this? Because he who knows his own heart knows the heart of all beings, and he whose heart is pure, to him the heart of every being is pure. (Daisogonhōmonkyō)

Buddha said, "O my Disciples, refrain from **Guard** meaningless words, be always on guard as to **Your** what you say, know when to speak and when to **Speech** keep quiet, let your words conform unto the Law, and let your words always be edifying unto others even when making a joke. (Kegonkyō)

Men of this world are prone to use their tongue like a sharp knife; with their mouth they speak glibly about various poisons and evils, while it is the tongue itself that really poisons the body. (Chōseinponkyō)

Men who speak true words gain a boundless fortune; not through the gifts they may receive, nor through their ascetic practices or profound learning, but solely by being truthful. (Chidoron)

Do not use many words and put a watch upon your lips that you use no violent language, for this is what is meant by True Words. (Daishūkyō)

Foolish utterances are the affliction of all mankind, and they live in darkness. Life they have but it is like unto death. (Shōhō-nenjokyō)

Be Patient   Patience is the source of all happiness. (Rokudoshūkyō)

The happiness born of patience brings peace, prosperity and endless joy. (Ninnikukyō)

If one tries to end strife by strife, there will be strife forever. Forbearance alone can end strife, and this is truly a precious law. (Chūa-gonkyō)

Nothing is so strong as patience; and where patience dwells malice takes flight. (Shijuni-shōkyō)

Patience is the real cause which brings true deliverance. The understanding of the ultimate rightness and equality of things is but the fruit of patience. (Ubasokukaikyō)

Be Diligent   O Monks, be diligent in your work and then nothing will be difficult. Wherefore, O Monks, consecrate yourselves earnestly to your work; for even little drops of water, falling ceaselessly, will finally make a hole even in a rock. (Yui-gyōkyō)

It is not necessary to wait several Kalpas to obtain the reward; the greater the consecration the sooner the reward. (Kegonkyō)

Negli-gence   Negligence is the enemy of all discipline. In the case of laymen negligence leads to want, and industry lags because of it. With monks negligence hinders the work of deliverance from suffering and blocks the entrance to the Way. (Hon-gyōkyō)

Licen-tiousness   Licentiousness is the fountainhead of all evil; sobriety, the source of all good. (Nehankyō)

Licentiousness stands foremost in the rank of sins. (Shōhōnenjokyō)

Licentiousness is the taproot of all suffering and sorrow; if, then, you desire to escape from suffering, fling away licentiousness. (Shōhōnenjokyō)

O my Disciples, flee from fornication, know how to be content with your own wife, and do not even for a single moment lust after another woman. (Kegonkyō) **Guard Chastity**

Fornication is an act of impurity. He who falls into this temptation loses the straight Way, ruins his own life and early ends in the grave. His sin will lead to obstinacy and stupidity, and in the next world he will be doomed to the evil way. Wherefore be careful that you do not get entangled in sensuality. (Hasshikyō)

Buddha said, "Sell not your love for gain, O Men and Women, for this cannot lead to a righteous life. (Bonmōkyō)

A sense of shame is a garment for all goodness. (Daiunkyō) **Have a Sense of Shame**

If the dirt and filth (of the heart) is washed off with tears of penitence, both body and soul will become vessels of cleanliness and purity. (Shinji-kankyō)

He who has a feeling of shame and humiliation shall have his sins wiped out and he shall become as clean and pure as before. (Nehankyō)

There are two wonderful laws in the world which shield man; namely, the feeling of shame and the feeling of humiliation. Without these two laws mankind would be on a level with the beasts, whether one is a father or mother, older or younger brother, wife or child, wise man or teacher, great or small. (Zōichiagonkyō)

Honesty is the Paradise of the Bodhisattva. (Yuimakyō) **Be Honest**

The Way is born of the heart; if the heart is upright, the Way will be open. (Butsuhatsu-hannehankyō)

O Disciples, shun every kind of theft, know that you shall not lack any of the necessities of life; and take nothing which belongs to others unless it is given to you. (Kegonkyō)

The Nyōrais of the Ten Regions pass through life and death by the one road of honesty. (Engakukyō)

Be Not Drunk with Wine Wine is the source of vice and all evils. He who avoids wine shall be saved from many a sin. (Nehankyō)

He who henceforth makes me his master must avoid tasting even so small a drop of wine as the dewdrop falling from a blade of grass. (Shiburitsu)

Know How to be Content He who does not know how to be content with what he has is poor however rich he may be; but he who has learned to be content is rich even though he may have very little. (Yuigyōkyō)

Buddha said, "O Monks, excessive wants are the seat of suffering; and the labor and weariness of this world of Life and Death arise from covetousness. Remember that he who wants little and so is above the concerns of this life is perfectly free both as to body and mind. (Hachidaininkakukyō)

Contentment is the domain of wealth and pleasure, of peace and rest. The contented man is happy and at peace even though his bed is the bare ground; while the man who knows not the secret of being content is not satisfied even when dwelling in heavenly places. (Yuigyōkyō)

Cultivate Wisdom Wisdom is the strong ship which carries us across the sea of life and death. It is the lighthouse which lights up the encircling darkness; it is the good medicine for all patients, and the sharp ax which cuts down the trees of passion. (Yuigyōkyō)

The advent of truth and wisdom is like the sunrise which drives away darkness, no one knows whence. (Ajaseiōkyō)

Even if one commits a serious crime, its traces **Repent** will be wiped out if one repents. If one repents daily with all one's might, the root of sin will forever be torn out. (Zōichiagonkyō)

A man may commit a grave sin, but if he takes himself seriously in hand and truly repents so that he desires to sin no more, the effects of his sin shall be eradicated. (Gōho)

If you would repent, call upon all the Buddhas of the universe, read the scriptures, make vows with a sincere heart, and seek to destroy every evil deed of body and soul; for thus shall your sins be blotted out moment by moment. (Kanfugenkyō)

Gratitude is the foundation of great mercy and **Know How** the door which leads to good deeds. A grateful **to be** **Thankful** man is beloved and esteemed by men, his name will be made famous, after death he will be born into heaven and at last he will be perfect in the ways of Buddha. An ungrateful man is even lower than the brutes. (Chidoron)

A state without a ruler is like a body without **Be Loyal** a head; it cannot exist very long. (Bussetsu- **to Your** jiaikyō) **Lord**

Prosperity and happiness of the people depend upon the king. (Shinjikankyō)

The king looks upon his subjects with a heart of mercy as if they were his children; and the people regard the king as their father. (Skōgunōshomonkyō)

Great and wide are the mercy and virtue of a righteous king. He who knows no gratitude towards the king shall suffer for it. (Shinjikankyō)

When you see the king, entertain a feeling of

U

reverence in your mind; and when you are in the presence of your parents, show affection. (Myōhōshōnenjokyō)

Obey Your Parents Nothing is greater than filial piety, for it is the culmination of virtue. The culmination of all wickedness is ungratefulness to parents. (Ninnikukyō)

A devotional service to parents is more noble than giving alms, even though the pile of treasure disbursed should reach from the earth into the twenty-eighth heaven. (Matsuramatsukyō)

Filial piety is more noble than devotion to the spirits and gods that inhabit heaven and earth; for parents are indeed the highest gods. (Shijūnishōkyō)

If there is no Buddha in the world, be good to your parents; for to be good to one's parents is to minister unto Buddha. (Daishūkyō)

Food, drink and treasures are not sufficient to express one's gratitude for the love of parents; the best expression is shown by turning them to the right doctrine through Indō (saying mass for the spirits of ancestors and so guiding them on the Way). (Fushigikōkyō)

Duties of Parents The duties of parents towards their children are five, namely: To see to it that they shun all evil and do good, to teach them how to read and write, to teach them to observe the doctrines and commandments (of Buddhism), to see to it that they get married, and to pass on to them the property of the family. (Ropporaikyō)

Relation of Master and Disciple The disciple, in following his master, should be careful not to tread upon his master's shadow. (Shamiigikyō)

He who knows gratitude towards his teacher pays heed to the teacher's words when he is in his presence; and in his teacher's absence he meditates upon his teachings. (Chūshingyō)

There are five things which a disciple observes
in his devotion to his teacher: He supplies his
wants, does him homage and bestows upon him a
devotional service, honors and reveres him, gives
implicit and respectful obedience to his com-
mands, gives heed to his instruction in the Law
and observes the teaching, never forgetting it.
(Chōagonkyō)

The teacher should observe the following five
rules towards his disciple: He should train him
in accordance with the teachings of the Law,
teach what his disciple has not yet learned,
make him appreciate the moral value of the
doctrines, choose good friends for him, and
give him his best and fullest knowledge. (Chōagonkyō)

Honor the Wise and Holy

The virtuous man should be regarded as a
Buddha. (Kikkyōkyō)

Be not haughty in the presence of a wise man,
nor slander the good man. (Kikkyōkyō)

For an evil man to slander a wise man is like
spitting at the heavens; the spit will never reach
the heavens but only fall on the face of the spitter.
And again, it is like throwing dust against the
wind which ends in being blown against the one
who tries it. He who reviles the wise only brings
calamity upon himself. (Skijūnishōkyō)

Choose Your Friends

If a man has wise and good men for friends, his
heart and body will be made clean both inwardly
and outwardly. Such men are the really true
and good men. (Daisōgonkyōron)

Wise men are the source of all bliss; in this
world they help us escape from the prisons of
kings, and after death they protect us from the
gates of the Three Infernal Regions. Thus our
ascending into heaven and our entering upon the
Way are made possible through the help of good
friends. (Tanyokyō)

Rules of Friendship   There are three rules which a friend should ✓ observe towards a friend, namely: He should admonish him when at fault, cherish with a deep joy whatever good there is in him, stand by him in time of trouble. (Ingwakyō)

A friend should not be forsaken simply on the strength of some other person's evil report. If you hear your friend evilly spoken of, be all the more careful to find out the truth in the matter. (Komponbinakyō)

The Family   Let father and son, brother and sister, husband and wife, all the members of the family and all relatives love and respect each other; and never let them entertain a feeling of bitterness and hatred. Those who have great possessions should not be avaricious towards those who have little. Word and conduct should harmonize, and all inconsistency in dealing with one another should be avoided. (Muryōjukyō)

If all are faithful, there will be peace in the home, and fortune will smile upon the family naturally and without there being any need to have it bestowed by the gods. (Ananfumbe-tsukyō)

Duties of Husbands and Wives   A husband should support and please his wife by observing the following five points: He should respect her with a sincere heart, never bear any ill-will against her, love her with a pure affection, give her whatever food and clothing she may need, and from time to time present her with gifts to adorn her person. (Zenshoshikyō)

A good wife spares not her own life, and under no circumstances does she do anything contrary to her husband's will. (Zōichiagonkyō)

Only a chaste, wise and clever wife is fit to bring up children; and children who have such a mother cannot fail to become men and women of great character. (Zōichiagonkyō)

All the doctrines of Buddhism are grounded **Mercy** in mercy. (Kegonkyō)

Every virtue has mercy as its root. (Nehankyō)

The heart of mercy is the primary and secondary cause of all peace and pleasure. (Ubasonkukaikyō)

He who shows pity towards a beggar opens the prison gates of Hungry Spirits. (Bosatsuhongyōkyō)

He who gives alms shall receive a blessing; he who shows mercy shall never be hated; he who does good destroys evil; and he who conquers evil desires shall be free from all trouble. (Chōagonkyō)

He who gives alms with a view of obtaining birth into heaven, or does it in order to make a name for himself and receive a reward in return, or again is kind, being prompted only by a feeling of fear, shall in no way obtain the pure fruit. (Fumbetsugōhōkyō)

He who walks in the way of benevolence and **Love All** shows mercy, loving all and saving many, shall obtain the Eleven Blessings and shall always be attended by fortune. These Eleven Blessings are: A restful sleep, peace when awake, without bad dreams, protected by Heaven, beloved by men, immune to poison, not in danger of water, not in danger of fire, always prosperous, and after death birth into Heaven. (Hōkukyō)

Do nothing unto others which you would not have done unto yourself. (Gokushōkukyō)

Nothing lives that does not fear the sword and rod, and that does not love life. Therefore treat others as you would yourself. Do not kill or wield the big stick. (Nehankyō)

To spare not yourself in saving others is the noblest. The second grade of nobility is to save others and yourself. The third grade in point of nobility is to save yourself when you cannot save others; and the lowest is to save neither yourself nor others. (Hōshakukyō)

Men Should Always Pray

He who with a steady heart raises his voice and without ceasing prays the prayer, Namu Amida Butsu, "I adore Thee Thou Buddha of Boundless Light and Life," shall be free from his sins committed during eighty Kalpas of Life and Death and he shall obtain birth into Paradise. (Kwammuryōjukyō)

CHAPTER VII

THE PLACE OF BUDDHISM IN JAPANESE LIFE — PAST, PRESENT AND FUTURE

A. *The Influence in the Past*

AN interesting but exceedingly difficult problem is the one as to what place Buddhism has had in the life of the Japanese people. The answer to this question is peculiarly difficult because Buddhism is not and has not been the sole religion of Japan, but during the greater part of its long history in this land it has been closely bound up with Shintō and Confucianism; so that even to-day, though it is officially separated from Shintō, a great many Japanese are Shintōists, Confucianists and Buddhists at one and the same time. Some writers speak of Shintō as the root, Confucianism as the branches and leaves, and Buddhism as the flowers and fruit of the tree of Japanese civilization. This conception is not altogether wrong, for it is true that historically Shintō comes first, and that in organizing legal and educational institutions Confucianism has played a prominent part, and that finally the chief contribution of Buddhism lies in the realm of art, philosophy and religion. But since art, philosophy and religion are not only the flower and fruit of a civilization but also in turn become the root and branches of the succeeding stages, Buddhism from the ninth century on has been a real part of the roots, branches, leaves, flowers and fruit of the Japanese tree of life. That is, its influence has been so profound that there is no aspect of Japanese life which has not been greatly modified by it. This influence cannot be measured by enumerating simply the major points, though this is all that we can do here, but so far-reaching has it been that one can see it also in countless minor ways which apparently have little to do with religion as such.

Among the major contributions which Buddhism made to Japanese life we must place first and foremost the fact that it has been a vehicle of the higher civilization of the continent. This was true not only during its beginnings in this land when it so obviously was the means of bringing in the wealth of Korean and Chinese culture, but down to the Tokugawa period the Buddhist monks and priests continued to be the chief means by which Japan kept in touch with the rest of the world. The point cannot be overstated, for just as truly as Christian missionaries from Europe and America have been the apostles of a superior civilization to the backward nations of the world, so have the Buddhists often been to Japan the messengers of progress and light. In a real sense has Buddhism been the "Light of Asia," and perhaps no part of Asia has received as much through it as has Japan. In saying this we do not wish to imply that Japan would have remained in darkness if it had not been for the religion of the Buddha. It is naturally impossible to say just what would have taken its place. Perhaps Shintō, though a very primitive religion, would have developed into a higher, and on the whole, a more satisfactory religion. Nor do we wish to imply that Buddhism is not to-day an actual hindrance to the coming of the "Greater Light," the "Light of the World." But the history of Japan having been what it was, it is correct to say that Buddhism has been a determining factor, and that the sources of Japanese culture have been either directly or indirectly mainly Buddhist.

As Buddhism was both a vehicle of a higher civilization and itself the expression of such a civilization naturally its influence on the intellectual life of the nation was incalculable. Shintō was the religion of an immature people, Buddhism a philosophy of life as worked out by a profoundly meditative and speculative India. Thus the first really deep-going influence which Buddhism exerted upon Japan was that it led the people to think more profoundly upon the problems of human life. This intellectual stimulus extended in all directions. First of all it affected the native religion, and Shintō was raised from a jumble of contradictory legends and myths into what was at least the semblance of a reasoned philosophy of life. The various legends were systematized and built up into a more or less connected whole. The Japanese began to work out a connected account of the past and wrote the first history of their race. It is true that the Kojiki and Nihongi are not real histories, but they are attempts to weld together in some way the traditions of the past into a historic narrative. Then further, this intellectual stimulus soon showed itself in its effect upon the language. With the coming of Buddhism the Japanese language was raised into a real medium of education and culture. A very large per cent of the present vocabulary came either directly from Buddhism or was added from the Chinese to give an adequate expression of the new ideas which came in the train of the new religion. The spread of the art of reading and writing, and thus education in general, was largely due to the influence of the Buddhists. Buddhism taught Japan the elements of logic, psychology, natural sciences as then known in India and China and the subtleties of philosophy and metaphysical speculations. The first sects introduced laid special stress on dialectics and psychological analysis, and this certainly had a great deal to do with sharpening the intellectual powers of the people. And what was true in the early days remained true for centuries; namely, that whatever the Japanese knew of philosophy and science they owed largely to Buddhism. This intellectual development accounts for the fact that when Western culture came to Japan in the modern period the Japanese were able to assimilate it in such a surprisingly short time, and that to-day there are Japanese scholars in every field of learning who can hold their own with the scholars of any nation. In short, Japan has been a cultured nation for centuries and she owes to Buddhism a great debt for the major part of this culture.

Now this spread of general culture and this development of the intellectual powers of the people naturally had a profound effect on every phase of life. Thus *e.g.*, in the political world it helped create a new Japan. When Buddhism reached these shores, as we saw in Chapter III, Japan was not yet a real nation. It was rather a land inhabited by various tribes with the tribe in the Kyōtō-Osaka region gradually gaining the ascendancy. Buddhism enlarged the horizon of the people with its constant emphasis on universals, so that the tribe-idea naturally had to give way to the national ideal. It is true, as we said above, that the organization of the political institutions came from Confucianism, but it came largely through the Buddhist missionaries and educators. And again it is true that Shintō has been the political weapon through which patriotism was cultivated and the various tribes subdued and unified, but, after all, it was a Shintō profoundly modified by Buddhism, and it was the Buddhist philosopher who laid the real foundations of the Japanese state by inspiring the early historians to build up the myths and legends of prehistoric times into a more or less concatenated whole. Even to this day the Japanese state has for one of its main pillars the legendary history of the Kojiki and Nihongi which, in an indirect way at least, owe their very existence to the impact of Buddhist culture upon early Japan. Then further, the part which Buddhist monks and priests played in the actual political development of the nation through the centuries is beyond measure. It is true that this was far from being a noble part in all cases. In fact there were times when the rulers of the nation were little more than mere puppets of ambitious priests who shielded themselves behind the sacred mantle or the hallowed walls of a powerful monastery. What we wish to point out, however, is that whether for good or evil the part which Buddhism has played in the political life of Japan has been not only an indirect influence but often a very direct and decisive one.

But not to claim for Buddhism too much either of good or evil in a field usually claimed for Shintō and Confucianism,

let us come to the sphere in which the influence of this religion is self-evident, we mean the field of art, philosophy
and religion.

In the field of art it is more correct to say that Buddhism
created certain branches of Japanese art than simply that
it influenced them.   Thus Japanese architecture, sculpture
and painting are what they are because Buddhism has made
them so.   Music and poetry have also been influenced,
though perhaps to a lesser degree.

If in the field of architecture we were to remove from
these pine-clad hills and valleys the Buddhist temples, monasteries and flights of stone steps leading up to them, very
little of grandeur or beauty would remain.   The average
Japanese house seems to be a development of the primeval
hut and as a work of architecture it cannot claim a very
high place.   What makes it attractive is not any architectural feature but rather the cleanliness, neatness and
simplicity of the interior; or it may be its picturesque environment.   The Shintō shrine, too, cannot be said to rank
very high, though the shrine entrance, the Torii, may be
regarded as a real work of art.   But it is really only when
we come to Buddhist buildings that Japanese architecture
can make any claims.   We are not saying that these measure
up to the architectural monuments of the West, but only
that whatever there is in Japan that merits any attention
along this line belongs to Buddhism.

In the field of sculpture Japan is relatively much richer,
and this is almost purely the product of Buddhism.   What
existed of this art before the introduction of Buddhism may
be classed with the crude clay figures produced by most
primitive peoples.   It is surprising in what a short time really
world masterpieces in bronze, clay and wood were produced.
As we saw in Chapter III, within a hundred years after
Buddhism had reached these shores, the Buddhist sculptors
were doing wonders.   The world's largest bronze statue
belongs to Japanese Buddhism of the eighth century.   It is
true that this does not rank so very high as a work of art,
but there are many smaller relics of that period which do

rank high. And not only during that first period did the Buddhist sculptor carve his ideals in wood and bronze, but all down through the centuries he dominated this art. The thousands and tens of thousands of images and statues which are to be found in temples, temple grounds, along the highways and byways, in cities, towns and villages, in valleys, on hills, mountain sides and mountain peaks, — all these are the handiwork of the Buddhist artists. And not only is the Buddhist pilgrim surrounded on his journey through life by the symbols of the things invisible, but when he is dead and buried Buddhist art in stone and bronze marks his resting place and "implores the passing tribute of a sigh."

And if Buddhist ideals have guided the chisel and the knife, they have also inspired the pencil and the brush. Here the influence, though perhaps less evident to the casual student, is equally striking. In a land of such natural beauty as Japan one would naturally expect the painter to be inspired largely by his wonderful environment, but instead of that, practically all the older schools of painters were inspired by Indian and Chinese masterpieces introduced by Buddhism. Thus one student of the subject says that "it may safely be asserted that not one in twenty of the productions of these painters, who to the present day are considered to represent the true genius of Japanese art, was inspired by the works of nature as seen in their own beautiful country." In fact the very neglect of perspective in landscape paintings and the "impossible mountains" in these are well-known characteristics. It may be that the very exquisiteness of the scenery in Japan has made the artist despair of ever producing it on canvas, and so instead he seeks only to suggest it, leaving everything but a few bold strokes marking the outline to be supplied by the imagination. The oldest Japanese painting, dating as it is believed from the seventh century, is a mural decoration in Hōryūji, a Buddhist temple near Nara. Practically all the leading schools down to the present day had their birth in a Buddhist atmosphere. Thus the great painters, Chō Densu and Jōsetsu, the most famous names in the most glorious period of Japanese painting, were Buddhist priests. The great men who succeeded them and founded independent schools, all kept true to the old traditions and preferred the models introduced from China by the Buddhist monks from century to century to the infinitely more perfect models which nature itself supplies to every artist in Japan. Thus while Buddhism has created and nurtured the art of painting in Japan, it may also be said to have hindered the highest development in that it has imposed a slavish adherence to classic Buddhist models, and only occasionally have artists been able to break away from this tyranny, and paint as they really saw with their own eyes.

The influence of Buddhism on music, the most subtle of the arts, it would be difficult for any one not a real student of oriental music to estimate. And for a Westerner the subject is practically impossible, for there is nothing among things oriental which seems more weird. It takes years for one whose ears are attuned to the harmonies of our Western masters to be willing to admit that Japan has anything worthy of the name. It often seems more like the twang of loosely strung chords terribly out of tune. One of the best authorities on the subject of the scale in Japanese music says that it consists "of five notes of the harmonic minor scale, the fourth and the seventh being omitted, because, as there are five recognized colors, five planets, five elements, five viscera and so on, there must also be five notes in music." Being written in the minor key its dominant note is that of melancholy and despair, and not that of joy and victory. Because of this, Japanese music, whether influenced by Buddhism or not, is after all a real expression of that pessimistic philosophy of life of which Buddhism is the best formulation. As one's understanding of this philosophy of life grows, one's ears also become more sympathetic with the music of it, and especially do one's ears respond to the one distinctively Buddhist instrument of Japan, namely, to the rich, mellow tones of the temple bell. In the words of Captain Brinkley, "The suspended bell of

Japan gives forth a voice of the most exquisite sweetness and harmony — a voice that enhances the lovely landscapes and seascapes, across which the sweet solemn notes come floating on Autumn evenings, and in the stillness of Summer's noonday hazes. The song of the bell can never be forgotten by those that have once heard it. Their notes seem to have been born amid the eternal restfulness of the Buddhist paradise, and to have gathered, on their way to human ears, echoes of the sadness that prepares the soul for Nirvāna."

Japanese poetry, to continue the Hegelian order of the arts, also shows the influence of Buddhism. It may be difficult to prove that the form of poetry has been much influenced but its contents reflects every aspect of Buddhist thoughts and ideals. This is peculiarly true of the short stanzas called Tanka, consisting of not more than five lines and thirty-one syllables, and still more of the Hokku, consisting of only seventeen syllables. These short poems are really more like epigrams and so are apt vehicles of sentiments too deep for thought, or ideals too lofty for many words. The favorite subject matter of these short poems are "the flowers, the birds, the snow, the moon, the falling leaves in autumn, the mist on the mountains . . . and the shortness of human life," but the point of view from which these are treated is usually the Buddhist. Thus the favorite cherry blossom is the symbol of the brave knight who does not cleave selfishly to this life; the moon is the symbol of the change to which all things are subject, the falling leaves in Autumn point the way of all life, and the shortness of human life is, of course, an ever-recurrent note in Buddhism; and the short stanza is especially well suited to give expression to a sigh over life's fleetingness. Even the subject of love is dealt with in Japanese poetry from the standpoint of the Buddhist doctrine of Karma. Thus lovers imagine themselves to be destined for each other because in their Karma preëxistence they had loved; and the conjoint suicides so popular in this land are often inspired by the thought that the law of Karma will bring the lovers together in a future existence under more favorable conditions than the present.

Then a form of poetry which is distinctively Buddhist is the Wasan or Buddhist hymn. Though the Wasan is not ordinarily ranked very high as literature, occasionally these hymns rise to high levels and compare not unfavorably with our Christian hymns and songs.

But if the influence of Buddhism on Japanese life has been strong in the field of art, it has been perhaps even greater in the realm of philosophy and religion. It is true, of course, that it had to divide the field with Shintō and Confucianism, but largely on terms laid down by itself. In fact, it is very doubtful whether Shintō would have survived at all if it had been opposed by Buddhism, and not incorporated into it; for Shintō was entirely too primitive to have satisfied much longer the growing intelligence of the Japanese. Buddhism's victory might have been delayed but it would have been inevitable. And Confucianism, too, gained its hold in Japan largely because Buddhists propagated it. It was fostered by them because it supplemented the Buddhist teachings, especially in the field of practical ethics. Thus, as we have said, both Shintō and Confucianism had their place in Japanese life largely on terms laid down by Buddhism. This, of course, in turn affected Buddhism and made it quite different in Japan from what it was in other lands. But still the genius of the religion of the Japanese people, especially in its higher intellectual and philosophical aspects, has been for centuries and still is to-day, more Buddhist than anything else.

What, then, are the chief contributions to the distinctively religious life of Japan which Buddhism has made?

First of all, Buddhism elevated and enlarged the conception of the Divine. Shintō was a rather puerile animism and crude polytheism, and the Japanese had not yet advanced to the idea of the universal or the monistic whole. The elements of monism or monotheism found in present-day Shintō were not there when Buddhism first reached these shores; for, as we have said above, not until Buddhism had made itself felt was there even an attempt made to build up the various legends and myths of the native religion into a connected and reasoned whole. But it is the very breath of the philosophy of Mahāyāna Buddhism to reduce the plurality of being to an all-embracing Divine Whole, and to regard the myriads of gods and individual beings as in some way the expression of the All-One. It is true, of course, that in popular Buddhism the gods of polytheistic Shintō and other cults have always played a prominent part; and, on the other hand, it is true that the conception of the Divine All in philosophic Buddhism frequently faded away into thin mist or the "Unknowable" of agnosticism; but even so, it must be admitted that Buddhism did give the Japanese a loftier conception of the ultimate source of all reality than Shintō had. In fact, as we have seen, Amida Buddhism in particular entertained a conception of the Divine which did not differ very far from the Christian conception of God.

Secondly, Buddhism greatly enlarged the conception of man's destiny. The early Shintō ideal went very little beyond the conception of man as a creature of sense-experience. The gods were implored or propitiated in order that they might bestow upon the suppliant what he wanted for a prosperous and happy existence. And the happiness of existence lay not so much in the realm of an enriched personality, as in the realm of those things which satisfy the desires of the senses. What lay beyond the realm of sense or the point in time when the sense organs are dissolved in death, did not concern the early Shintōist so much. Buddhism, however, taught Japan that man's present life is but a moment of his existence and that the real life is more than the life of the body. In spite of the doctrine of the non-reality of the self, Buddhism has impressed, through its doctrine of Karma, the thought of the far-reaching effects of the psychic forces in human life. It taught the Japanese to think of all things *sub specie æternitatis* and to regard especially the individual human life in its relationship to the past and the future. Thus it both minimized and mag-

nified the place of man in the universe. It minimized man
in that it exhibited him as but a fragment of the Whole.
But it also magnified human life in that it showed that
however small this fragment might be its destiny is wrapped
up with the destiny of the Great All. To be sure, Buddhism
did not always have a very clear idea as to what this destiny might be, and often it seemed to be the destiny of Vacuity, but occasionally at least it held out to man a hope of a
future life which was truly inspiring. And even in quarters where the hope of a larger future was not emphasized,
or where it was left among the great uncertainties, the
emphasis which such Buddhist thinkers placed on self-culture carried with it by way of implication the thought of a
higher destiny; for what would self-culture mean if at the
end of the road lay no real positive goal? That is, the
schools in Japanese Buddhism which apparently denied
the future life, after all, held out some sort of desired future
to the individual and so ennobled the conception of man's
destiny.

A third great contribution which Buddhism made to the
religious life of Japan is the conception, or conceptions, regarding the way by which man can reach his higher destiny.
Whatever have been the perversions of these conceptions —
and they have been gross and many in popular Buddhism
— the higher Buddhism has always insisted that it must be
by way of obedience to the truth. Man must know the
truth, and the truth shall set him free from the bondages of
his little self into the liberty of the greater Something. The
doctrine of Karma, which runs all through Buddhist thought,
on its better side means that this universe is under law. To
know this law is to know the truth, and to obey the truth is
to become superior to the law, or rather to direct the operations of the inexorable law in such a way as to bring man
into a better and fuller life. Even the schools which teach
the doctrine of salvation through faith in Amida do not deny
the necessity of obedience to the law of Karma, only they
hold that the obedience was rendered once and for all by
Amida. Thus as we have said, whatever perversions there

x

have been in popular Buddhism, and whatever superstitious practices of magic the ignorant masses may indulge in, the higher side of Buddhism has always stood for the conception of a universe of rational laws which man must obey if he would advance into a larger and nobler life.

This thought of obedience to the truth naturally leads us to the moral and ethical side of the religious life. We saw in the preceding chapter what the moral ideals of Buddhism are. There may be nothing distinctive in these ethical teachings when compared with the ethics of other advanced religions. But when seen in the light of Shintō ethics — if it is possible to speak of such a thing — it will be realized what a great contribution Buddhism has made. And when it is further remembered that Buddhist priests were largely the medium through which Confucian ethics were made known in this land, we will have to say that practically all the moral training which the people of Japan have had up to the modern period they owe either directly or indirectly to Buddhism.

Not only did Buddhism influence the thought side of religion and the practical working out of this in ethical conduct, but also in the less important side of the outer trappings of religion did it exert a great influence. One reason why Buddhism appealed to the ancient Japanese was the fact that it had much more elaborate and impressive outward settings than their native religion had. It brought with it images, statues, pictures, bells, incense and all that goes to make an impressive ritual; and, in the course of time, it developed in Japan a complex ecclesiastical machinery. So rich in these outward things is Buddhism that even a Roman Catholic might feel perfectly at home in these surroundings. A few years ago a writer in one of the leading Christian papers made a comparison between Buddhism and Catholicism, and he showed over thirty points in which the two were in agreement in these externals of religion. It is not strange that when Xavier and his fellow workers came to Japan they were regarded at first by the Buddhist priests as but one more sect of their own religion.

Such, then, are some of the main influences which Buddhism has exerted upon the life of the people of Japan. In some fields these have been so determining that of the major Asiatic states Japan is most Buddhist, and certainly in no other land has Buddhism so much to its credit. It has been the dominant religion in this land for about a thousand years, and during that time Buddhism has developed aspects which make it more nearly an adequate religion for an advanced people than the forms it has taken in other Asiatic countries. That is to say, Buddhism has not only exerted a great influence on Japan, but the Japanese genius has also in turn impressed itself upon Buddhism.

But after we have said this much about the influence which the religion of Buddha has exerted upon Japanese life in the past, we must now come to the question as to what place it has in present-day Japan, and then the still more difficult question as to what its place will probably be in the future, for no one is more ready to admit than educated Buddhists themselves that a new day has arisen for the old religions of this people, and that, though the past may have belonged to Buddhism, the present and especially the future are problematic.

B. *The Place of Buddhism in Present-day Japan*

The Japanese saying that "what goes before becomes master" gives us in part the clue to this question. The fact that Buddhism has dominated the life of Japan in the past means that the present, too, belongs largely to it in spite of the outward appearances to the contrary; for as has been pointed out in the introductory remarks, a nation cannot suddenly cast off its old religions as a worn-out garment; and even this rising generation of Japanese, which laughs at the superstitions and beliefs of its fathers and glibly denies that it is Buddhist, after all, breathes the Buddhist atmosphere much more than it realizes. By this we do not mean to say that Buddhism has not lost much ground in the modern period and that there are not forces at work now which seem destined ultimately to undermine the old founda-

tions of the religion of the Buddha in this land. We simply
wish to express it as our conviction that present-day Japan
still belongs largely to the religion of the Buddha; or if not
to the religion which the Buddha proclaimed, at least to the
religious complex which looks to him as its founder.

Perhaps the simplest way to answer this question as to
what place Buddhism has in modern Japan is to ask the
reader to keep in mind what we have said in the preceding
section as to its place in the past and here show simply to
what extent Buddhism has lost this place.

We have already given in the latter part of Chapter III
a partial statement of the situation, and what we give here
is to be regarded as supplementary. The great fact to
remember is that the whole movement, which prepared the
way for the Restoration in 1868 and all that this implied
and brought with it, was from the beginning not a movement of the Buddhists but rather of the Neo-Confucianists
and Neo-Shintōists. To be sure, both Neo-Confucianism
and Neo-Shintō owed much to Buddhism, but when these
reached the self-conscious stage they drew their main strength
from the spirit of opposition to the latter. It is not strange,
therefore, that when this movement was crowned with success Buddhism was disestablished as a state religion and the
Buddhist priests, who for centuries had basked in the sun-
shine of Government favor, were thrown out into the cold
and forced to shift for themselves. Not only was Buddhism
disestablished as a state religion, but there was even an attempt made to suppress it altogether. Many temples were
denuded of their precious statues and decorations, the
priests were evicted and forbidden to propagate their teachings. These drastic and high-handed measures were, of
course, doomed to fail, for Japan was too thoroughly devoted
to its past. After a few years of mild persecution the priests
were allowed to keep their ecclesiastical organization and
propagate their views, but they were compelled to stand on
their own feet and to work under certain limitations.

This apparent hard fate was, however, not an unmixed evil,
for it served to waken at least the leaders from the lethargy

which had befallen not only them but the whole Buddhist world of Japan. Early in the seventies signs of new life began to manifest themselves, and a spirit of union among the various sects arose. This was further quickened by the impact of Western civilization which from that time on poured into Japan. At first this influx was met with a spirit of opposition by the old-time leaders. Not only did they stand against Christianity but also against Western science and philosophy. Especially was this true in the early eighties, when the Japanese official world seemed to swallow wholesale everything that came from abroad. But as the Buddhist leaders became better acquainted with Western thought, and especially when they perceived that in the West itself there was a keen conflict between the newer philosophies based upon Darwinian evolution and Christianity they soon sought to form an alliance with Western science and use it as their chief weapon against the religion of the West. As the time went on this union between progressive Buddhists and certain schools of Western philosophy became closer and closer and the teachings of Buddhism were restated in such a way as to appear that parts of the Kantian philosophy, the Hegelian dialectics, Spencerian agnosticism, etc., were but Western forms of the cardinal elements of Buddhism. In short, the progressive Buddhist used from Western philosophy and science what suited his purpose to fight the religion of the West.

Towards the end of the eighties and early in the nineties came the reaction against everything Western, and the conservative Buddhists sought to profit by this. They were loudest among those who pointed out the self-sufficiency of everything Japanese. Did not Buddhist thought antedate the highest development of Western science and philosophy by centuries? Why, then, should Japan learn from the West? So strong was this movement for exalting everything Japanese that some Buddhists were quite ready to forget their differences with the Shintōists and Confucianists at whose hands they had suffered so recently, and unite with them in one "Great Way" of things Japanese. The motto of a leading Buddhist, "Defense of the country and love for the truth," crystallizes this spirit in a sentence. For a while the conservatives had their way but Japan had, after all, put too much of the new wine into the old wine skins. They had to burst; or rather some of them have burst and others will do so as the new wine continues to ferment. Not only is this true in the general field of education and politics but also in the field of religion. The students who studied abroad in the eighties and nineties are now the leaders in the thought life of Japan. They are imbued with the scientific spirit and devoted to the historico-critical method. The Neo-Confucianists and Neo-Shintōists had begun to use this method and this had led to the Restoration and an attack upon Buddhism as a foreign religion. But now this deadly weapon, in a more perfect form, is being used by the more advanced Buddhists themselves and the results are beginning to show. Just what the results will be in the long run is hard to tell, but the first effect of a wide application of this method is bound to give a tremendous shock to the ordinary claims of Japanese Buddhists. It is bound to show that the whole fabric of Japanese Buddhism cannot possibly stand as a consistent whole, and certainly not as all being either the direct or indirect teaching of the founder of Buddhism. It is nine tenths historical development, and in many of its cardinal points this development runs counter to the teachings of S'akyamuni. To be sure, these views are not very widespread yet and the great masses of the uneducated do not question the authority of the priests, but every year's work of Japan's great educational system is bound to help undermine the present basis of Buddhism in Japan.

While the advanced Buddhist scholars are occupied with the perplexing problems raised by modern thought and methods, the common Buddhist is left to go his own way. On the one hand he is being taught in the public schools the new learning of the West, and on the other hand the great hordes of ignorant priests seek to continue to rivet upon him all the superstitions and worn-out forms of the past.

Very little has been done by Buddhists to bridge effectively the chasm between the old and the new. The result is disastrous. The old women in the country and some of the old men are still earnest followers of things as they were. The younger generation, though nominally Buddhist, is utterly ignorant of and indifferent to the religion of their fathers. The interest they have in the temples of their neighborhood does not usually extend beyond the occasional festival and street fair held in the temple precincts. And, of course, as all men must die, and the priests have the monopoly on funerals, even the indifferent youth of to-day must occasionally have their attention directed to things which transcend temporal interests. This indifference to Buddhism so characteristic of the rising generation does not mean that there is not still a strong unconscious influence exerted by it upon young Japan, but only that young Japan does not consciously and with zeal identify itself with the religion of the Buddha. Rather is the present generation, especially the illiterate class, turning to the old religion of Japan, *i.e.* Shintō in the form of such new sects as Tenrikyō, which counts its adherents by the hundreds of thousands. It is true, of course, that Tenrikyō and the other popular Shintō sects are as much Buddhism as Shintō, but they regard themselves as pure Shintō and rather emphasize their difference from Buddhism. At any rate, they are forces which in an increasing manner Buddhism must reckon with if it would continue its sway over the hearts of the people.

This is beginning to be recognized by the more progressive priests. Not only are they being stung into activity by their enthusiastic Shintō rivals but also by the growing influence of Christianity, from which latter they borrow various methods of propaganda. Thus at last Buddhists are really making an effort to make their sacred scriptures accessible to the common reader. The leading sects are circulating what might be called "Sectarian Bibles"; namely, volumes bound in convenient form which contain the chief scriptures of the sect with standard commentaries on the same. One of these published first in 1911 passed through 45 reprints in three years. Biographies of Buddhist saints, catechisms, expositions of Buddhist philosophies, essays and sermons on various moral and religious topics are appearing in greater number from year to year. Monthly magazines are issued by all the leading sects and through these a rather large section of the more intelligent public is reached. Then further, Buddhists are organizing themselves into various societies and organizations. Thus we find Young Men's Buddhist Associations, Women's Buddhist Societies, Buddhist Sunday Schools and similar organizations patterned after Christian models. Thus one branch of the Shin Sect, the Higashi Honkwanji, claims to have over 100,000 children enrolled in 680 Sunday Schools. Even the popular summer schools and Chautauquas have their counterpart in modern Buddhism. Street preaching and special "evangelistic" campaigns are not unheard of. An increasing number of temples are holding regular preaching services several times a month and really are trying to instruct the people. This revival is strongest among the Zen, Nichiren and Shin sects, though the Jōdo and Shingon are also being affected, and it is not wholly absent from the Tendai. The awakening in the Zen Sect seems more of the nature of a "thing fashionable," whereas in the Nichiren and Shin sects it seems to have a genuine religious basis. Especially in the latter is it sufficiently religious and vigorous to lead to a missionary propaganda extending to outlying portions of the empire, to China and even to the Japanese settlers in Western lands.

Another symptom of new life is seen in that movement among the so-called Neo-Buddhists which is looking towards the union of all the sects; a union which if it stops short of actual organic oneness, should at least result in one great coöperative enterprise which it is hoped by its promoters will make the religion of the Buddha once more a living force in the life of Japan. This, like most of these newer activities, draws its chief inspiration from the union movements in Christian circles, though it also owes something to those more enlightened leaders who are pointing out that the numerous divisions of the past have lost their *raison d'être.* A beautiful white brick structure in the grounds of the famous Asakusa Temple in Tōkyō is a monument to these would-be reformers, but any one visiting those grounds will usually find the doors of this architectural gem closed, while the filthy old Kwannon temple close by with its well-worn idols and fortune-telling priests seems as popular as ever. If it has lost its hold on the hearts of the people at all, it is because adjacent to the temple grounds is Tōkyō's center for the "movies" which offer to modern Japan far greater attractions than the simple side shows of popular temples. As the crowds surge back and forth between the old temple and the "movies" they pass in front of the union preaching hall of the Neo-Buddhists, but it hardly receives even a glance from these pleasure-seeking pilgrims, and one wonders whether this is not very much the attitude of the rising generation towards all these efforts among Buddhist reformers. At any rate, is it true that thus far they have not succeeded in raising up a body of intelligent followers conscious of their mission as a constructive force in the life of modern Japan. Rather is it true, as one of the older Buddhist scholars has recently said, that these Neo-Buddhists and would-be reformers are loud in what they are *going* to do, but thus far they have only torn down the old, and have accomplished nothing along constructive lines. It still remains true in spite of all these activities that the average Buddhist believer belongs to the most ignorant sections of society, and that he is also shockingly ignorant even in matters of the religion he professes.

When, therefore, one would measure in a few words the place which Buddhism occupies in the life of modern Japan, the conclusion seems inevitable that while its hold on the ignorant masses is still very strong, especially in the more backward parts of the empire, it does not occupy a very conspicuous place among the forces which are making for progress. No one in Japan would think of looking to the Buddhists for leadership. As a matter of fact Buddhist priests, with a few exceptions, are notoriously behind "in education, character, morals and influence." That is, they are unfit as leaders, not only in secular matters, but also in things which make for individual and social uprightness. One cannot but be impressed with the contrast between the present-day situation and the early days of Buddhism in Japan when the Buddhist priests and monks were the apostles of the superior civilization of China, or the days of the great religious awakening in the twelfth and thirteenth centuries when Japan had religious leaders of real power and influence. To-day the leadership is in other hands. The apostles of the new civilization of the West are, as a rule, those on whom Buddhism has the lightest hold, and the leaders in the realm of things spiritual are decidedly those who have drunk most deeply from the fountains of Christianity. Almost every movement of any consequence in Japan to-day which is making for individual and social righteousness has Christian men and women as its leaders. The best that can be said for the Buddhists is that they occasionally attempt to imitate these movements, but an imitation is seldom equal to the real thing. The truth of the matter is that the great days of Buddhism in Japan, the days when its power and influence counted for progress, lie in the distant past. The present, and even more the future, belong to others. But this brings us to the third aspect of our subject, viz., the question as to what place Buddhism will probably occupy in the future in Japanese life.

C. *The Place of Buddhism in the Future*

Just what place Buddhism will occupy in the future is even more difficult to determine than what place it holds to-day. We shall try to answer the question more from the standpoint of its adequacy as a religion of the future than speculating as to what place it will really hold. Only the future can answer the latter question, for it does not at all follow that though Buddhism is inadequate as a religion, it may not dominate the life of Japan for decades and even centuries. We can only point out why it is not an adequate religion for the highest development of Japanese life.

One of the striking differences between Japanese Buddhists and Japanese Christians is their attitude towards the future. It would be difficult to find a real Christian in Japan who does not hope and believe that Japan will some day be a Christian land. However small the mustard seed may be it will some day grow into a large plant and give shelter. The leaven will ultimately leaven the whole lump. In short, the Christians of Japan have absolute confidence in the future of their religion, and it is this faith that overcomes the world.

Among Japanese Buddhists it would be difficult to find such confidence in their own future. There are many Buddhist parents to-day who, though clinging to their old faith, have little hope that their children will do the same. They vaguely feel that "the old order changeth, yielding place to" what they know not. This lack of confidence has been increased in recent years by the discovery that those very sects which have shown the most marked symptoms of revival have been almost made bankrupt by the dishonesty of their leaders. And rightly does the anxious believer conclude that "if they do these things in a green tree, what shall be done in the dry?"

It is, of course, true that some Buddhists have confidence in the future of their religion, but it is not a widespread characteristic. In fact, even the optimists hope for little more than that the future will be as the past in which Buddhism divided the field with others and by clever compromises maintained its dominance. There is a growing number among the liberals who would unite Buddhism with other religions and make one new and all-inclusive system. That is, they are not looking for a reformed Buddhism, a Neo-Buddhism, but for a new religion in which the Buddhist elements shall be, perhaps, the most prominent.

But if Japanese Buddhists themselves have little confidence in the future of their own religion, there are good reasons for it. A statement of these reasons is virtually an answer to the question, What are the great defects in Japanese Buddhism which make it inadequate as the religion of the future?

Before answering this most interesting of all questions from our own Christian standpoint, we shall give what is at least a partial answer made not long ago by one of Japan's most enlightened thinkers; namely, Professor Inouye Tetsujiro of the Tōkyō Imperial University. Writing on the subject of Religious Reform in Japan, and especially on the need of reform in Buddhism, this learned author points out what he considers the great defects in this religion.

The first outstanding defect is the character of the priests. "Buddhist priests, in spite of a few notable and brilliant exceptions, which however only serve to make the general darkness more visible, are behind the rest of the world in education, character, morals and influence; and though Christian rivalry has stirred some of them to emulation in educational and charitable enterprises of recent years, these works of charity have been far from vigorous." That this adverse judgment is not an overstatement of the case is clear to any careful student. In fact many Japanese writers express themselves with less restraint when dealing with this subject. One naturally wonders what future a religion can have when its leaders are behind those whom they seek to lead.

The second reform needed according to Professor Inouye is the abolishing of idols, and the substitution of the Japanese language for the unintelligible Sanskrit and Chinese in the Buddhist ritual and scriptures. Idols may have had their place in the past, says this critic, but the modern Japanese ought to be beyond these crude representations of the Divine. And equally important is "the abolition of the practice of reading and chanting the sūtras in a language which, practically, neither the priests nor the congregation understand." It is true that modern Japan should be beyond these crutches of religion, but popular Buddhism is still so bound up with idolatry that the abolition of idols would mean to many the giving up of their gods. Not that the idols should not be abolished, but that it must be accompanied by a constructive work. The substitution of Japanese for the unintelligible Chinese is finally being tried, but Japanese Buddhism has a long way to go before it can make up for the neglect in the past.

The third great defect pointed out by Professor Inouye is even more serious, and if the reform suggested by him were carried out, it would not leave enough of the Buddhist elements in the reformed religion to enable even a Bodhisattva to recognize it as Buddhism. The proposal is so naïve that we must give the full text on this point. "The pessimism of India, which is of the essence of Japanese Buddhism, is not suited to our needs. Pessimism is the creed of a decaying nationality in the hour of adversity, when this world looks dark and life has no hope to offer us. Then in despair, we turn from this miserable world, and seek comfort in the hope of something better after death. In ancient India pessimism was perhaps natural, but pessimism can never raise a nation to a higher life, and what Japan, with its new hopes and aspirations, requires is a religion of hope, full of noble ideals and aspirations. Buddhism must shed its pessimism or lose its hold on the people." This may not be a new estimate of the spirit of Buddhism but it is a true one. It is in the last analysis a philosophy of defeat, and therefore cannot satisfy the "hopes and aspirations" of an awakened nation. But when the suggestion is made that "Buddhism must shed its pessimism or lose its hold on the people," one wonders how a professor of philosophy in a great university could think out anything so naïve. For Buddhism to "shed its pessimism" is not like a snake shedding its skin but rather like shedding its backbone. It is like the night shedding its darkness, for just as the night ceases to be night when the darkness is gone, so Buddhism without its pessimistic spirit would no longer be Buddhism. To be sure, the night sheds some of its darkness when the moon shines with its light borrowed from the sovereign of eternal day, and so Buddhism, in the future, may illumine its pessimism by borrowing elements of "hope and aspirations" from sources other than its own. But for it really to "shed its pessimism" and for it to become "a religion of hope, full of noble ideals and aspirations" seems impossible without becoming a religion fundamentally different from what it is and has been.

It is true, of course, that Japanese Buddhism has tried to shed the pessimistic philosophy of India, and in the development of Amidaism with its semi-theistic God-idea it has in a measure laid hold on elements of hope and aspiration; but, after all, this reaching out for the living God has always been hindered by the agnostic philosopher who reduces Amida and his salvation to mere ideals which have no real ontological reference. And furthermore, just in proportion as Buddhism has succeeded in shedding its pessimism it has departed from the religion of the founder. If it is ever to shed its pessimism entirely, and become truly a religion of hope and aspiration suited for an awakened people, it will have to cease being Buddhism in its cardinal elements, whatever name may be attached to it. Of course the Buddhist might say that such a change would be a "developed Buddhism." That might be so, but would it not be more correct to say that it would be a new religion rather than a "developed Buddhism"? The generic elements of a religion may undergo some outward changes, and the religion remain essentially the same, but for a religion to abandon its generic elements and build itself upon others is really to become a new religion even though the old name be continued.

The fourth reform suggested by the above-mentioned critic is equally sweeping and would leave very little of the old if carried out. To give his own words, "There are countless superstitions in Buddhism, practices and doctrines which the ignorant accept blindly and the educated laugh at. We will take but one instance, that of Shumisen, the fabulous mountain which Buddhist cosmology places at the center of the world. We might mention others, transmigration, the six spheres of sentient existence, Paradise, Hades, the innumerable Buddhas and Bodhisattvas. The world has progressed since the days of S'akyamuni, still more so perhaps since the days when the Mahāyāna sūtras were written. Can we of the Meiji period (this was written at the close of the Meiji era), with our modern education in the principles of science, be expected to accept these anti-quated superstitions?"

The fifth defect in Japanese Buddhism pointed out by Professor Inouye refers to Buddhist ethics. He points out that the ethical ideals of Buddhism are those held in India over two thousand years ago, "and the men who live by them unfit themselves to become the ethical teachers of a modern, commercial and industrial generation of men. Japan wants a system of religious morals, but it must be one suited to her present needs. Buddhists may yet be the moral teachers of this nation, if they will bring their ethical system into harmony with present-day needs." But, as has already been pointed out in Chapter VI, the philosophical basis of Buddhist ethics is inadequate for a real vital moral life. On the one hand the spirit of agnosticism which is the dominant current in all Buddhist thought forever cuts the nerve of any vigorous morality in that it makes good and evil, right and wrong but mere "practical differences" which, however, have no basis in reality. A mere "practical difference" which is not a real difference is in the last analysis vicious and anything but practical in the long run. It may be practical for me to lie, and tell the truth at another time, but unless my truthfulness is based on something more firm than on what seems merely practical it will fail to be even that, for surely no one could be expected to put much confidence in my words if convenience, or the merely practical, were the measure of my veracity. And further, Buddhist psychology runs absolutely counter to the higher ethical ideals, as we also pointed out in Chapter VI. Buddhist psychology has ever asserted that the self has no real existence and it has contented itself with a "provisional self," and yet Buddhist ethics claims as its highest goal the "intellectual and moral development of the personality." Surely for one to strive to achieve a goal which one knows to be an illusion is the grossest sort of folly. It is no wonder if the followers of such an ideal should be found rather indifferent in their pursuit. No, if Buddhists would "bring their ethical system into harmony with present-day needs," as Professor Inouye suggests, they will have to do more than make simply a few alterations here and there.   They will have to change above all else the basis of their ethical system.

Surely if Buddhism is what the above-mentioned critic says it is, and if it has these great defects, there is not only a need of reform, but there is need of a revolution in the very fundamentals; and this when accomplished would mean practically a new religion, no matter what its name might. be.   Can this change be made, and has modern Buddhism sufficient vitality to attempt the undertaking? It is one thing to recognize the defects, but quite another to overcome them.   If Japan needs, *e.g.* "a system of religious morals" suited to her present needs, and Buddhism has not such a system, can it set to work to evolve one?   Can it create a vital ethical system which will give the coming generation that moral stamina so much needed?   Can this be done by a religion which has never given the human personality its proper place and whose spirit of pessimism forever cuts the nerve of aspiration and achievement?

But these defects in Japanese Buddhism pointed out above are not the only ones which in our judgment prevent it from being an adequate religion.   When we say this we are not contradicting what we have said in the beginning of this chapter where we have spoken of the many things Buddhism contributed to Japanese civilization.   At this point we are measuring Buddhism by Christian standards and not by Shintō or Confucian.

The most fundamental defect in Buddhism as we see it, and a defect which has almost endless ramifications and accounts largely for its spirit of pessimism and other defects mentioned above, is the Buddhist conception of truth. Not to repeat here what we said in Chapter V on this subject, but simply to point out again in a few words the baneful and blighting effect which such a thoroughgoing agnostic philosophy has upon life and how it cuts the very nerve of all truth.   For it must be remembered that while Buddhism has much to say theoretically about truth, *i.e.* Absolute Truth as known by the Enlightened One, it regards all truth known to man and even all explanations of the Absolute Truth as not differing essentially from error. However profoundly an explanation has been worked out and the student is given to feel that now at last he has something which he may regard as really true, at the end of the explanation usually comes the agnostic touch reminding one that the truth explained is only an "accommodation to human ignorance" and that real truth cannot be known.

It is this essentially agnostic attitude which in the first place accounts for the conglomerate nature of Buddhism as a philosophy or a practical religion in which the nobler elements are so often buried by the accumulated rubbish of passing centuries. It accounts for the fact that in Buddhism can be found every shade of thought common to man, and why the most contradictory doctrines and practices can exist side by side without any one thinking it strange. Contradictions become but two sides of the same thing, and from this viewpoint a system with the greatest contradictions is *ipse facto* the most comprehensive statement of the full truth. Thus it is the boast of Buddhism that its philosophy is much more profound than that of Christianity because where the latter teaches certain definite views as true, Buddhism teaches both these views and their opposites and every shade between. And so if it be asked what Buddhism teaches on this or that point, it can be said that it teaches almost anything you please. Or to put it in the true Buddhist way, Buddhism teaches This from one point of view and the Opposite from the opposite point of view. (And since both are equally true or good there is good reason for following neither very seriously.)

But if it be asked, Which is the true Buddhist point of view? the answer is that Buddhism views truth from every angle and so gets an infinite variety in its statements of the truth. Thus it is customary to speak of the 84,000 doctrines of Buddhism. Are then these various statements of the truth taken together to be regarded as the full statement of the truth and all to be regarded as true? Yes and No, is the reply, for this again depends upon what point of view

Y

you take of the matter.   And so the dialectics goes on *ad infinitum,* and the upshot of the matter is that he who has gone furthest in the search of truth knows best that he really knows nothing.   It is this agnosticism among the thinkers in Buddhism which begets in their ignorant followers often the most astounding credulity and superstitions, for the heart of man demands something to which it can cling.   If the leaders hold out nothing positive to which the mind can cling, then the ignorant follower invents something, and usually something crude.

The reader may feel that we have overstated the case, but to show that we have not we refer him to Chapter V, in which we have given an outline of Buddhist teachings on the main points of religion.   Not to repeat what was said there, we simply point out how great is the variety of answers given to the central question in religion.   Can any Japanese Buddhist say, *e.g.* what is the answer which his religion makes to the great questions about God?   The best he can do is to say that Japanese Buddhism presents a bewildering variety in its conceptions of the Divine.   These conceptions range all the way from the "Unknowable Absolute" of the philosopher to the crude and extremely realistic gods of popular polytheism.   As polytheism becomes a reasoned belief it changes in some sects into a semi-theism; in others it dwindles into what is virtually atheism, but in most cases it becomes what we describe by the vague term of Pantheism.   But all of these fade, in the last analysis, into the conception of the Divine as the "Great Unknown."

The most satisfactory God-idea in Japanese Buddhism is that held by the Amida sects.   It approaches in the minds of some writers the monotheistic conception.   But even here there is nothing very positive, for as we have shown in Chapter V, the answer to the question as to whether Amida is a personal being or not depends upon the "point of view."   In one sense Amida is said to be personal, but in what is apparently regarded a higher sense he is not personal.   The believer may take his choice and answer the question by either Yes or No, for whether Amida is personal, or whether he has any real existence is really beyond the power of man to know. Or to put it in the strictly Buddhist fashion, Practically Amida should be regarded as a personal god, though from the standpoint of "Absolute Truth" he cannot be said to be personal or have any real existence.

But why Amida should be regarded as a personal God "practically" when in reality he is not personal may not seem clear to the reader. The Buddhist answer to such an objection would be that it is an idea which is suited to man's need and so to that extent it should be accepted as true even though it is not really true. But whether such a "practical" idea will continue to function "practically" when it is known to be not "really true," we leave for the Buddhist psychologist to answer to his own satisfaction. We have, however, our own suspicions that "practical" ideas which are not "really true," found so frequently in Buddhist thought, account for the fact that Buddhism is losing its hold on an awakened people, and that the average Japanese of to-day is not over-zealous about the things of God. And it is also perhaps no wonder that some of the Neo-Buddhists would eliminate everything pertaining to the Divine from their religion and build up something like Comte's religion of Humanity which is made by man, for man and leaves man worshiping himself.

If the conception of the Divine in Japanese Buddhism is inadequate, no less is this the case with the Buddhist view of man and his destiny. On the one hand Buddhism apparently denies the very existence of the self, regarding it as but an epiphenomenon resulting from the play and interplay of the Karma-energy, which latter eludes any possibility of a consistent conception, and on the other hand Buddhist ethics teaches that the development of the personality is the highest aim of life. In fact some sects hold out to the believer a very realistic picture of the future life in which man is apparently to enjoy all that he loves in this life. Amida's Paradise is indeed a very concrete heaven to the average believer. But as the believer grows in intelligence and begins to delve in the deeper teachings of his sect his vision of Paradise begins to fade. He learns that for "practical" purposes he should act and live as if the achievement of an enriched personality were the goal of all our striving and the one value which abides the wreck of time, but in reality personality and all individuality cannot be a permanent state. Just as the idea of a personal God is regarded as being only "practically" true, but not "really" true, so it is with the human personality. Both ideas are to be accepted as "provisionally" true because they function practically, but they are not to be regarded as actually true.

Again do we raise the query: If the achievement of an ideal personality is only an "idea of an ideal," and in reality there is no such thing as personality, or no permanence to an "achieved ideal personality," how long will such an idea function practically? Why should man strive to achieve an enriched personality when this lofty goal confessedly has no existence? Nothing can be "practically" true which is not really true. Thus again we see how the Buddhist agnostic attitude cuts the very nerve of human achievement.

But what are we to say to some of our modern Buddhists who would eliminate the idea of the Divine and the problem of human destiny in the larger sense from religion altogether and reduce religion to a mere matter of present human relationships? To sum up the position of these men in a few words: Let the modern man give up his quest for the Divine and the problems which deal with man's relationship to the "unseen world," and let him confine his strivings to the things of the present and to the destiny of the nation or the race rather than to the destiny of individual personalities. Let Buddhism become simply a moral philosophy. Japan needs "a system of religious morals." That is, she needs a system of morals which has the religious spirit, for during the Meiji era a system of morals, devoid of the religious tone, has been tried and found wanting. So the religious tone or flavor must be brought back into ethics, but brought back without any entangling alliances with ideas regarding the Divine or man's relationship to the Divine. For has not the highest philosophy of Buddhism held for centuries that all such speculations really lead only to the abyss of the "Unknowable Absolute"? Let the modern Japanese confine his activities to the cultivation of a "practical moral life," and especially let him confine himself to such "practical moral principles" which will fit him to live among a "modern, commercial and industrial generation of men." While he may have a certain reverence for the "Mystery of Reality" which lies hidden in the "bosom of the Absolute," he should not worry his mind about the real nature of that reality or what will become of him when the time comes for him to sink back again into the unfathomable One-All.

This is in short what some of our enlightened Buddhists are advocating. We realize, of course, that in this they are not very different from some of our Western moralists who would have a moral philosophy with the religious flavor but with the heart of religion left out. And it is also true that such a step would be rather in harmony with the spirit of the founder of Buddhism. Gautama, too, felt that the one thing needful was for man to walk in the path of practical ethics — an ethics with a religious flavor but with God left out. The goal, however, at which the founder's ethics aimed was quite different from the goal which these moderns have in view. For him this ethical path was a way out of this world of evil, while to these later Buddhists the walking in the path of practical ethics is a means by which man may become master of his environment and so satisfy his present desires. But both agree in that they regard the deeper religious question, namely, the question of God, as impractical. That is, both seek to build up a practical ethics without a true religious basis.

One wonders how any one with a glimpse of psychology could be so short-sighted. The core of morality must always be the achievement of a moral or ideal personality. And if this is so, then the question as to the final value of such an "achieved personality" or the conservation of such values cannot be avoided. And in answering this question it is impossible to avoid the further question as to whether

personality has a place in the universe, not only as goal but
also as source, *i.e.* the question as to whether there is a Personal God and man's relationship to Him.

Furthermore, the futility of trying to build up a vital ethics
without a true religious basis ought to be evident to these
Neo-Buddhists from Buddhist history itself. The very
fact that Gautama left the great religious questions about
God and the soul unanswered resulted, as we have seen in
the preceding pages, in his followers trying to answer these
questions for themselves. And the answers given in the
course of the centuries were so varied that the religion of
Gautama became one great jumble of contradictions which
have buried the "practical ethics" of the Middle Path.
The lesson from Buddhist history is unmistakable. The
heart of man demands an answer to the question about God
and man's relationship to Him. The answer which agnosticism makes and which Buddhist philosophy has tried to
make will not permanently satisfy, and man will continue to
demand some answer more positive. This is the meaning of
the prevalence of polytheism all through Buddhist history,
and it is also the meaning of the nobler answer to the great
question which we have in the semi-theism of the Amida sects.
The "practical ethics" without a true religious basis has not
satisfied men in the past, and it cannot satisfy them in the
future. And if modern Buddhists ignore this lesson of history, they will find that Japanese Buddhism will continue to
be grossly polytheistic and that their proposed "practical
ethics" will be swamped by the superstitions of credulity,
just as Gautama's "practical ethics" were.

We repeat, the great question about God and man's relation to Him must be answered. The Amidaists have
caught a glimpse of this great truth and that is why on the
whole Amidaism has been and is to-day the most vital religious force in Japanese Buddhism; but it, too, is inadequate, for the agnostic philosopher has also cut the roots of
this promising tree of life. We have seen how again and
again this brightest star of hope and aspiration in Buddhism
appears only to disappear again in the mists of doubt and

despair which continually rise from the fathomless depths of Oriental agnosticism. It is because of this recurrent note of skepticism all through Buddhist history that it has been a philosophy of "pessimism and defeat" and not a religion "of hope and aspiration." For Buddhism to now rise up and cast off its pessimism, as Professor Inouye suggests, is impossible unless it can somehow or other lay hold on the Living God.

But can Buddhism do this? Can it lay hold on a faith in God the Heavenly Father? No, it cannot and at the same time remain true to its generic elements, for it was founded on the thought of man's inability to know the "Unknowable Absolute," and through all the centuries, in spite of the various counter currents in the Buddhist stream of life, this has been the dominant current; this has been the generic element of Buddhism, North and South, Mahāyāna and Hīnayāna.

If Japanese Buddhism cannot lay hold on the Living God without undergoing a radical change in its fundamentals, it does not follow that Japanese Buddhists cannot fling away their pessimism and lay hold on Him and so find satisfaction for their hopes and aspirations. That this is possible is best shown by what is taking place to-day in Japan. But this is another story; it is the story of Christianity in this land. Of this story only the first chapter is history; the remainder is written in the hearts of the rising generation and will be written in the lives of the generations to come,

"For the old order changeth yielding place to the new,
And God fulfills himself in many ways."

NOTES

Chapter I

1. It would seem that even before the rise of Buddhism and that religious complex which we call Hinduism, the general characteristics of the religious life of India were essentially what they have been all through the centuries. That is, on the one hand we have the philosophers' profound speculative thoughts about the deeper realities of life, and on the other hand we see the very crude and naïvely realistic conceptions as held by the common people. There is always a wide gap between the two. India has apparently never been very successful in formulating the results of its speculative efforts in such a way that they can be applied by the common man to life as he must live it. Buddhism was an attempt to brush aside the vain and impractical speculations of the old-fashioned philosophers and to fix men's attention on a practical course of conduct which should lead him from a lower into a higher and better life, but it, too, failed in the end; for one of the most outstanding characteristics of Buddhism throughout the centuries has been just this wide chasm between the ideals and thoughts of a few leaders and the life of their ignorant followers.

2. The date of the Buddha, according to Buddhists themselves, is placed all the way from the eleventh to the sixth and fifth centuries before the Christian era. Northern Buddhists, desiring to have their master antedate Confucius and Lao-tse, give the day of his birth as belonging to the latter part of the eleventh century B.C.; 1026 B.C. being the date accepted by many in Japan. The date generally accepted in Burma, Siam and Ceylon is 623 B.C. for his birth and 543 B.C. for his death. Western scholars and modern scholars in the Orient are fairly at one in putting the date of his birth about the middle of the sixth century B.C. and the date of his death somewhere about the year 480 B.C. This conclusion is reached from the fact that King Asoka's inscriptions on certain stone pillars mention cer-

tain Greek kings who reigned during the middle of the third century B.C., and from the fact that the Ceylon Chronicles state that between the accession of King Asoka and the death of the Buddha 218 years elapsed. As it is therefore impossible to fix exactly the date of the accession of Asoka, and especially since the statement in the Ceylon Chronicles is not altogether clear, we cannot be too positive in fixing the date of the Buddha. The truth of the matter is that it is almost next to impossible to fix any dates in early Indian history.

3. The names under which the Buddha is known are numerous. Not only are the forms of the word Buddha many, as S. Hardy has pointed out, but he is given many different appellations by his followers in the various Buddhist lands of Asia. Of course, the name Buddha is really not a proper name, but a generic name. There have been many Buddhas, according to Buddhists, and so one should prefix the proper name Gautama or the definite article "the," if one is speaking of the Buddha who lived in India about the sixth or fifth century B.C. Perhaps the most common term under which the Buddha is known is S'akyamuni, *i.e.* the Teacher of the S'akyans. In fact, in Japan one seldom hears him spoken of as "the Buddha" (Jap. Butsu), but usually as Shaka, Shakasama, Shaka Butsu or Shaka Nyōrai. A term in Buddhist literature much in use is this word Nyōrai (Sk. Tathāgata). In early Buddhist literature the Tathāgata frequently means Gautama Buddha, though it is not exclusively applied to him. The Tathāgatas are many. In later Buddhist literature the Nyōrai often means one of the great Buddhas of Northern Buddhism. Amida especially is often designated by this term. Japanese Buddhists are accustomed to speaking of the Ten Names of Buddha, the first being the name Nyōrai, which probably means the Perfect One, or the One Who Comes in the Likeness of the Truth. It is the highest term applied to a Buddha. The other nine names are likewise descriptive of some attribute characteristic of a Buddha. Thus he is spoken of as the one filled with all virtue and wisdom, the supreme Lord, the Teacher of heaven and earth, the world-honored One, etc. Beyond these expressions there are others less technical, but also more or less descriptive of the true characteristics of a Buddha.

4. The Three Conceptions (Sk. Trividyā), namely, Impermanence (Sk. Anitya), Suffering or Misery (Sk. Dukha) and Non-Ego (Sk. Anātmā), may be regarded as the three axioms of

Buddhism. These are essentially the same as the so-called Three Law-Seals, and these latter may be said to be the three characteristics of Buddhism which distinguish it from other religions; they are the three tests by which heretical views can be distinguished from the orthodox view. These Three Law-Seals (Jap. Sambōin) are: All Work is impermanent (Jap. Shōgyō mujō), All Laws are without an ego principle (Jap. Shōhō muga), and Nirvāna is Tranquillity (Jap. Nehan Jakujo).

5. The Four Noble Truths (Sk. Āryāsatyāni or Āryānisatyāni, Jap. Shitai) stated in a word each are as follows: Suffering (Sk. Dukha, Jap. Ku), Accumulation (Sk. Samudaya, Jap. Shū), Extinction (Sk. Nirōdha, Jap. Metsu) and Way (Sk. Mārga, Jap. Dō).

6. The Noble Eightfold Path (Sk. Mārga or As'thanga Mārga, Jap. Hachi Shōdō) is the following:

  a. Right Views (Sk. Samyagdrichti, Jap. Shōken).

  b. Right Aspirations (Sk. Samyaksamkalpa, Jap. Shōshiyui).

  c. Right Speech (Sk. Samyagvāk, Jap. Shōgo).

  d. Right Conduct (Sk. Samyagādjīva, Jap. Shōgō).

  e. Right Mode of Livelihood (Sk. Samyagvyāyāma, Jap. Shōmei).

  f. Right Effort (Sk. Samyaksamādhi, Jap. Shōjōjun).

  g. Right Mindfulness (Sk. Samyaksmriti, Jap. Shōnen).

  h. Right Rapture (Sk. Samyakkarmānta, Jap. Shōjō).

7. For the meaning of the word Tathāgata see note 3 above. This is probably the term which the Buddha used most frequently of himself when speaking to his disciples of his own inner experience and the nature of true enlightenment.

8. The second and third of the Four Noble Truths, viz. the truth as to the origin of suffering and the truth as to the cessation of suffering, were stated more fully in a sort of double formula known as the Causal Nexus of Being, or what might be called the Twelve Links of the Karma Chain, the twelve Nidanas. These formulas read something as follows: "From Ignorance come Latent Impressions; from Latent Impressions comes Thought-substance; from Thought-substance come Name and Form; from Name and Form come the Six Roots (i.e. the sense organs, Buddhism recognizing six); from the Six Roots comes Contact; from Contact comes Sensation; from Sensation comes Desire; from Desire comes Clinging to Existence; from Clinging to Existence comes Becoming; from Becoming comes Birth; from Birth come Decrepitude and Death, Pain and Lamenta-

tion, Suffering, Anxiety and Despair. This is the origin of the whole realm of suffering.

"But if Ignorance be removed by the complete extinction of Desire, this brings about the removal of Latent Impressions; by the removal of Latent Impressions, Thought-substance is removed; by the removal of Thought-substance, Name and Form are removed; by the removal of Name and Form, the Six Roots are removed; by the removal of the Six Roots, Contact is removed; by the removal of Contact, Sensation is removed; by the removal of Sensation, Desire is removed; by the removal of Desire, Clinging to Existence is removed; by the removal of Clinging to Existence, Becoming is removed; by the removal of Becoming, Birth is removed; by the removal of Birth, Decrepitude and Death, Pain and Lamentation, Suffering, Anxiety and Despair are removed. This is the removal of the whole realm of suffering."

This statement is incidentally a very good example of the style in which the Buddha's teachings were cast as a rule, namely, what to a Western mind would be a weary form of repetition.

9. There are several reasons why the careful student must hesitate in saying with most writers on early Buddhism that the Buddha denied the existence of the self. Of course, every one must admit that he did not accept the soul theories current in India at that time, but as most of these conceived of the soul as a refined substance which passed over from one body to another it does not follow that the Buddha, in rejecting such theories, rejected every soul-theory. The very fact that he put the question as to whether the Arhat continues beyond death among the great Indeterminates should make us hesitate to say that he positively denied his continued existence. In fact, if this question belongs to the great Indeterminates, then there is as much reason for saying that the Buddha believed in the continuity of the soul as that he did not.

Even if it is admitted that his primary interest was in freeing man from the bondage of existence and the Arhat's chief joy consisted in the consciousness that at death the empirical ego would come to an end because its Karma had been exhausted, it still remains possible that the Buddha could have believed in the continuity of the higher ego, one that is not to be conceived of in terms of the empirical ego, but for all that be a true self. Kant has accustomed us to the conception of a distinction be-

tween the "empirical ego" and the "transcendental self,"
though we must admit that at first sight it is difficult to understand just what the "transcendental self" as distinguished from
the "empirical self" might be. For if the self known in self-
consciousness is not the real self, then it is difficult to see how
one can assert even the existence of another self which is the
real self. Of course, it is true that the self is greater and more
than what appears in self-consciousness from moment to
moment. That is, every man feels that the flow of consciousness is never the full expression of his entire self. Thus when a
bank clerk is adding up columns of figures from day to day and
this work represents the stream of his consciousness for six or
eight hours every day, it is not true that the whole self is expressing itself in this operation. And that is true more or less with
the life of every man. In fact every one has experiences in
which a depth of his being is revealed to himself of which he
had never dreamed. And great crises in men's lives often bring
out qualities which are startling, not only to their friends but
also to themselves. All of this simply goes to show that there
is room for the distinction between the ego of the ordinary stream
of consciousness and the full ego, or the real ego of which even
we ourselves get only glimpses as it were from time to time.

Now may it not be that the Buddha had in mind some such
distinction, and that when he said that the ego was an illusion
and fell apart at death, he meant this empirical ego whose life is
made up of the world of sense, the world of physical pleasures
and pains which for the average man makes up almost the whole
life, but that he did not deny the existence and continuity beyond death of a higher and deeper self ? The successive taber-
nacles which Karma creates constituted the seat of the successive empirical egos, and these were the fetters of the higher ego
from which it could only be freed after the higher ego was perfectly enlightened and saw that the life of the senses and the
pleasures of the empirical ego were not the core of its real life.
That is, it is Ignorance which somehow attaches itself to
the higher ego which gives rise through the twelve links of the
Karma chain (the twelve links of the Karma chain, or the
twelve segments of the Wheel of Life, are : Ignorance, Latent
Impressions, Thought-substance, Name and Form, the Six
Roots, Contact, Sensation, Desire, Clinging to Existence, Becoming, Birth, and Decrepitude and Death. For a fuller statement of this with some slight changes see note 8 of Chapter I

and Chapter V, Sect. B) to the life of the body and the experience of the empirical ego and the whole chain of future rebirths. Only after this Karma chain is broken by a dispelling of the initial ignorance does the higher ego gain its freedom. It is true that if the Buddha believed in the existence of this higher ego, one would expect him to have laid greater stress on the state of this ego beyond death, and one would think that he would have made salvation less negative, *i.e.* not a mere "escape from evil," but rather a future positive good. In answer to this objection it may, however, be said that the early Buddhists did use rather positive terms to express the conception of salvation. If the Buddha himself did not use these terms, it may have been because he sought to avoid filling the conception of Nirvāna with the contents taken from the experience of the empirical self. Of these things Nirvāna was void, but nevertheless it may have had a content which transcends human experience and so could not be expressed in terms of this experience. Even union with the Brahman was inadequate to express the thought, for the Brahman was regarded as the unitary ground of all empirical existence, and so union with the Brahman savored too much of the things of this world to be acceptable to the Buddha as an ideal of salvation. No, salvation was to be a deliverance from the bondages of the empirical-existence self, and therefore when spoken of in terms of this self, Nirvāna must be regarded as absolutely void. But the Arhat may nevertheless continue in the realm of the "transcendental self," and his Nirvāna is therefore a state which is beyond human language to express.

Now in saying all this we do not wish to state positively that the Buddha held such a view, but the facts known thus far as to the core of his teachings should make one hesitate to say that he denied the reality of the self in the above sense. The "illusion of the self" may have meant the illusion regarding the sense-life of the body and the craving thirst for earth's fleeting pleasures as having real content for the deeper self. At any rate inasmuch as the Buddha put the continuation of the Arhat in a future state among the great Indeterminates there would seem to be as much ground for holding that he believed in such a continuation as that he did not. Even among Christians of our own day there are those who have no positive convictions about the nature of the spiritual self and its destiny. They say these things belong to the realm of speculation and that they are interested primarily in the practical life, the things which concern our present daily life. Like these good people, the Buddha, too, as we have said, was more interested in freeing men from the lusts of the flesh by showing them how to walk in the Noble Eightfold Path than in spending his time in answering the great questions as to the real nature of the spiritual self and its destiny. He was positive in asserting that life as lived by ignorant humanity is not worth living, and that a knowledge of its nature and the cause of its sufferings constituted true wisdom; and further, that the truly wise will seek to end such a life by walking in the Middle Way, the Noble Eightfold Path. Everything beyond these practical and immediate interests he regarded as belonging to the realm of the unknown, about which speculation is futile.

10. The very fact that we have no English or Western equivalent for the word Karma is due largely to the difficulty of getting at its real meaning. In Japanese the expression "Ingwa ōhō" is used to express the general Causal-Nexus law, while the term "Gyō" designates more specifically the ethical aspect of Karma in the life of an individual.

11. The Five Aggregates (Sk. Skandhas, Jap. Goun) are the following:

    a. Bodiliness or Form (Sk. Rūpa, Jap. Shiki).

    b. Sensation (Sk. Vēdana, Jap. Shū).

    c. Perception (Sk. Samdjnā, Jap. Sō).

    d. Predisposition or Action (Sk. Karman or Samskara, Jap. Gyō).

    e. Consciousness or Knowledge (Sk. Vidjnāna, Jap. Shiki).

12. To say that Karma is like Schopenhauer's "Blind Will" or "Will-to-be" is really putting things upside down, for Schopenhauer was a student of Buddhism and so it is more correct to say that his "Blind Will" is like that mysterious energy which Buddhism designates by this word Karma.

13. The Middle Way is the way midway between the two extremes of a life of sensual enjoyments and a life of asceticism. The Buddha had experienced both. As a young nobleman he had lived the life of the world; and while he probably never was a sensuous man, he must have experienced the pull of the lower passions. When he began his great quest, he went to the other extreme and for about six years lived the life of an ascetic, but this, too, proved a disappointment. It is only when he lived a life of moderation and walked in the Middle

Way that he attained enlightenment. Of course, to men of the world even this life of moderation seemed like an ascetic life, and that is why he was often called the Great Ascetic. And it is also true that many of his followers were real ascetics and clung tenaciously to the time-honored way of trying to achieve spiritual enrichment by mortifying the body. But the Buddha himself had risen above this method and advocated the Middle Way, the way of moderation. The Middle Way in Chinese and Japanese Buddhism has a wider meaning. In ethical contexts the term means very much the same that it meant in primitive Buddhism, but more frequently it stands for the general Mahā-yāna world view as over against other world views. It stands for a world view which holds that reality is neither what it appears to be to the unenlightened masses, nor is it an absolute void, as is held by some philosophers. For a fuller statement see Chapter V, Sect. C.

14. There were at least six new sects that came into existence about the time that Buddhism arose. Of these only one be-sides Buddhism has survived, viz. the Jaina Sect. The rest, apparently, were absorbed into that all-inclusive system we call Hinduism to-day.

CHAPTER II

1. It is customary to speak of four Great Councils of Bud-dhism. These are: (1) The Council of Rajagriha called soon after the death of the Buddha. (2) The Council of Vaisālī called about one hundred years after the first council. (3) The Council of Pātaliputra called by the great Buddhist King Asoka in the eighteenth year of his reign (about the year 245 B.C.). (4) The Council of Jalandhara called by the Indo-Scythian King Kanishka. The first and second councils are recognized by all Buddhists. The third council is regarded by Southern Bud-dhists as being on the same plane with the first two, while the fourth is not admitted to have had any real authority. On the other hand, Northern Buddhists look upon the fourth council as being next in importance to the first council of Rajagriha; for it may be said that King Kanishka plays in Northern Buddhism much the same rôle that Asoka plays in Southern Buddhism, both being regarded as great defenders of the faith.

2. When we say that Southern or Hīnayāna Buddhism re-mained more or less true to the teachings of original Buddhism, the statement should not be taken too strictly. It is true only

in a very general way. In its popular form Southern Buddhism is every whit as much of a perversion of Gautama's religion as is the popular form of Northern Buddhism.

3. Compare Chapter V, Sect. D and note 3 of Chapter V.

4. Asvaghosha (Jap. Memyō), Nāgārjuna (Jap. Ryūjū), Asanga (Jap. Mujaku), Vasubandhu (Jap. Seshin).

5. It is customary to speak of twelve Chinese sects in Buddhism, though their number changed somewhat from time to time. The following nine were introduced into Japan : Jōjitsu, Sanron, Jōdo, Zen, Tendai, Kegon, Hossō, Ritsu and Shingon. We have given them in the order in which they arose in China and not in the order in which they were introduced into Japan. The following four sects also flourished in China, but were never introduced into Japan, though their teachings were transmitted in one way or another : Bidon, Nehan, Chiron and Sōron.

CHAPTER III

1. While this was the first public and successful introduction of Buddhism into Japan, it would seem that it was not the first attempt of Buddhists to get a hold in the island empire. We are told that about 25 years earlier a Chinese priest had come to the southern shores with an image which he set up in a grass hut ; but the record goes on to say that the people among whom he worked did not understand what it meant and none were led to follow the new faith.

2. The southern portion of Japan had long since been cleared of the aborigines and occupied by the Japanese, but it can hardly be said to have come completely under the control of the Yamato chieftains of central Japan. Even for a considerable length of time after this, southern Japan continued to be a rival of central Japan rather than subject to it.

3. The word Shintō is a Chinese word and means "the Way of the Gods." Obviously this name was given to the native religion after Japan had come into vital contact with China. Before that time there probably was no such thing as a Shintō Religion, but rather only a number of primitive local cults which were gradually being welded together into a sort of connected whole as the nation was being welded together politically. That is, the native religion developed *pari passu* with the state from disconnected elements into at least a semblance of unity.

4. The monistic and theistic aspects of some of the modern Shintō sects are of comparatively late development.

5. As a matter of fact the imperial family, according to Shintō (and this every loyal Japanese is supposed to believe, even to this day), is descended from Amaterasu, the chief Shintō deity.

6. Yamato Damashii was first largely a product of Shintō, but in its modern characteristics it owes perhaps just as much to Confucianism as to the old native religion.

7. Whether these masterpieces of the seventh century were really produced by Japanese or whether they are the work of Koreans who were residing in Japan at that time is difficult to determine. We know, *e.g.*, that in the latter part of the seventh century, as a result of the fall of the Korean kingdoms of Kudara (660) and Koma (668), a great many refugees came to settle in Japan; and, of course, long before this many Koreans had crossed over to the islands to serve as teachers in the various arts and handicrafts.

8. The great aim of the Taikwa reformers was the real unification of Japan and the establishment of a central government which would have real authority over the various sections of the empire. How successful they were in this may be seen from the fact that when the reformers of 1868 looked around for a model, they turned back to this period of Japan's history for inspiration and guidance. And furthermore, Emperor Tenchi, who as Prince Naka-no-Ōye was one of the leaders in these reforms, is regarded to this day as one of Japan's three greatest emperors.

9. For the chief differences between the three great divisions of Buddhist philosophy, • viz. Hīnayāna, Provisional Mahāyāna and True Mahāyāna, see Chapter V, Sect. C.

10. When we say that the Kegon Sect belongs to the Mahāyāna School and as such belongs to that type of Buddhism which won Japan, we do not mean to say that later Buddhist sects were all more or less like the Kegon. As a matter of fact there are as many types of sects in the so-called Mahāyāna division as there are in Buddhism as a whole; especially is this true if one considers the popular religious teachings of these sects. The Mahāyāna sects agree with one another only in a very general way, viz. in the philosophical basis of their teachings. The religious application, however, that is made of these general teachings differs very widely in these sects.

z

11. There are, of course, larger bells in existence to-day. The great Moscow bell, *e.g.*, is much larger, as is also the one at Tennōji in Osaka; but these, it must be remembered, were cast many centuries later, and besides, the Moscow bell has never been hung successfully.

12. It is only by accommodation that one can speak of the Kojiki and Nihongi as histories. The best that can be said about them is that their authors meant them to be received as faithful accounts of what had transpired. These writers, or rather the authorities who inspired them, were more concerned with "the correct interpretation of the facts" than with the facts themselves, and so one should not be surprised if one finds occasionally choice bits of Chinese history incorporated bodily in the annals of the simple islanders. And yet as these two works are the oldest Japanese records in existence they must be regarded as our chief sources for early Japanese history.

13. The great Taikwa reforms, *e.g.*, were made possible largely because of the knowledge of things Chinese which these reformers possessed. As a matter of fact the "brains" of the reforms were really the two so-called National Doctors who had resided at the Chinese court for some thirty years. One of these was the Buddhist priest Bin.

14. Compare Chapter IV, the section which deals with the Five Periods of the Buddhas ministry.

15. As a matter of fact no Buddhist sect with the exception of the Nichiren Sect would regard the teachings of other sects, however contradictory to its own teachings these might seem, as false. The philosophers of almost all sects would hold with the Tendai Sect that all contradictions are but opposite sides of the same reality. The only claim that one sect would make for itself is that it stresses a certain truth more strongly than other sects.

16. As we pointed out in Chapter II, it is very difficult with our limited knowledge of the history and life currents of Central Asia to determine whether Buddhism in its passage from India to China came into contact with Western thought-currents.

17. While magic and mystery are very characteristic of the Shingon Sect, we do not wish to imply that this sect has a monopoly on such things. As a matter of fact the priests of all sects have exercised authority over not only the ignorant masses, but also statesmen and rulers because of their supposed powers with demons and offended spirits of the dead. It is amazing

to see how comparatively strong this hold is even to-day in circles where the higher grade of intelligence, one would think, should make this sort of thing impossible.

18. "It not only became the religion of the court," says Murdoch, "but in course of time we actually read of an emperor of Japan making solemn public profession of being the humble servant of the three sacred things, — Buddha, the Law and the Priests, to wit. In 900 the abdicated sovereign received the tonsure, and this practice soon became customary; and a century or two later it was not the titular reigning emperor, but the Hō-Ō — or Cloistered Emperor — who really ruled."

19. By this time Japan had become a real land of soldiers. The great Fujiwara family, which had been virtually the dominant force in the empire ever since the reforms of the seventh century, and which had ruled not with the sword but with the more refined methods of diplomacy, was being compelled to give way to the famous Tairas and Minamotos. This struggle kept the land in constant turmoil until finally the illustrious Yoritomo of the Minamoto family succeeded in bringing the conflicting elements under one strong hand, viz. through the establishment of the Kamakura Bakufu.

20. Compare Chapter V, Sect. G, Subsect. 2.

21. Kwannon (Sk. Avalokitesvara) is usually spoken of by Western writers on Chinese and Japanese Buddhism as feminine, but this is not exactly accurate. Avalokitesvara probably means "The One Who Looks Down from Above," i.e. one who looks down upon suffering humanity with compassion. Whether this Bodhisattva is masculine or feminine is really beside the mark, for all beings that have reached the Bodhisattva state are above sex distinctions. Kwannon, or Kwannon-sama, plays a very big rôle in Japanese Buddhism, and perhaps no temple in all Japan is as popular as the famous Kwannon temple in Asakusa, Tōkyō. The distinctive attribute of this deity, viz. mercy and compassion, is usually represented in a very realistic way by an image with many hands, hands that are ever ready to help the needy.

22. The Bosatsu Hōzō is said to have lived about ten Kalpas ago. Now the length of a Kalpa is variously estimated. One way to measure it is to think of a castle 10,000 miles in cube filled with mustard seeds. A little bird comes once every three years and takes out one grain. When this huge storehouse has been emptied in this way then one Kalpa has elapsed. Or an-

other way to measure the length of a Kalpa is to imagine a mountain of granite. A little bird occasionally flies over it and accidentally touches it with its wings. When the mountain has thus been worn away to the level of the surrounding plain then one Kalpa has elapsed. It is perhaps needless to say that Hōzō Bosatsu has not a shred of historicity about him, but is purely the invention of the pious imagination.

23. This great vow is really only one of forty-eight which Hōzō is supposed to have made. It is the famous eighteenth vow and reads as follows: "If when I have attained Buddhahood, all beings in the Ten Quarters (*i.e.* the universe), who with a heart of faith desire to be born into my country and call upon my name, do not attain their desire, then I shall not enter [the joys of] full enlightenment."

24. Buddhist psychology usually speaks of six organs of sense, adding to the five senses ordinarily recognized the Will, or something which corresponds roughly to what Western psychologists mean by the Will.

25. The Zen Sect is not the only one which holds this view of human knowledge, but the true Zen follower, at least in his moments of silent meditation and contemplation, is perhaps more consistent in his religious application of this theory of human knowledge than are the adherents of other sects.

26. This statement is a good illustration of how in Zen thought and in Buddhist thought generally the human self merges with the Universal Self. The individual begins his meditations by getting rid of all individual objects of thought until he finally is supposed to lay hold on the one and only object of thought. It is, however, no longer the individual mind that does this, but it is rather the Universal Mind in the individual that becomes conscious of itself. "The Entity that never changes will appear." It will appear not to the individual mind as such, but only as the individual mind has become the Absolute Mind.

27. The reason the Zen leaders made the military capital of Japan the center of their activity is because the Kamakura authorities encouraged them to do so by showering all sorts of substantial favors upon them. Just as Emperor Kwammu when he built his new capital at Kyōto had encouraged a new type of Buddhism in the form of the Tendai and Shingon sects in order to play them off against the old Nara sects and their power, so Yoritomo and his successors at Kamakura were care-

ful to provide themselves with priests and diviners who would be loyal to them and their ambitions as over against the Kyōto authorities who had on the whole the older Buddhist sects as their supporters. It must be remembered that in the great political struggle of the twelfth century, which resulted in shifting the real administrative power of the empire from Kyōto to Kamakura, the Buddhist priests and monks played a big part. This was so not only because the leading monasteries controlled considerable military power, but because even the most blatant and high-handed warriors of that age believed firmly in the magic powers of the clever and unscrupulously ambitious priests. Hence temples had to be built in order that unholy ambitions and selfish schemes might be sanctified through the good offices of the priests, who alone had access to the superhuman powers which overrule the affairs of men.

28. When Nichiren arose, the work of Yoritomo had been accomplished. The Kamakura shōgunate was firmly established and the emperor at Kyōto had been deprived of all but nominal authority. On the other hand, it should be said that if Nichiren had been better acquainted with the history of his country, he would have known that in a true sense the country was more united in his day than it had been for centuries. The Kamakura shōgunate had succeeded in unifying at least the military strength of the nation and in giving the land an administrative system which was effective and on the whole a blessing.

29. This is one of the few cases in the long history of Japanese Buddhism where a religious leader was condemned to death; and it should be observed that even in this case the condemnation was not so much for his religious views as for his supposedly dangerous political views. Religious persecutions in the severe forms which medieval Europe witnessed were practically unknown in Japan. The most severe form was usually banishment to some remote part of the empire which, as we saw in the case of Shinran, e.g., was not always an unmixed evil. On the other hand, it must be confessed that the causes which led to persecution were usually far less noble than in Europe, and frequently were of a very sordid nature. "But what was known as a 'persecution' in medieval Japan," writes Murdoch, "was of a comparatively mild nature. Into the punishment of heresy, the rack, the stake, and the faggot never found any entrance; banishment to some remote part of the empire was the severest penalty inflicted; and it was inflicted, not so much

for preaching new and strange doctrines, as for provoking popular tumults and breaches of the peace. It is true that for generations the priests had been the most turbulent class in Japan, and that when the Great Monasteries in the Home Provinces were not at actual warfare with each other, their mutual relations were little more satisfactory than those of an armed truce. But to dignify their broils and squabbles with the name of religious wars would be entirely beside the mark. Such bloodshed as there was took place, not in defense of disputed points of doctrine, or of any abstract theological propositions whatever. From first to last, in some shape or other, it was all merely a question of loaves and fishes, for the considerations that provoked these armed ecclesiastical debates were generally of the earth earthy, and not infrequently sordidly so."

30. The Zen, Shin and Nichiren sects in particular preëmpted the Kwanto; the Jōdo, for some reason or other, failed to get much of a hold here for several centuries but found its great following among the cultured civilians of the Kyōto region. Emperors Shirakawa II., Takakura and even the astute Toba II. were followers of Hōnen, though this may have been due simply to the fact that they sought thus to develop a new force which they might play off against the powerful Hieizan priests when occasion demanded it. At any rate their names gave prestige to the Jōdo Sect and enabled it to gain very speedily a strong hold in the territory of the older sects. The influence of the Jōdo Sect in the Kwanto became marked with the rise of the Tokugawa shōgunate.

31. This tolerant attitude of the Buddhist philosophers was not exactly a characteristic of the average Buddhist monk of this period. Or if it is true that they were tolerant of doctrines that differed from their own, they certainly showed a different spirit when their economic interests clashed with those of their brethren in the faith. Compare note 29 above.

32. Hideyoshi does not only compare favorably with the military statesmen of his own land, but some would even class him with Cæsar and Napoleon. As a matter of fact his ambitions, if not his ability, were apparently no less than theirs; for the pacification of Japan was to have been only the beginning of his program. Standing beside the image of the great Yoritomo one day he expressed his ambitious dreams as follows: "You are my friend. You took all the power under Heaven [*i.e.* Japan]. You and I, only, have been able to do this; but you

were of an illustrious family, and not like me, sprung from the tillers of the earth. My ultimate purpose is to conquer not only all that is under Heaven [Japan], but even China. What think you of that?" While he was unable to make good this boast, he did succeed in giving China cause for anxiety, and his power was felt along the entire coast of Eastern Asia, and even the Spaniards in the Philippines were made to realize that he was a man with whom they had to reckon.

33. Occasionally individual Buddhists like the Tendai priest Tenkai or the Zen priest Takuan exerted great influence in the affairs of state, but this was nothing in comparison with the influence exercised in the days when even the emperors preferred the cloister to the throne and from these places of retirement wielded their power.

34. A point which Western students of things Japanese usually overlook is that the formalism and that strict observance of all the niceties of an elaborate etiquette which often seems to put a straight jacket upon the normal and free development of human personality, is really no more inherently natural to the Japanese than to any other people. It is largely the product of a studied effort on the part of the leaders in the Tokugawa period. What strikes the student of Japanese history is that the men and women back of that period seem more like the free Westerner in their spirit than like the older Japanese of the present generation. We say the "older Japanese" of the present generation advisedly, for any one acquainted with the younger elements must know that the love for freedom and untrammeled self-expression is as strong with the young men and women of Japan as it is even with Americans.

35. This statement may seem to be contradicted by what was said about the constructive influence which Buddhism exerted during the great reconstruction days of the Taikwa reforms, but there is really no contradiction involved. The constructive influence which Buddhism exerted in those days did not spring from the forces inherent in Buddhism as such, but rather from the fact that Buddhism was the vehicle of the superior continental civilization whose chief elements were other than Buddhist.

36. The attempt on the part of the Government to foster patriotism by forcing teachers and pupils in the primary schools to visit and make obeisance at the National Shrines from time to time has led to real difficulties. No matter what the official world may say about the clear distinction between these National

Shrines and the ordinary Shintō shrines, the people in general do not make such a distinction; and therefore to make obeisance at the National Shrines is regarded by them as having a real religious significance. It is more than merely showing respect for national heroes; it is real religious worship. Not only do Japanese Christians object to being compelled to worship at such shrines but the Buddhists, too, feel that it interferes with their religious liberty. Of course, both Christians and Buddhists are as loyal Japanese as are the Shintōists and they do not hesitate to show all due respect to national heroes, but they feel that the distinction which the Government is trying to make is really an absurd one. It is absurd for the simple reason that many of the national heroes of Japan have in the course of the centuries been deified, and religion and patriotism from a Shintō standpoint have been one. If the Government really wants to be consistent and make its position rational, it will have to go one step further and say that these national heroes who in the past have been deified are really only great men and not gods, and that they should receive only such reverence as is due to great men. Japanese Christians yield to none in true loyalty to their country and the country's great heroes, but they shall ever insist that there must be a distinction between the respect and reverence given to great men and that reverence and worship given to God and to God only. The truth of the matter is that this attempt on the part of the Government to make this separation between National Shrines and the ordinary Shintō shrines is simply one of those naïve efforts which are being made by statesmen to-day to bridge the chasm between the old and the new. It is an effort which seeks to preserve the old spirit of loyalty and patriotism and at the same time shift it from its old basis of the traditional emperor- and hero-worship to a new basis of loyalty to human rulers and institutions; and in making this shift they are trying to occupy first a halfway position. A halfway position, however, cannot satisfy either the adherents of the old nor the advocates of the new, and so more or less friction over this point may be expected for some time to come.

CHAPTER IV

1. The Tōkyō edition of the Buddhist canon contains about 400 vols. and the Kyōto edition about 250 vols. Another series,

of about 750 vols., published in Kyōto contains the Chinese commentaries and exegetical works. But in addition to these presentations of works in Chinese, two other series are being published containing the literature of Japanese Buddhism, each series having about 200 vols.

2. The writings of the founders of Japanese sects are sometimes of greater importance to the average adherent than are the regular canonical books. Thus, e.g., the writings of Shinran mean far more to the Shin Sect than all but three or four books of the official canon as received from China.

3. The Pali canon is really only a canon of one of the earlier sects and not of Southern Buddhism as a whole. It is quite likely that each of the various schools in early Buddhism had its own arrangement of the scriptures and that these differed somewhat from each other. But if this is the case, then all these various redactions have been lost except in so far as they may be preserved in the voluminous Northern canon.

4. The Chinese canon has as its core the older Sanskrit canon, i.e. translations from the Sanskrit pure and simple. But it has also a great many books written originally in Chinese. And the canon in Japan in the wider sense has in the same way many books written originally in Japanese.

5. Compare H. Haas, *Der Kanon des Buddhismus in Japan. Mitteilungen der Deutschen Gesellschaft für Natur- und Völkerkunde Ostasiens.* Band x, Teil 1, pp. 106 ff.

6. Even conservatives regard Asvaghosha as the one who really made Mahāyāna Buddhism known, and they look upon his "Awakening of Faith" as the real cornerstone of this type of faith. But, of course, they would insist that this was not really original with him and that he simply transmitted what he had received in secret. The liberals, on the other hand, would say that the work was original with Asvaghosha, but that it was really only an elaboration and development of S'akyamuni's teachings.

7. About one hundred years after the Buddha's death Buddhism had divided into two great divisions with various subdivisions. The two great divisions or schools were the Mahāsamghikāh (School of the Great Assembly) and the Sthavira (School of the Chairman). From the first of these there developed in the course of time the following eight branches: Ekavyāharikāh, Lokottaravadināh, Kukkulikāh, Bahusrutiyāh, Prajnāptivādināh, Jetavaniyāh, Aparasailāh, Uttarasailāh. From the Sthavira developed Sarvāstivādāh and from this came

first the Vastiputriyāh which in turn divided into four branches, viz., Dharmottarāh, Bhadrayānikāh, Sammitiyāh and Sannagarikāh. A second branch of the Sarvāstivādāh was the Malūsasakāh which gave rise to the Dharmaguptāh. And after this there arose still two further branches from the Sarvāstivādāh, viz., Kāsyapīyāh and Sautrāntikāh. These divisions and subdivisions are what is meant by the so-called eighteen or twenty sects of Hīnayāna Buddhism which were in existence at the time of the second Great Council of Buddhism, the Council of Vaisali. But it is hardly correct to designate them as sects of Hīnayāna Buddhism, for the term Hīnayāna was probably not coined till several centuries later.

CHAPTER V

1. The Twelve Links of the Karma-chain are known in Japanese by various terms, such as : Jūni Inen, Jūni Inshō, Jūni Yushi, Jūni Engi and Jūni Enmon. These terms differ a little in the atmosphere that surrounds them, but all are attempts to express the meaning of the chain of existence. Sometimes the order of these links is inverted, so that the first link of Ignorance is given as the last link, and the last link as the first. The order depends upon whether one reasons from effect back to cause or starts with the cause and proceeds to the effect. Following the order we have given, the Sanskrit and Japanese terms are as below:

    (1) Ignorance (Sk. Avidya, Jap. Mumyō).
    (2) Latent Impressions (Sk. Samskāra, Jap. Gyō).
    (3) Thought-substance (Sk. Vidjnana, Jap. Shiki).
    (4) Name and Form (Sk. Namarūpa, Jap. Myōshiki).
    (5) The Six Roots (Sk. Chadāyatana, Jap. Rokusho).
    (6) Contact (Sk. Sparsa, Jap. Shoku).
    (7) Sensation (Sk. Vedana, Jap. Ju).
    (8) Desire (Sk. Trichnā, Jap. Ai).
    (9) Clinging to Existence (Sk. Upādāna, Jap. Shu).
    (10) Becoming (Sk. Bhava, Jap. Yu).
    (11) Birth (Sk. Djāti, Jap. Shō).
    (12) Decrepitude and Death (Sk. Djarāmavana, Jap. Rōshi).

2. Compare note 11, Chapter I.

3. This division of every universe into three realms, or classes of beings, like so many other things in Buddhism, was borrowed from Brahmanism. It is an imitation of the Brahmanic Four

Worlds (Bhuvanatraya); only that Buddhists substitute for the physical categories, Earth, Heaven and Atmosphere of the Brahmans, the ethical or spiritual categories of Desire, Pure Form and Formlessness.

4. In addition to these eight Hot Hells and eight Cold Hells one finds mention of eight Dark Hells, ten Larger Cold Hells with a hundred million smaller hells attached to each, and 84,000 Smaller Cold Hells. In no sphere has the Indian imagination been more extravagant than in this. Japan has taken on some of this rubbish as may be seen especially from such a writing as Genshin's description of the Buddhist hells; but, after all, the Japanese mind has never lost itself very seriously in such morbid speculations.

5. Zendō is regarded as the fifth of the seven great Church Fathers of the Shin Sect who preceded Shinran. These seven are the two Indians, Nāgārjuna and Vasubandhu, the three Chinese, Donran, Dōshaku and Zendō, and the two Japanese, Genshin and Genku.

6. The Six Virtues (Sk. Paramita) are known in Japanese as the Roku Baramitsu (Baramitsu is simply a transliteration of Paramita), or Rokudo (Six Crossings). These Six Virtues are the following: Charity (Sk. Dāna, Jap. Fuse), Morality, *i.e.* Keeping the Commandments (Sk. Sīla, Jap. Jikai), Patience and Forbearance (Sk. Kchānti, Jap. Ninniku), Exertion or Diligence (Sk. Vīrya, Jap. Shōjun), Meditation (Sk. Dhyāna, Jap. Zenjō) and Wisdom (Sk. Pradjna, Jap. Chie).

Sometimes four other virtues are added to these six, making thus the so-called Ten Virtues, or Ten Crossings (Jap. Judo). These added four are: Use of Proper Means (Sk. Upāya, Jap. Hōben), Knowledge or Science (Sk. Djnāna, Jap. Chi, or Jakuna), Pious Vows (Sk. Pranidhana, Jap. Gwan) and Force of Purpose (Sk. Bala, Jap. Goriki; literally meaning, Five Powers). Compare Chapter VI, Sect. B, Subsect. 2.

7. The Four Great Vows (Jap. Shiguseigwan) must be made and fulfilled by all Bodhisattvas. Some Bodhisattvas, however, bind themselves by even more self-sacrificing vows than these. Thus we have the famous Forty-eight Vows of Amida made by him before he entered the Buddha state, and especially the famous Eighteenth Vow of these forty-eight in which this unselfish Bodhisattva declared that he would not enter the bliss of Buddhahood until he had worked out a way of salvation for all beings.

8. Though the Paradise, doctrine is a very popular one with the masses in Japan, there are some Buddhists who regard this desire to be born into Paradise as the worst kind of evil Karma, which really lands the one who has it in Hell. "The heart that desires Paradise is already in Hell. In the case of Shaka (S'akya-muni) or a deity there is no Paradise."

9. There are some Buddhist scriptures which may not categorically deny the possibility of salvation to all men but which nevertheless seem to hold out very little hope to the masses that are lost in sin and misery. Thus we read, "A blind turtle and a floating tree are more likely to meet and see each other than ignorant and stupid humanity is to obtain the body of a man." That is, the ignorant masses in their next incarnation stand very little chance of being born as human beings but will be born in one of the lower four realms. Their salvation then from the bondages of this evil world seems almost hopeless. It is only when one measures time by Kalpas that one can speak of such beings as attaining salvation ultimately.

CHAPTER VI

1. Compare Chapter V, Sect. D, Subsect. 5.

2. Compare Chapter II, Sect. B.

3. For a fuller statement of this Noble Eightfold Path see Chapter II, Sect. B, Subsect. 2.

4. For a list of the Ten Virtues which differs a little from this one, see note 6 of Chapter V.

SELECTED BIBLIOGRAPHY OF WORKS IN JAPANESE

Dictionaries.

1. Bonkan Taiyaku Bukkyō Jiten . . . Dr. U. Hagiwara
   Sanskrit-Chinese Buddhist Dictionary.
2. Bukkyō Daijirin . . . . Hompa Hongwanji
   Great Dictionary of Buddhism.
3. Bukkyō Jirin . . . . Fujii and Shimaji
   Buddhist Dictionary.
4. Bukkyō Daijiten . . . . Tokunō Ōta
   Great Dictionary of Buddhism.
5. Tetsugaku Daijishō.
   Great Dictionary of Philosophy.
6. Zenshū Jiten.
   Dictionary of Zen Sect.

Texts and Commentaries.

1. Dai Nippon Bukkyō Zenshō.
   Collected Literature of Japanese Buddhism. (This great
   series when completed will contain about 200 large volumes.
   It will comprise the Chinese Tripitaka, original Japanese
   works and standard commentaries.)
2. Kokuyaku Daizōkyō.
   The Canon Translated into Japanese. (This is a work of
   twelve large volumes containing translations into Japanese
   from the leading Buddhist scriptures.)
3. Bukkyō Seiten . . . . . Drs. Murakami and Maeda
   Buddhist Bible. (Selections from the leading scriptures arranged topically.)
4. Jōdoshu Seiten.
   Bible of the Jodo Sect. (Containing the "Basal Scriptures"
   of the sect and standard commentaries.)
5. Nichirenshu Seiten.
   Bible of the Nichiren Sect.
6. Shingonshū Seiten.
   Bible of the Shingon Sect.
7. Shinshū Seiten.
   Bible of the Shin Sect.
8. Zenshū Seiten.
   Bible of the Zen Sect.
   (The material in numbers 3–8 is contained, of course, in
   number 1, but here it is in more convenient form for a study
   of the particular tenets of the respective sects.)

349

Histories.

1. Indo Bukkyō Shikō . . . .   Tetsu Sakaino
   Historical Outline of Indian Buddhism.
2. Shina Bukkyō Shikō . . . .   Kōyō Sakaino
   Historical Outline of Chinese Buddhism.
3. Nihon Bukkyō Shikō . . . .   Dr. S. Murakami
   Historical Outline of Japanese Buddhism.
4. Daijō Bukkyō Shiron . . . .   Dr. E. Maeda
   Historical Essays on Mahāyāna Buddhism.
5. Shinshū Zenshi . . . .   Dr. S. Murakami
   Complete History of the Shin Sect.

Biographical.

1. Shakamuni-den . . . . . Profs. T. Inouye and K. Hori
   Life of S'akyamuni.
2. Shakamuni-den . . . . Daijo Tokiwa
   Life of S'akyamuni.
3. Nihon Bukka Jimmei Jishō . . . . . . Junkei Washio
   Biographical Dictionary of Japanese Buddhist Monks.
4. Hokke Gyōja to shite no Nichiren . . . Dr. M. Anezaki
   Nichiren as a Follower of the Lotus of Truth. (The English
   volume is called "Nichiren, the Buddhist Prophet.")
5. Shinran Shōnin Den . . . . G. Sasaki
   Life of Shinran Shōnin.

Essays and Studies.

1. Butten no Kenkyū . . . . Dr. B. Matsumoto
   Studies in Buddhist Canons.
2. Bukkyō Gairon . . . . Dr. S. Murakami
   Outline of Buddhist Doctrines.
3. Bukkyō Tōitsuron . . . . Dr. S. Murakami
   Buddhism Unified. (Vol. I, Daikōron, Main Outline;
   Vol. II, Butsudaron, Buddhalogy; Vol. III, Genriron,
   Fundamental Principles.)
4. Kompon Bukkyō . . . . Dr. M. Anezaki
   Fundamental Buddhism.
5. Daijō Busseturon Hiban . . . . . . Dr. S. Murakami
   Critical Essays on Mahāyāna Buddhism.
6. Genshin Butsu to Hōshin Butsu . . . . Dr. M. Anezaki
   Buddha Revealed and Buddha as Law.
7. Amida Butsu no Kenkyū . . . . . . Ryūkei Yabuki
   Studies on Amida Buddha.
8. Jōdokyō no Kenkyū . . . . . . Shinkyō Mochizuki
   Studies in the Pure Land Teachings.
9. Mikkyō Kōyō . . . . Raifu Gonda
   Outlines of the Mystery Teachings.
10. Tendaishū Kōyō . . . . Dr. E. Maeda
    Outlines of the Tendai Sect.

Lectures and Comments.

1. Hekiganroku Kōwa . . . . Sōen Shaku
   Comments on the Hekiganroku.

Lectures and Comments — Continued.

2. Hokkekyō Kōgi . . . . Tokunō Ōta
   Lectures on the Hokkekyō.
3. Shōshinge Kōwa . . . . Tei Tada
   Comments on the Shōshinge.

(The classical commentaries and comments by Japanese
writers of the past are contained in Dai Nippon Bukkyō
Zenshō mentioned above.)

INDEX